BISEXUAL
LOVE

BY

DR. WILHELM STEKEL
(VIENNA)

Authorized translation by

JAMES S. VAN TESLAAR, M.D.

Fredonia Books
Amsterdam, The Netherlands

Bisexual Love

by
Wilhelm Stekel

ISBN: 1-4101-0378-1

Reprinted from the 1933 edition

Fredonia Books
Amsterdam, The Netherlands
http://www.fredoniabooks.com

Preface

The present work is the English version of a part
of one of the volumes in the author's massive series
of clinical studies bearing the generic title, *Disorders of the Instincts and Emotions* and covering the
whole range of the so-called *Parapathic Maladies.*
The translation represents approximately one-half
of the *Homosexualität* of the volume entitled *Onanie
und Homosexualität,* and bearing the sub-title, *Die
Homosexuelle Neurose.* The balance of the *Homosexual Neurosis* and the author's clinical study of
Autoerotism are also translated and will appear
shortly.

It is the author's intention, and mine as his translator, to issue an English version of all the volumes
in this comprehensive series. In addition to the
subjects covered in the present volume and in the
two volumes to follow shortly, the *Disorders of the
Instincts and the Emotions* include the *Anxiety
States, Female Frigidity, Male Impotence, Infantilism* (including *Exhibitionism* and *Fetichism*), the
Compulsion Neuroses and *Morbid Doubts.* The
range of the subjects and the plan of the volumes
already published show that the series as conceived

iii

by the author forms a complete clinical account of the psychogenetic disorders, and represents the most recent development of scientific research. Since the genetic study of these parapathic maladies involves a thorough understanding of the facts of sexual life Dr. Stekel's works on the _Disorders of the Instincts and the Emotions_ constitute incidentally the latest practical reference Handbook of Sexual Science in the light of our newer knowledge and should prove also on that score of inestimable value to the medical and the allied learned professions.

The absence of formal systematic instruction in the Principles and Practice of Psychoanalysis in spite of the wide interest that the subject has deservedly aroused in our midst is highly regrettable, the more so since the lack of systematic instruction in our country deprives the older practitioners as well as the oncoming generations of physicians of an opportunity to familiarize themselves with this most important branch of therapy. Even though the curriculum of instruction in our schools, and particularly in our medical colleges, is admittedly burdened with a bewildering plethora of other branches of instruction, it is inconceivable that our colleges, our hospitals and psychiatric institutes, and our other institutions of higher learning will long continue to neglect a subject of such vital importance as psychotherapy and re-education, now that the subject has been placed, at last, upon a solid basis through the application of the psychobiotic and genetic methods of approach. But it will probably take considerable time before competent instruction to fill the need will be available.

It appears therefore highly desirable that an English version of Dr. Stekel's works should make their appearance at this time. For in the absence of formal instruction his clinical studies form an excellent substitute, perhaps the most suitable means available for post-graduate instruction in the clinical aspects of Psychoanalysis. And should systematic courses be made available in the near future, in response to the urgent need, our instructors and students alike will undoubtedly find the Stekel series most valuable aids for study and guidance.

In a letter received from Dr. Stekel while this work was going through the press he states that a new edition of *Onanie und Homosexualität* is being issued in the original, bearing a dedication to the present translator.

Van Teslaar.

Brookline, Mass.

CONTENTS

vii

I

Leben—ist das nicht gerade ein Andersseinwollen, als die Natur ist?—Nietzsche.

BI-SEXUAL LOVE

I

*Living,—is it not the will to be otherwise
than nature is?—Nietzsche.*

That there are preeminent physicians who
earnestly look upon masturbation as the cause of
homosexuality seems hardly believable. It would
be as proper to consider masturbation the cause of
sexuality. We have shown elsewhere that onanism
may be the result of ungratified homosexual trends.
At times it may stand as a substitute for some
homosexual act. It then replaces for a time the
adequate temporary form of sexual gratification.
I state "temporary form," because the sexual
object itself does not remain permanently the same
and the sexual directive goals,—to use the excellent
expression of *Hans Blüher* [1] are often abandoned.
The false notion that onanism is responsible for
homosexuality has been preconized by *Krafft-*

[1] Hans Bluher: Studien ueber den perversen Charakter.
Ztrbl. f. Psychoanalyse, Oct., 1913.

11

Ebing, whose great authority in matters of sexual psychopathology persists to this day. His services are significant, indeed, and we must observe that he has at last accepted the view of *Hirschfeld* that homosexuality is inborn,—that there is an acquired and a hereditary homosexuality.[1] But in the last (14th) edition of *Krafft-Ebing's* work, which has appeared in 1912, his editor, *Alfred Fuchs,* preserves the statement about onanism at the head of the chapter and he even underscores the contentions of his great teacher on this particular subject.[2]

---

[1] *Neue Studien auf dem Gebiete der Homosexualitaet. Jahrb. f. Sexuelle Zwischenstuffen,* vol. III, Leipzig.

[2] This view of *Krafft-Ebing* is by no means "antiquated." It is still maintained by *Stier* (Zur Aetiologie des kontraeren Sexualgefuehls. Monatschrf. f. Psych. u. Neurol., vol. XXXII, 1914) and very energetically criticised (ibid.) by *Hirschfeld and Burchard.* "It is inconceivable," state the above named authors, "how *Stier* can ascribe an etiologic significance to onanism in connection with homosexuality. Its distribution, ubiquitous—in the opinion of most specialists, would permit one to hold masturbation responsible for any other sexual development as well." According to *Stier,* early and long-continued onanism (especially mutual) is harmful because "it does away with the feeling of shame in connection with one's sexual organs and makes for readier handling even by the uncorrupted adult." *Fleischmann* also finds 33 excessive onanists among 60 inverts and concludes (Beitr. zur Lehre der kontraeren Sexualempfindung, Zeitschr. f. d. ges. Neur. u. Psychol., vol. VII, 1911) that "like alcoholism, masturbation must influence the development of the perversion." Many of his patients mentioned the habit in a casual relation. We know well that the sense of guilt is attached to the habit of masturbation. But *Fleischmann* sees in that a proof. "Onanism plays a role in the development of the sexual perversion," he argues, "because it rouses an increased sexual excitability while the will power is weakened by it at the same time and

My work proves that we must abandon the merely descriptive method of sexual research. The subject's first account is only a statement of the manifest content of his consciousness concerning his paraphilia. We must look into the latent content, into the unconscious and quasi-conscious forces involved. The descriptive form of sexual research must be replaced by the psychological, in keeping with the spirit of our times. In no other field does analysis so convincingly and completely prove its claims.

What was the status of the subject before the advent of analysis? *Krafft-Ebing* originally looked upon homosexuality as the result of a hereditary transmission, a hypothesis not corroborated by the observations of subsequent investigators. Certain circumstances favor an outcropping in manifest form of the latent homosexuality common to all persons,—a fact which complicates this problem. Environment also comes into play. An environment such as is furnished by some nervous or psychopathic parents naturally plays a role. This subject we shall take up later. The alleged hereditary transmission is supposed to show itself in the homosexual through the early awakening of the sexual instinct and by the appearance of masturbation during early childhood. But we know that

there follows a progressive wandering of the sexual instinct away from the normal sexual aim and object."

the homosexuals share this peculiarity with all
others, especially with neurotic persons. A strong
flaring up of instinct is not the consequence but the
cause of the neurosis. But according to *Krafft-
Ebing* masturbation during childhood is the cause
of homo- or pseudo-homosexuality breaking forth
at a later period. "Nothing is more likely," he
states, "than masturbation, so to disturb and occasionally thwart all noble emotions at the source
as they arise spontaneously out of the sexual feeling.[1] The habit robs the nascent feeling of charm
and beauty leaving behind only the husk of grossly
animal craving for sexual gratification. An individual, so thwarted, attains the age of maturity
lacking the esthetic, ideal, pure and undefiled longing
which leads to the other sex. At the same time the
heat of sensuous passion cools off while the inclination towards the other sex is significantly
weakened. This deficiency embraces the morals,
the ethics, the character, the phantasy and the disposition of the youthful masturbator as well as his
emotional and instinctive life and holds true of both

---

[1] This contention is altogether wrong. I have never seen so
many and such pronounced idealists as among masturbators.
Young artists, poets and musicians in particular often show,
I have found, a strong tendency to masturbation, and this
agrees with the pronounced bisexuality of all artists, which has
been particularly pointed out by *Fliess*. The youths of this
type are often so delicate and sensitive that they see in the
sexual act only animal brutality and hide their own sexuality
from the whole world. Among masturbators we find the
champions of truth, the over-moralistic preachers, the ethical
reformers and dreamers.

sexes, occasionally reducing to zero the yearning after the opposite sex, so that in the end masturbation is preferred to every other form of gratification."

Imagine the injurious effect of such statements upon the masturbating youth; particularly when he reads that the best way to combat homosexuality is to fight against masturbation (p. 336, *loc. cit.*).

The great investigator has confused here cause and effect. The masturbators avoid the path leading to woman not because they masturbate. They indulge in the habit because the path towards womanhood is closed to them. For many persons masturbation is the only available method of sexual gratification. Persons with a strongly accentuated homosexual tendency often find no other path open at all, particularly when the intercourse with woman becomes impossible for them on account of some definite traumatic incidents, such as we shall discuss fully later.

Masturbation is never *the cause* of homosexuality. Homosexuals do not contract the habit early, as *Krafft-Ebing* claims,—it is an early, a very early habit of all persons—and that without any exception. The homosexuals do not forget their childhood onanism because there are other, more painful memories for them to repress and drive out of memory. Again we shall speak fully of that

later. More important for the present is the
question: how does homosexuality arise? Is the
condition hereditary or acquired? Is it something
fatally predetermined or is it only the result of
certain definite constellations of the family circle?
May it be ascribed to a hereditary taint? *Krafft-
Ebing* was at first of the latter opinion and propounded the thesis that "we may doubt whether a
person of the same sex ever has a sensuous attraction for a normally predisposed individual," but
later he changed this opinion fundamentally and
expressed the conviction that there is an inborn
homosexuality though the condition is found only
among the hereditarily predisposed.

He propounded the following theses:

"1. The sexual life of such persons manifests
itself as a rule very precociously and consequently,
is of abnormal strength. Not rarely the peculiar
attraction for members of the same sex which in
itself marks the abnormal direction of the sexual
instinct is associated with other perverse manifestations.

"2. The spiritual love of these persons is frequently an exalted dreaming just as their sexual
instinct as a whole penetrates their consciousness
with a peculiar and even compulsive strength.

"3. In addition to the functional signs of degeneration manifested in the contrary sexual instinct often there are found also other functional

and frequently also anatomic stigmata of degeneration.

"4. Neuroses are present (hysteria, neurasthenia, epileptoid states, etc.). Neurasthenia, transitional or chronic, is nearly always manifest. This is usually a constitutional state induced by inborn conditions. It is awakened and sustained through masturbation or compulsory abstinence." [1]

These statements are relatively milder and here the ideal traits of homosexuality are also given some recognition, although—as we know well—all without exception are addicted to masturbation. *Krafft-Ebing* does not know that all artists are neurotics and that neurosis stands in intimate connection with creative ability. He also makes a distinction between true and false homosexuality,— bisexuality (psychic hermaphroditism) and other forms, as described by *Hirschfeld*.[2]

[1] Cf., on the other hand, the views of *Bloch:* "That the contrary sexual instinct-feeling in itself is not a sign of psychic degeneration and need not be looked upon at all as morbid, is shown among others, by the fact that the condition is often associated with spiritual superiority. As proof we find, among all nations, men of proven homosexuality, who are the pride of their respective people as writers, poets, artists, military strategists, or statesmen. Further proof that the contrary sexual feeling is no disease and does not necessarily lead to immoral tendencies may be seen in all the noble qualities of heart which it is capable of generating, precisely as the heterosexual attraction, such as courage, self-sacrifice, altruism, artistic feeling, creative energy, etc., just as it may be responsible also for any of the morbidities and failings of heterosexual love (jealousy, suicide, murder, unhappy love with its deleterious effects on mind and body, etc.)

[2] It was clearly the duty of the new editor of Krafft-Ebing's

Krafft-Ebing points out a certain relationship between homosexuality and neurosis. But since he still preserves the concept of degeneration, he is forced in the end to admit that homosexuality may also appear in the normal and is not necessarily a morbidity.

Moll, to whom we owe the first great comprehensive work on homosexuality, is of an entirely different popular work to have recorded therein the author's latest views. In his *"Neuen Studien auf dem Gebiete der Homosexualitaet,"* he states: "In contrast with the conception that contrary sexuality is an inborn anomaly, a disorder in the evolution of the sexual function of monosexuals and of the glandular development of the sex glands, *the conception of 'morbidity' is untenable.* We may rather speak in this connection of a malformation and compare the anomaly with bodily malformations,—for instance, with the anatomic deviations from the average type. But the concept of a simultaneous psychopathic state remains a legitimate assumption, because subjects presenting anatomic as well as functional deviations from type (*stigmata degenerationis*), *may preserve good physical health for a time, and may even show points of superiority.*

"At the same time so tremendous a deviation as contrary sexual feeling must have a far wider influence upon the psyche than many of the anatomic or functional stigmata of degeneration. That is the reason why any disturbance in the usual development of a normal sexual life reflects so commonly in an unfavorable sense upon the harmonious psychic development of personality. *Victims of contrary sexual feeling often show neuropathic and psychopathic predispositions,* such as, for instance, a tendency to constitutional neurasthenias and hysteria, milder forms of periodic psychosis, inhibitions against the unfoldment of psychic energies (intelligence, moral sense), including moral inferiority, especially associated with hypersexuality, eventually leading to most serious disorders of the sexual instinct. At any rate, it can be shown that, relatively speaking, heterosexuals prove greater cynics about sexual matters than the homosexuals. Also that other degenerative signs upon the field of sexuality, such as sadism, masochism, fetichism, etc., are much more commonly found among the former. . . ."

ent opinion. He states: "Considering the sexual instinct not as a means for the attainment of pleasure but as standing in the service of procreation we must look upon exclusive homosexuality as belonging to the realm of pathology." (*Die kontraere Sexualempfindung*, Berlin, 1899, 3rd edn.) This is an untenable argument. *For there is no procreative instinct as such, only a sexual instinct.* Science is not concerned with the study of purposiveness, it is interested in the ascertainment of facts. Science must not and cannot be placed in the service of teleology. At any rate *Moll* is inclined to look upon homosexuality as a neurosis: he claims to have found in recent years a growing tendency among investigators to establish a border province between mental health and disease, "and into that realm have been relegated many cases of psychic degeneration—I may mention, for instance, certain compulsory neuroses. I believe it is proper that we should place in the same category the contrary sexual feeling." (*Loc. cit.* p. 435.) He refers here to *Westphal* who compares homosexuality to moral insanity.[1]

Notwithstanding *Moll's* opinion we must state that most modern investigators declare that they have examined many homosexuals whom they have found normal or have at least designated as normal.

---

[1] *Die kontraere Sexualempfindung, Symptom eines neuropatischen (psychopathischen) Zustandes. Arch. f. Psych. u. Neurol., vol. II*, p. 106, 1870.

Havelock Ellis and *Albert Moll* [1] very appropriately
state in their last joint work:

"*Naecke* has repeatedly maintained that the
homosexuals are perfectly healthy and aside from
their specific deviation may be normal in every
respect. We have always maintained this view although, contrary to *Naecke*, we assume that *homosexuality is very frequently found in intimate association with minor nervous states.* We agree
with *Hirschfeld* that heredity plays a rôle in no
more than 25 per cent of the cases of homosexuality
and that, although a neuropathic background may
be present in homosexuality, the degenerative factor
plays but a small role." These authors find the
hypothesis that every person's constitution combines the male and female elements a keen concept
though rather hypothetical. "But still it is undoubtedly justified, if we look upon homosexuality
as an inborn anomaly or, to speak more correctly,
as an anomaly resting on constitutional traits,
which if morbid, are so only in *Virchow's* sense, according to whom pathology is not the science of
diseases but of deviations, so that the homosexual
may be as healthy as the color blind. Inborn
homosexuality ranks on the level of a biologic
variation: it is a variation, representing perhaps
an incomplete phase of sexual differentiation, but

[1] *Handbuch der Sexualwissenschaften (Die Funftionsstœr-
rungen des Sexuallebens.)* Leipzig, Verlag F. C. W. Vogel,
1912, p. 652.

bearing no discernible relationship to any morbid condition of the individual."

I am inclined to doubt this view. What proof have we that the homosexual is perfectly healthy when any criterion of health we may accept must be artificial? On this point we have only the statements of the involved persons to rely upon. All describe themselves as healthy. Do not advanced psychopaths do the same? They lack any feeling of illness. This seems to be characteristic of homosexuals in particular. They want their condition to be looked upon as normal. They claim to be in good health, seldom wish to change their condition, and usually do not call for medical advice unless they come into conflict with the law and find themselves in danger. The authors themselves very properly remark: "As to the men, the homosexuals prefer to hold themselves as normal and endeavor to justify that contention. Those who struggle against their instinctive craving, who look upon their conduct as peculiar or so much as entertain any doubts about it, are in the minority,— less than 20 per cent."

Naturally the large number of homosexual physicians have always tried to convince their observers that they are normal and that they do not differ from other persons in any other way. But all unprejudiced observers have to admit the presence of numerous neurotic traits in connection with homosexuality. This I have undertaken to prove *sine ira et studio* having met numberless homosexuals and having become very closely acquainted with many of them. *I have never yet found a homosexual who was not a neurotic.* He is necessarily that, as I shall later prove. He must be neurotic, the same as the heterosexual, who struggles to overcome and repress a vast portion of homosexual longing with him. *Havelock Ellis* and *Moll* as well as *Krafft-Ebing* also lay stress upon the tendency to neurasthenia. But who nowadays is not neurasthenic? is a question frequently heard. Such an unprejudiced investigator as *Iwan Bloch* becomes convinced and recognizes an inborn homosexuality which must not be conceived as a morbidity. For a long time *Bloch* preconized a different view but changed his opinion convinced by *Hirschfeld's* work and through his own professional contact with homosexuals. He is now a believer in the theory of inborn homosexuality having been led to this view particularly by the statements of the homosexuals. Later we shall prove how unreliable such statements must be. At any rate so keen an observer as *Bloch* could not fail to note the striking percentage of neurotic homosexuals. But he thought they were nervous because "homosexuality acts upon them as a psychic trauma." Further he states: "According to my investigations and observations the *relationship between*

*health and disease among homosexuals is originally
the same as among heterosexuals* and in time, on account of the social and individual isolation of the
homosexuals, acting like a psychic trauma, morbidity becomes accentuated; usually we encounter
nervous complaints and difficulties of an acquired
character, and we note the development of a typical
'homosexual neurasthenia,' which may readily
enough lead some superficial observers to confuse
post hoc with *propter hoc.*" Undoubtedly the
dangers of homosexual activity favor the development of anxiety states. But such nervous states
are found also in cases showing no predisposition
towards anxiety, and anxiety states are encountered without any relation to homosexuality.

Magnus Hirschfeld places himself with all the
weight of his personality and experience squarely in
favor of the contention that homosexuality is a
normal state. His investigations touching upon
this field are numerous. We also owe to his labors
that great work on the subject: *Die Homosexualitaet des Mannes und des Weibes.* (The Homosexuality of Man and of Woman, Verlag L. Marcus,
Berlin, SW, 61.) No investigator interested in
this subject can neglect this fundamental and exhaustive treatment of it. Subsuming the views of
Hirschfeld we may state: There is a genuine inborn
homosexuality which must not be looked upon as
a morbidity. This homosexuality should be con-

fused neither with bisexuality nor with pseudo-homosexuality. *Hirschfeld*, too, has changed his views in the course of time. He had conceived homosexuality as a sexual intermediary stage between man and woman and proposed the famous term: *the third sex*. As is well known all persons are bisexual. *Hirschfeld* looked for the well known physical stigmata of bisexuality among the homosexuals. He found among men enlargement of the breasts, female hips, delicate skin, etc., and among women growth of facial hair, male, energetic traits, etc. In his work entitled, *Der Urnische Mensch*, he maintained: "A homosexual not differing bodily, physically and mentally from the full grown man I have not found among 1500 subjects and I am therefore disposed to doubt the occurrence until I shall meet such an individual." But in his more recent work he declares: "The androgynic type of man and the gynandric type of woman are not necessarily homosexual. There are types of persons which may be described as eunuchoid,—they give the impression of castrated persons without having undergone the operation,—they possess female bodies, high voice and beardless face. Generally there is azoospermia, frequently anorchia. There are corresponding types in the female sex,—persons with bodies showing many masculine traits. These marked womanly men and mannish women are often considered homosexual, but it is not uncommon to find them completely heterosexual inasmuch as they find complementary individuals among the types belonging to the opposite sex. The types which attract them are also androgynous." [1]

Hirschfeld does not admit the influence of latent homosexuality in the choice of this androgenic type. A homosexual whose condition is not manifest he does not recognize. His ground for diagnosis is no longer similarity of bodily traits when compared with the opposite sex. The determining factor for *Hirschfeld* is only the subject's feeling. *If he is homosexually inclined (particularly if so disposed from childhood), the subject is homosexual.* *Hirschfeld's* own statement is as follows: "The determining factor in the diagnosis of homosexuality remains as before the contrary feeling proper; the diagnosis is strongly supported by a negative attitude towards the other sex, as well as by alterosexual episodes, although these two features in

[1] I find a very interesting observation by *Bloch,* one which deserves to be widely circulated: "A final and not unimportant form of Pseudo-homosexuality is hermaphroditism (*das Zwittertum*). It is remarkable that science has concerned itself only in recent years with the close study of hermaphroditic conditions which have not received heretofore the attention warranted by their sociologic bearings and their frequency. It is a great merit of *Neugebauer* and of *Magnus Hirschfeld* that they have called general attention to these remarkable sexual *Zwischenstufen,* intermediary states, and have pointed out their great practical significance, a matter of which no one has thought before, as is shown by the significant fact that the new German civil code has done away with the legal proscriptions of the old Prussian law concerning the *Zwitter* (hermaphrodites), upon the contention that no person is of unknown or unascertainable sex.

themselves are not capable of establishing the diagnosis." Since *Bloch* also admits that there are many virile homosexuals with bodily structures wholly male, it follows that the organic diagnosis of homosexuality is altogether unreliable. *Hans Blüher,* a reliable expert on homosexuality, also recognizes the pure homosexual, which he calls the "male hero" type, whose character and habitus is completely male, thus differing from the second type, the "woman-like invert" (*invertierter Weibling*). The latent homosexual he considers a third type. (Vid. *Die drei Grundformen der Homosexualitaet: Eine sexuologische Studie.* Jahrbuch f. sexuelle Zwischenstuffen, vol. XIII).

Let us repeat and underscore the far-fetched feature of this method of diagnosis. According to it *there is no objective means for ascertaining homosexuality. The only diagnostic guide is the homosexual's declaration that he has always felt homosexually inclined and that he is indifferent towards the other sex.*

The analyst is well qualified to recognise the utter weakness of such a diagnostic guide. We meet continually persons who claim to know themselves thoroughly; they claim that they have investigated their own state very conscientiously but after a few weeks, often only after a few days (illustrations will be fully given in this book) the subject must admit that he did not know himself, that, in fact, he had avoided knowing himself. *All persons lie about sexual matters and deceive themselves in the first place.* All play *Vogelstrausspolitik*, the ostrich.

All neurotics falsify their life history or at least retouch it. They simply forget the facts which do not suit their system of thinking. We must also bear in mind *Havelock Ellis'* statement that the homosexuals prefer to consider themselves as normal. Similarly the childhood history is distorted consciously or unconsciously and a life history is reconstructed (in retrospect) from which all heterosexual episodes have been eliminated.

Psychoanalysis has proven that all homosexuals, without exception, shown heterosexual tendencies in early life. There is no exception to this rule. *There are no monosexual persons!* The heterosexual period stretches far into puberty. *All persons are bisexual.* But persons repress either the homosexual or the heterosexual components on account of certain motives or because they are compelled by particular circumstances and consequently act as if they were monosexual. Even the "male hero" (*Maennerheld*) type and *Hirschfeld's* "genuine" homosexual is only apparently monosexual. A glance through the confessions disclosed by all writers is enough to convince one of this fact. *Hirschfeld* himself points out that it is to the credit of psychoanalysis that it has revealed

the transitory heterosexual cravings of the homosexual.

*The instinct of the homosexual originally is not
exclusively directed towards the same sex. Originally the homesexual is also bisexual.* But he represses his heterosexuality just as the heterosexual
must repress his homosexuality. *Blüher* who is unwilling to recognise a pathogenesis of homosexuality
for the 'male hero' type, contends that one could
claim with equal relevance that there is a pathogenesis of heterosexuality.

That is a fact. Every monosexuality is other
than normal or natural. *Nature has created us bisexual beings and requires us to act as bisexual
beings.* The purely heterosexual is always a neurotic in a certain sense, that is, the repression of
the homosexual components already creates a predisposition to neurosis, or is in itself a neurotic
trait shared by every normal person. The psychology of paranoia, for whose investigation we are
indebted to the genius of *Freud*, shows us the extreme result of this process of repression on one
side, just as homosexuality shows us the other side
of the same process.

There is no homosexual who is not more or less
neurotic, that condition being due to the repression
of the heterosexuality. The repression is a purely
psychic process and has nothing to do with degeneration. Homosexuality is not a product of

degeneration in the ordinary sense. It is a neurosis and displays the etiology of a neurosis, as we shall prove later.

I revert to *Hirschfeld*. Regarding the relationship of neurosis and homosexuality he states:

"1. Pronounced physical and mental stigmata of degeneration are relatively rare among homosexual men and women; at any rate such signs are not more frequent in proportion to the total number of homosexuals than among the heterosexuals of both sexes.

"2. On the other hand we find frequently and not merely as a result of homosexuality, *a greater instability of the nervous system* (frequently shown in the periodic character of endogenous temperamental instability) (*endogene Stimmungsschwankungen*).

"3. The family of the homosexual often contains a larger number of nervous persons and such as deviate from the normal sexual type. (*Hirschfeld, l.c., p.* 338).

Hirschfeld also emphasizes the labile character of the nervous system among homosexuals pointing to the large number of abnormal sexual types in the family of the homosexual. That undoubtedly is a correct observation. It may be explained in two ways: (1) as the result of heredity; (2) as a consequence of a common environment. The extent to which these two factors are at work in particular instances may be ascertained only on the basis of specific inquiries.

I can state from my own professional experience that the parents of homosexuals always show abnormal character traits. With remarkable frequency male homosexuals have mothers who are melancholic, or subject to depressions or who are advanced hystericals. All gradations are found, from the emotional, domineering type of woman to the solitary, quiet, submissive woman who becomes a prey to melancholia and eventually must be interned in some institution. Urlinds show just as frequently a pathologic father, a home tyrant, a drinker, morphine fiend, dissolute fellow, 'lady killer,' epileptic or hysterical. We will determine later to what extent such parents influence psychically their offspring and the attitude of the children towards them. Careful investigation of life histories will make the subject plain.

How do the various writers explain the rise of homosexuality? We have mentioned already that *Hirschfeld* and all investigators deriving their inspiration from him hold to the theory that homosexuality is inborn. According to them, therefore, it is part of inexorable fate, like the law of the planets. . . .

But *Bloch* finds the condition baffling in spite of all the explanations furnished by *Hirschfeld* and reverting to the latter's chemical theory (*andrin* and *gynecin*) he concludes:

"(1) The so-called 'undifferentiated' stage of the sexual instinct (*Max Dessoir*) is often eliminated when the sexual instinct becomes directed towards a definite particular sex among heterosexuals or homesexuals before the advent of puberty. Homosexuality shows a definite, clear direction of the sexual instinct towards the same sex long before puberty.

"2. A comprehensive theory of homosexuality must also explain the extreme cases, particularly male homosexuality coupled with complete virility.

"3. Sexual parts and genital glands cannot determine homosexuality in those possessing typical normal male genitalia and testicles; neither can the brain itself be the determining factor in genuine homosexuality, because homosexuality cannot be rooted out by the strongest conscious and unconscious heterosexual influences brought to bear upon thought and phantasy,—the condition developing in spite of such influences.

"4. Since as a predisposition (not as sexual instinct) homosexuality appears long before puberty and before the actual functioning of the respective genital glands, it suggests that in homosexuals some physiologic action pertaining to 'sexuality' but not necessarily related to the functioning of the genital

glands undergoes some subtle change as the result
of which the sexual instinct is turned from its goal.

"5. The condition suggests chemical changes,
alterations in the chemism of sexual tension, the
latter being fairly independent of the activity of
the sexual glands proper, as is shown by the fact
that it may be preserved among eunuchs and others
who undergo castration." (*Bloch, loc. cit.* p. 589).

Further he states: "In my opinion the anatomic
contradiction, the biologic monstrosity of a womanly, or unmanly psyche in a typical male body or a
womanly-unmanly sexual psyche in the presence of
normally appearing and functioning male genitalia
can be solved only if we take into consideration this
intercurrent third factor. The latter may be
traceable to some embryonal disturbance in the
sexual chemism. That would also explain why
homosexuality often appears in the midst of
healthy families as a singular manifestation, having
no relation to any possible hereditary transmission
or degenerative taint. On the other hand, the contention of *v. Roemer* that homosexuality is a re-
generative process has hardly any points to support it. The root of the riddle of homosexuality
lies here. At least I conceive it to be a riddle.
With my theory I endeavor to cover merely the
facts and the probable physiologic relationship of
homosexuality with particular reference to the biologic aspect of the problem and to do it more closely

than the previous theories have done it. But my theory does not attempt to explain the ultimate origin of the relatively frequent condition known as homosexuality.

"I do not claim to be able to penetrate into the last ultimate causes. This remains a riddle to be solved. But from the standpoint of culture and procreation homosexuality appears to be a meaningless and purposeless dysteleological manifestation, like many another natural appearance, such as, for instance, the vermiform appendix in man. In a former chapter I have already pointed out that the progress of culture has been in the direction of a sharper differentiation of sexes, that the antithesis male and female, becomes progressively sharper. Sexual indifference, genital transition-forms are of primitive character and *Eduard v. Mayer* is correct when he holds that homosexuality was much more widespread during the prehistoric age than it is today and considers it as common, genetically, as heterosexual love. Through heredity, adjustment and differentiation, culture has progressively repressed the homosexual leanings." (*Bloch, loc. cit.* p. 590.)

Concerning these novel theories of homosexuality I must remark: *It is not correct that the homosexuals before puberty show an exclusive definite inclination towards their own sex and only towards their own.* The truth is that like all other persons, the homosexuals show a bisexual period (the undifferentiated stage of *Max Dessoir*) before puberty. Only they forget their heterosexual experiences. The truth is that a comprehensive theory of homosexuality ought to explain also the extreme cases, specifically male homosexuality coupled with complete preservation of vitality and female homosexuality with the preservation of all feminine characters. Such cases are covered neither by *Hirschfeld's* theory nor by that of *Bloch*. The third point is equally pertinent. It cannot be a question of brain and genital gland. Chemical influences are likely, but difficult to prove.

The baffling feature of the problem is due to the fact that the attempt has been made to explain all cases of homosexuality on the basis of a single plan.

As a matter of fact homosexuality may develop in a number of ways and each one must be taken into consideration. That the genital glands play a role in homosexuality seems to me very likely. But while these influences may be suspected they cannot be proven. What I am able to prove on the basis of my data are the psychic factors.

Nor must we forget that not only does the body influence the mind, but that the reverse is also true: the psyche builds up the body in accordance with its predispositions. We find that the artist's physiognomy differs from that of the artisan, and the physician's differs from that of the attorney.

The mind also models the body. A man who feels himself woman-like and who longs to be a woman will unconsciously adopt woman's ways and imitate woman. In the course of time even his appearance will be womanly. Possibly—that agrees with my view—the transformation is conditioned by glandular changes. We may presuppose that, but the notion appertains to the realm of hypothesis, which I prefer to avoid.

All writers sem to neglect the powerful role of the psychic factors. These factors may seem unreal to the upholder of mechanistic theories. Unfortunately most physicians underestimate the power of the unconscious wish as a plastic and synthetising energy within the human organism. The wish to be a man may raise boys to manliness; the wish to remain a child hinders development towards adulthood; the wish to be a woman makes for femininity. Any one familiar with *Pawlow's* investigations of the 'conditioned reflex' will readily see that certain particular wishes may exert a definite influence upon the activity of the genital glands. The wishes are certainly capable of influencing the appearance, action, activity and features of the individual.

When a boy acts like a girl, it does not necessarily mean that he has that kind of a predisposition. It may only signify his identification with his mother or with a sister.

Very clearly on this point is the testimony of a case of which I find an account in *Hirschfeld's* book.

A homosexual woman writes: "I was born in the country, where my father owned a large estate, and there I was brought up till my 14th year. I was the youngest. My oldest brother had girlish ways about him and was mother's pet rather than father's, whose favorite child, in turn, was my eldest sister. On my part I am the thorough image of my father in all character traits and in my sensuous predisposition as well. In later years father had often said: 'With you and Ludwig (the elder brother) nature made a mistake; you should have been a boy and Ludwig a girl.' Nevertheless I am certain that father knew nothing about homosexuality, also that my brother was not homosexual. My peculiar predisposition showed itself already while I was a child, for it was always my greatest desire to be a boy. As a child two or three years of age, I put on some of father's clothes, played with his cap and promenaded around the yard with his walking stick." (*Hirschfeld, loc. cit.*, p. 43).

We see clearly that this young woman identified herself with her father. She wanted to be a man like her father.

The remarks of *Ulrichs* (*vid. Inclusa*, p. 27 ffl.) may be understood in the same sense: "As a child the urning shows an unmistakable predisposition towards girlish occupations, intercourse with girls,

girlish games, and playing with dolls. Such a
child is very sorry that it is not 'boy-like' to play
with dolls, that Santa Claus does not bring him also
dolls and that he is not allowed to play with his
sister's dolls. Such a child shows interest in sew-
ing, knitting and cutting, in the soft and delicate
texture of girls' clothes, such as he, too, would like
to wear, and in the colored silks and ribbons of
which he delights to abstract some specimens as
keepsakes. He avoids contact with boys, he avoids
their plays and games. The play horse leaves him
indifferent. Soldier games, so much in favor with
boys do not attract him. He avoids all boyish
rough plays, such as snow-balling. He likes ordinary ball games but only with girls. He throws
the ball with the girl's light and stilted arm movement not with a boy's free and powerful arm swing.
Any one who has occasion to observe a boy urning
and does it carefully may verify these or similar
peculiarities. Is that all only imagination? I
had observed in myself long ago the peculiarities
mentioned above and, moreover, they always impressed me, although I did not at first recognize
their female character. In 1854 I related the facts
to a relative of mine, intimating that they must
have some bearing on my sexuality. He scorned
the idea and I yielded to his opinion at the time.
But in 1862 I took up that matter again with him:
meanwhile I had had opportunity to observe other

urnings and I noted that the female *habitus* re-
curred in every one, although not precisely with the
same particular features. But the female *habitus*
differs also among women with regard to certain details. In my case, as a boy of 10 or 12 years of
age, how often my dear mother sighed as she exclaimed: 'Karl, you are not like other boys.' How
often she warned me: 'You will grow up a queer
fellow, if nothing worse!' " (*Hirschfeld, l. c.* p.
117).

What do these fine observations prove? Any
one who understands the playful character of
children, their early directed psyche, must recognise that such conduct results through the influence
of a wish.

No—these observations do not prove at all that
the contrary sexual feeling is innate. *Hirschfeld*
contends: "these accounts (referring to previous
statements) show a remarkable absence of tenderness among the urning girls. An expert thoroughly familiar with their psyche, not without reason
states that we must watch the girl who passes
carelessly by a looking glass without stopping in
front of it when dressing and we must watch the
boy who clings with pleasure to the looking glass
returning to it again and again, for thereby both
betray early their homosexual nature." (*Hirschfeld, loc. cit.* p. 119). I see nothing in these state-

ments but an attempt on his part to differ from the other colleagues.

Finally I turn to my own conception of homosexuality, formulated, on the basis of psychoanalytic data and as an outgrowth of the teachings of *Freud*.

All persons originally are bisexual in their predisposition. There is no exception to this rule. Normal persons show a distinct bisexual period up to the age of puberty. The heterosexual then represses his homosexuality. He also sublimates a portion of his homosexual cravings in friendship, nationalism, social endeavors, gatherings, etc. If this sublimation fails him he becomes neurotic. Since no person overcomes completely his homosexual tendencies, every one carries within himself the predisposition to neurosis. The stronger the repression, the stronger is also the neurotic reaction which may be powerful enough in its extreme form to lead to paranoia (Freud's theory of paranoia). *If the heterosexuality is repressed, homosexuality comes to the forefront. In the case of the homosexual the repressed and incompletely conquered heterosexuality furnishes the disposition towards neurosis. The more thoroughly his heterosexuality is sublimated the more completely the homosexual presents the picture of a normal healthy person. He then resembles the normal heterosexual. But like the normal hetero-*

sexual individual, even the "male hero" type displays a permanent latent disposition to neurosis.

The process of sublimation is more difficult in the case of the normal homosexual than in the case of the normal heterosexual. That is why this type is extremely rare and why a thorough analysis always discloses typical neurotic reactions. The neurotic reactions of repression (Abwehr, Freud) are anxiety, shame, disgust and hatred (or scorn). The heterosexual is inspired with disgust at any homosexual acts. That proves his affectively determined negative attitude. For disgust is but the obverse of attraction. The homosexual manifests the same feeling of disgust for woman, showing him to be a neurotic. (Or else he hates woman.) For the normal homosexual—if there be such a type—would be indifferent towards woman. These generalisations already show that the healthy person must act as a bisexual being.

We know only one race of people who recognised formally the bisexual nature of man: the Greeks. But we must recognise also that the Greeks had attained the highest level of physical and cultural development. We shall have to inquire into the reasons why homosexuality fell into such disrepute and why the example of the Greeks found no imitation among the moderns, despite the recognition accorded the tremendous cultural achievements of the ancient Greeks. That will be done later. We conclude:

There is no inborn homosexuality and no inborn heterosexuality. There is only bisexuality.[1] *Monosexuality already involves a predisposition to neurosis, in many cases stands for the neurosis proper.*

The theory is not a novel one. New is only its association with neurosis. The merit to have been the first to express it belongs to *Kiernan* (*Medical Standard,* 1888). *Kiernan* started with the fact that all lower animals are bisexual and conceived homosexuality as a retrogression to the primitive hermaphroditic form of animal existence. We must note this theory as we shall have occasion to revert to it when discussing the predisposition to neurosis. *Chevalier* (*Inversion Sexuelle,* 1893) also begins his inquiry with a consideration of the aboriginal bisexuality of the fœtus. Two other investigators may be mentioned in this connection: *Lombroso,* to whom belongs the credit of having called attention to the manifestations of retrogression (*atavism*) and *Binet,* who maintains that homosexuality arises when the aboriginal undifferentiated sexual instinct (consequently the bisexual instinct) is aroused through some early experience in

[1] Hirschfeld emphasizes the fact that homosexuality has nothing to do with organic bisexuality. He states:

"I deem it important to point out this fact: *The most extreme* deviation of sexual type approaching the opposite sex, such as hypertrophy of the clitoris and full facial hair growth in the female, or hypospadia penis-scrotalis and gynecomasty in the female are found linked with heterosexuality more often than with homosexuality."

assoc'ation with a person of the same sex. Here
we have an adumbration of the theory of infantile
trauma which plays such a tremendous role in
Freud's work. In the following chapters a number of cases will be recorded clearly illustrating the latent influence of infantile experiences.

But we must guard against assuming as true all
the traumas which are reported to us. Some of the
incidents are interpolated into the life history and
only subsequently assume significance. But nothing
is so dangerous in psychology as one-sidedness.
The etiology of homosexuality is a particularly
fruitful field in which to prove, here and there, the
role of infantile traumatic experiences. *Krafft-
Ebing* holds that *Binet's* theory will not stand close
critical analysis but expresses himself very unfav-
orably regarding the importance of psychologic relations as a whole. He states: "Psychic forces are
not sufficient to explain so serious a degenerative
process." This depreciation of psychic influences
was not very surprising at a time when the prevalent tendency was to explain nearly everything
through heredity or taint.

Before attempting to give an exposition of the
psychologic theory of homosexuality I must discuss
the relations between homosexuality and neurosis.
All investigators, we have already seen, agree that
a relationship exists between them. The question

is: does the homosexual become neurotic because he
fears coming into conflict with the penal laws, because he feels his unfortunate predisposition is
something contrary to nature (to adopt his own
expression),—briefly because he is homosexual, or
is he homosexual because he is neurotic?

Here we naturally encounter the need of defining
the meaning of neurosis. What is neurosis and
who is neurotic? I call neurotic the person who
has not successfully overcome the asocial cravings
which he perceives to be unethical. I call asocial
cravings all instincts which society rejects as con-
flicting with its cultural demands. That in itself
shows that the essence of neurosis must differ in
different countries. In one instance we find repression of normal sexuality, because sexual
activity itself is considered unmoral. (Example: the
properly brought up girl in good society who must
remain coy.) In another, we find a struggle with
instincts which society decrees as morbid. (Example: the actress who maintains many friendships
and must suppress her homosexual longings.) In
the same way criminal tendencies may play a role
in the development of a neurosis. The neurosis is
the result of the struggle between instinct and inhibition. There are, therefore, two paths for the
development of the neurosis: a strong instinctive
craving which naturally endeavors to break through
the inhibitions and powerful inhibitions which re-

duce to a minimum the voicing of sexual needs even under the impulsion of strong instincts.

The predisposition to neurosis, therefore, is intimately linked with our instincts. The progression of the human race requires the frequent suppression of certain instincts and every step in ethical and cultural progress involves giving up some portion of instinctive cravings. The laws are a protection of society against the instinctive cravings of its members. Society tolerates but a portion of the instincts to a certain extent and all others it outlaws as asocial. The evolution of the race may eventually reach a stage wherein the instincts will have been placed altogether at the service of society: the domestication of the instinctive cravings. This is the meaning of the struggle of centuries between brain and spinal cord. The results of this struggle may be determined only if we contrast a truly aboriginal man with a typical representative of culture. What remarkable progress has been attained in the conquest of instinct! Society goes a step further. It takes care that individuals possessing asocial instincts should be unable to propagate their kind. Criminals are rendered innocuous, the asocial person finds the environment unfavorable and disappears.

But—as I have already stated in my book, *Die Träume der Dichter* [1]—the creative urge of nature

[1] English version by J. S. Van Teslaar, in preparation.

does not mollify man's asocial requirements. The struggle between nature and culture keeps up unabated and the result is neurosis. All paraphilias are a compromise between instinct and repression.

I must revert here to my theory of neurosis which I have expressed first in my work entitled, *Die Träume der Dichter*.[1] The neurotic is a retrograded type. He represents a conquered stage of human evolution. He must personally undergo the struggle through which the human race as a whole has already passed. The ontogenesis of culture! Whenever nature attempts the creation of something great, powerful or sublime it turns to the great reservoir of its past. Recessive types manifest more powerful instincts. The neurotic, criminals and the specially gifted persons have that in common. Three paths are open to the man with heightened instincts: he sublimates his selfish tendencies, his criminal cravings, his asocial attitude derived from previous epochs and becomes a creator (poet, painter, sculptor, musician, prophet, inventor, etc.); he works out his instincts untrammelled and becomes a criminal; or the sublimation is but partly successful and he becomes a neurotic.

My theory of homosexuality thus links itself to the view of *Lombroso*. The homesexual, in the first place, is a recessive character. He shows a precocious development of an instinct which does not

[1] Verlag J. F. Bergmann, Wiesbaden, 1913. Vid. note above.

fit the requirements of culture; but biologically he stands nearer the aboriginal bisexual predisposition of mankind than the normal person who is typical of the current age. This conflict manifests itself in various over-compensations, so that the neurotic advances beyond his age and becomes a creator of the future. I must ask my readers to consult my works quoted above for further details on this subject. I have here merely stated in brief what may have a bearing on our present theme.

The specially gifted, the artist, the criminal and the neurotic manifest the same characteristic: overstressing of instinctive cravings. The criminal carries out his promptings, the artist sublimates them in his works (*Shakespeare* conceived so many murders and that saved him from becoming a murderer . . . states *Hebbel*) while the neurotic meets in them his unsolvable conflicts. He is the criminal without the criminal's courage to commit asocial deeds. He is the Don Juan of phantasy, the Marquis de Sade of his own day dreams, the Jack the Ripper, without knowing it.

These considerations justify the assumption that poets, artists and neurotics must show a precocious development of the instinctive cravings, particularly of the sexual. That is in fact the case. With regard to artists this is well known,[1] the fact has

---

[1] *Cf. Dichtung und Neurose*, J. F. Bergmann. Authorized English version by James S. Van Teslaar.

been repeatedly mentioned as typical of criminals
and with regard to neurotics the analysts have been
able to prove it again and again.

We may now appreciate why all investigators
found that the sexual instinct awakens early in all
homosexuals. I want to make myself clear. We
owe to psychoanalysis the recognition of the fact
that the sexual instinct awakens early in all persons,
—a fact I have pointed out already during my pre-
Freudian period in my essay on *"Coitus during
Childhood."* But most persons repress their infantile memories and later recall nothing about these
occurrences dating from their childhood. The
homosexual remembers everything and that fact is
pointed out as proof of his sexual precocity. Already as a child he knew that certain things per-
tain to the forbidden realm of the sexual. He repressed from memory numberless particular incidents among the vast number his memory could hold.
The fact of his precocity, he does not forget. But
at the same time all memories which do not happen
to fit into his system of ideas are either bedimmed
in consciousness or lost from memory altogether.
Sexual precocity is a fact brought out in all life
histories and confessions of homosexuals. And that
very sexual precocity shows us that the conditions
which lead to the repression of heterosexuality, are
traceable far back into the past and stretch well
beyond ordinary memory recall. Therefore,

Krafft-Ebing finds: "The sexual life of persons of this type is usually manifest very early and is abnormally strong. Not infrequently it is associated with other perverse manifestations, in addition to the perverted direction of the sexual instinct peculiar to this type of sexual feeling."

Further in the same work: "There are neuroses present (hysteria, neurasthenia, epileptoid states, etc.). Nearly always there is also present either temporary or permanent neurasthenia." (P. 259.)

We see now that the two statements correspond. The individual becomes neurotic because he is unable to overcome the abnormally strong instincts. Epilepsy as well as grand hysteria serve as means for releasing the abnormally stressed instincts during slumber states.[1] It would appear therefore that a certain relationship must exist between homosexuality and epilepsy; in fact we shall take the opportunity later to report in full a case illustrating that relationship.

These instincts involve not only homosexual and heterosexual cravings. They include also sadistic tendencies and mysophilia, koprophilia, necrophilia and particularly the linking of sexual and criminal tendencies. Neurosis represents them under grotesque changes, attenuations, transformations, substitutions and exaggerations, all having counterpart

[1] *Nervöse Angstzustaende. Die psychische Behandlung der Epilepsie,* 2nd edition, p. 336.

in the homosexual neurosis. The relations between homosexuality and sadism are particularly interesting and will be considered fully in the following pages.

We may formulate our notion of the development of homosexuality as follows: *A person with abnormally strong instinctive cravings is induced early in life to surround these cravings with inhibitions. The early awakening of his sexual instinct and its precocious functioning bring him into conflict. The processes of repression and of sublimation set in to deal with these cravings much earlier than in other persons. For one reason or another the heterosexual components are repressed and the homosexual are evolved. The heterosexual cravings are hemmed in and rendered useless by disgust, hatred or fear.*

Homosexuality arises out of bisexuality as a result of certain particular attitudes which become determined very early in life. But not always. Such traits may appear also relatively late in life. Why and under what conditions does that happen? In the chapters next following we propose to take up this problem.

II

The development of Sexuality—The Bisexual Ideal of all persons—The fundamental Law of Sexuality—The role of homosexuality in Neurosis —Womanly men and mannish women—Gerontophilia—Love of Prostitutes—The significance of Sexual symbols—Various masks of Homosexuality — Transvestites—A case of Transvestitism—The significance of the hose as a Symbol—Love at first sight—The critical age—The pleasure Seeker—The case of a man passing through the critical age—Neurotic types of homosexuality—The Don Juan type— Psychoanalysis of a Don Juan—Passionate falling in love during advanced age, significant—Analysis of a Don Juan.

Das Christentum gab dem Eros Gift zu trinken:—er starb zwar nicht daran, aber er entartete zum Laster.—Nietzsche.

II

Christianity has given Eros a poison cup;
Eros was not killed thereby but has been
turned into a taint.—Nietzsche.

Freud who supports the theory of bisexuality
with all the weight of his authority, points out that
hitherto we have entertained wrong notions concerning the nature of the relations between sexual
instinct and sexual goal. The sexual instinct is
at first independent of its object and owes not its
origin to the excitations roused by the sexual object. The earliest stage of man he has designated
as autoerotic and he has described for us the infantile form of onanism.

The development of sexuality may be conceived,
broadly, as follows: the first stage is autoerotic, although allerotic stimuli are also present (suckling
at the mother's breast, caressing of the infant, etc.).
The child is more sensitive to all forms of excitation and all vegetative functions are surcharged
with pleasurable feelings more strongly in him than
in the adult. Sexual life is autoerotic, but it is bi-

53

sexually autoerotic. The child makes no distinction between the persons to whom it is attached. Young or old, male or female,—it is all alike to him. But autoerotism is characteristic of this sexual life. Gradually this feature is overshadowed by the appearance of the all-erotic tendency. At first the child seeks to find the goal for its sexuality among the possible objects of his limited surroundings. Just as the first period of autoerotism is overcome so the normal fixation upon one's family must be eventually outgrown. (Thou shalt leave thy father and thy mother and follow thine husband!) But even during the earliest period all libidinous excitations are distinctly bisexual. This bisexuality persists until the period of puberty, that is, throughout that stage of sexual indifference, of which *Desoir* also speaks. But the tendency to bisexuality is unable to withstand the powerful stress of puberty. The girlish boy becomes a man, the tomboy girl becomes a young woman. The development of the secondary sexual characters displace man's heterosexual characteristics with the stamp of monosexuality. Usually at this time there develops also a decisive struggle against homosexuality leading, sooner or later, to the complete suppression of that tendency. (Naturally there are exceptions, as some persons retain their bisexual character traits without trouble throughout life.) *I have not examined a person thus far in whom I failed to recognise clearly the signs of juvenile homosexuality.*

It is proper to hold that the neurotics show themselves functionally bisexual. Among the neurotics the males often have little or no beard growth, plump and roundish bodily figure, high voice and soft facial features, especially nose and lips; they have small hands, small feet, their penis is remarkably small, scant hairy growth upon their mons veneris, cryptorchism (undescended testicle), hernias. On the other hand neurotic women show hairy growth on face, flat chest, strong, male figure—more angular than is characteristic of women,—large, full hands, large feet, disorders of menstruation including amenorrhea (complete suppression), infantile uterus, male larynx and deep voice. I do not maintain that this is invariably the case. Now and then I have met with exceptions; but I believe that a thorough investigation would support this contention.

The tendency to neurosis is due to the strong instinctive cravings which manifest themselves bisexually.

There is a process at work which I am inclined to designate as the fundamental law of sex. According to this law every individual tends to sum up all his instinctive sexual cravings in one image. Every person seeks the sexual ideal capable of satisfying all his sexual longings.

The sexual ideal of the ancients was, clearly, a bisexual being. Divinity is the ideal erotic goal magnified. The first divinities were always bisexual. They were either women with a penis or men with a female breast. The longing for the bisexual ideal may be traced throughout humanity. In his Banquet, *Plato* has excellently expressed this longing in the well-known words of *Aristophanes*.

We feel that we are utilizing but a portion of our sexual energy and that the remainder is allowed to remain fallow. The various sexual trends are sometimes so split up in life that no part of them is sufficient alone to furnish the whole driving power for the proper sexual activity. This is the case with those who apparently manifest a diminished sexual craving, as *Freud* and *Havelock Ellis* have observed with reference to certain homosexuals. This condition is only apparent, however, and analysis discloses that it is not real. Persons of this type, apparently asexual, really vaccilate back and forth between various possible sexual goals never reaching the stage of aggression, because they are incapable of attaining a sufficient summation of sexual libido. Their libido splits up into a number of autoerotic acts, through which the fore-pleasure instead of centering on a focus is expended in small instalments, as I have pointed out when I described the various forms of cryptic onanism.

I repeat: the ideal of every person is to be able to concentrate all libido upon a single goal. That explains why the homosexual does not seek the typical male, except in the rarest instances. *Freud* has drawn our attention to this apparent contrast. Many homosexuals, particularly those who, themselves, possess strong virility, do not seek out the complete male for their ideal, but the womanly male. They prefer the female type of man, men in female clothes, or of female habitus,—a fact which has shaped a great deal the course of male prostitution. The male prostitute endeavors always to imitate the female through the use of trinkets, corset, the adoption of articles of female apparel, close shaving, peculiar gait and speech.

What the homosexual seeks consciously the latent homosexual, as we designate the neurotic and, in smaller measure, every individual who acts exclusively as a heterosexual, endeavors to attain through vague yearnings which he fails to understand but which are strong enough to break through.

Let us now turn our attention to these hidden forms of sexuality, before attempting to explain the rise of the manifest and of the overt forms of homosexuality. Among the latent homosexuals who struggle with all the problems of bisexuality which to them appear unsolvable and inscrutable, and who have recourse to various compromises which bring them some temporary relief, we may find the various transitional stages leading all the way up to the overt forms of homosexuality.

Latent homosexuality is a fact, not uncovered by analysis, but analysis has tremendously enlarged our understanding of the mental processes involved. The deeper we penetrate into the psychic mechanism of the neuroses and psychoses, the more vital appears to us the role of homosexuality. The difference between my method of analysis and the customary anamnesis is shown nowhere so clearly, as in connection with the disclosures of the neurotics regarding their hidden homosexuality. No other component of the sexual instinct undergoes repression to such an extent or shifts so far from the sphere of ordinary consciousness. I know persons who have frankly adopted a great many forms of paraphilia but have completely repressed the homosexual component of their condition. I have analysed, for instance, a young woman who had quite an eventful life history. She became neurotic because she could neither master nor suppress her homosexuality. Like all other neurotics she skilfully covered her homosexuality and this trait of hers remained unknown to her consciousness.

It will be helpful to the beginner, therefore, to know the various disguises which serve as masks for homosexuality. As is well known, all neurotic symptoms are the results of compromise and they cover, on the one hand, as much as they disclose, on the other. The tendency to adopt compromises, which is typical of the split personality, is a subject worthy of special consideration. The most antagonistic impulses are stressed and summed up under the same symptom. This tendency to adopt compromises governs the mental life of the neurotic. It is seen in dreams as well as in political life, in artistic products no less than in neurotic symptoms. If the need to adjust opposing tendencies under some compromise is not met successfully a condition of uncertainty arises,—of vacillation and doubt. Doubt is the result and the sign of unsuccessful compromises.

This superficial building up of compromises is seen most clearly in the case of homosexuality. The neurotic endeavors to focus the most divergent tendencies of his psyche upon the same goal. His ideal is a being at once male, female, and infantile (and perhaps also beast and angel at the same time).

The neurotics always describe their ideal in a way which corresponds to this polymorphous picture. The males rave about women of a strikingly manly bearing; heavy, angular figure, flat chest, energetic, bony facial features, short hair, deep voice, traces of facial hair or of a mustache. The hidden bisexual ideal is thus partially fulfilled (Woman with penis or man with vagina!). The repressed cravings, thus partly freed, serve during sexual agression and further the attainment of gratification.

When nature fails to meet these needs, external features, such as dress and ornaments are brought into play to enhance the illusion. The symbol is made to replace reality. Men fall in love with women who wear tights (or who sport mannish hats, officers' coats, walking canes, etc.) and consequently they are attracted by actresses, fencers, cycle-riders, mountain-climbers, horseback-riders, or by girls whom they chance to see in under-pants. Others require of their sexual objects the adoption of various male symbols before their libido is roused. The woman, appeals to them, for instance, at best, wearing a military blouse, a mannish hat, or in some male attitude or other, capable of yielding a suggestion of something genuine.

Women display parallel tendencies. They fall in love with men who are beardless, gynecomastic, men who have a large panniculus adiposus, broad hips, delicate throat, female voice, or who wear long coats and long hair. I will quote here only a few examples: the priest, the physician in his hospital coat, particularly surgeons with graceful arms, female impersonators, beardless men, or men with high voices who perfume themselves and wear bracelets, and artists with long, flowing locks of hair are likely to prove very attractive. (Perhaps the great erotic attraction exercised by all artists is due to their pronounced bisexual character.)

Physical factors are also of great significance.

Women who smoke, ride, go mountain climbing and who are generally aggressive, make a very strong impression upon the neurotic. This is true also about the influence of men with strong womanly features upon women. Many neurotic men dream of being overpowered. (The "pleasure without guilt" principle!). Energetic women fascinate them, just as delicate, sensitive men fascinate the hysterical woman.

Less known are other masks of homosexuality which I now mention. The love of old women (gerontophalia) and passion for children often covers a homosexual tendency. Persons deviating from the complete male or female type often prove irresistible for the same reason. Age eventually wipes out the typical secondary sexual characters. Man becomes like an old woman and old women acquire remarkable male features (including mustache) and male habits. Children also may figure as a strong bisexual attraction since they lack the secondary sexual characters.

A peculiar cryptic form under which male homosexuality manifests itself, is the love of prostitutes. The unconscious factor which here appeals to the homosexual component of the sexual libido is the fact that the body of the prostitute has been previously enjoyed by other men.[1]

[1] Hirschfeld relates several instances illustrating how heterosexual potence may be increased by the fires of homosexual

This process,—mediation through the other sex,—
plays a great role in homosexuality in various
other ways. The prostitute may be enjoyed only
in the presence of one or more male witnesses. The
carrying out of coitus jointly in one room, looking

passion: A merchant relates: "I am able to carry out sexual
intercourse with women, only if I keep thinking of the man
who possessed the woman before me." A young workingman
from Berlin relates: "When I was 17 years of age and I saw
young men of my age pick out sweethearts for themselves I did
the same. Later, as man, it seemed natural to me to get a
woman, although my own inclination had little to do with it.
The physical excitation necessary for the carrying out of the
sexual act I could rouse in myself only by thinking of some
male person. This sort of thing exhausted me and after a
time I decided to give it up. I felt myself strongly attracted
to a relative at that time. He was younger and as I had
greater influence over women I helped him by putting him in
touch with some and so we often carried out coitus together.
Seeing him [go at it so hotly] excited me tremendously and
then I carried out coitus without any difficulty." The proprie-
tor of a German hotel also relates that, before intercourse
with his wife, he was in the habit of rousing his passion by
kissing his head waiter. This furnished him the requisite sexual
preparedness and as quickly as possible he hurried to his wife,
whose bed was in the next room." Hirschfeld writes further:
"These sketches from life I want to conclude with the account
of a patient who consulted me for sexual hyperesthesia which
in his case was so keen that seeing the statuettes of naked
children ornamenting the Berlin castle bridge while crossing
it was enough to cause erection. He was a merchant, 42 years
of age. In order to obtain potentia coeundi it was necessary
for him not only to think, but also to speak aloud of some
pleasing man, in some such manner: "Did you notice that
servant of the count's, who called for a bundle this forenoon,
how did you like him? A neat boy, what? His livery seemed
quite new! Didn't you think it fitted him a bit too tightly?
How old should you say he was?" Only by carrying on such
talk with his wife, and he had to exercise the greatest in-
genuity in order to cover his object while doing so, was he
able to achieve ejaculation, and to beget children,—he was the
father of three."

on, or allowing onlookers, also betray this motive besides others.

In many cases the form of sexual intercourse preferred betrays a latent homosexuality. Men choose to lie underneath, or carry out coitus a posteriori, or per anum. Women show corresponding preferences. They attain supreme enjoyment only if they are on top during intercourse. Many paraphilias (fellatio, cunnilingus) betray a homosexual trend besides showing sexual infantilism.

Various external signs may betray a strong homosexual trend or mark a sudden outbreak of it. Men suddenly decide to cut or shave off their beard. They unexpectedly turn their interests to sports which give them the opportunity of watching men undressed. They become passionate fans around prize rings, are seen at sun bathing establishments and sporting places, or rave about the culture of nakedness as a hygienic fad, etc. Women suddenly find that they cannot possibly wear their long hair and decide to cut it short. Sometimes they do it without telling their husband so as to 'pleasantly' suprise him. They change fashions, take readily to English jackets, tight coats and Girardi hats and begin to show tremendous interest in the emancipation of women.

Joint suicide as a mask is a subject to which I can only refer briefly. Persons who do not have the courage to live together are the ones likely to commit suicide jointly. The suicide of two friends, male or female, is often due to unsatisfied homosexuality, however ideal, apparently, the motives may be. A life which does not yield to the full gratification craved by the unconsciously operating instincts, loses its zest. *Frenssen* states: "Sun, moon and stars no longer carry any message to one who has lost interest in them; a thing degenerates unless cultivated assiduously; it is so with everything. Indifference deadens; love breathes life into everything."

I have already pointed out in my treatise on Onanism that those who have not given up the habit may give expression to tendencies distinctly homosexual through their autoerotic acts. The feeling of guilt is due in part, although only in part, to this cause. The greater hold the habit has upon the individual the stronger also seems the homosexual trait back of it. Many onanists are asocial in their inclinations and avoid group life. But I know a number who are enthusiastic 'joiners,' belonging to numerous organisations and always eager to assume honorary membership in all sorts of clubs. That female lawyers are particularly apt to show homosexual tendencies is well known and the fact is often exploited in the comic papers under slight disguise.

Lastly, I must mention another important form of masked homosexuality: the artistic. Poets whose preference is the delineation of female characters are partly homosexual. They perceive accurately the female emotions, they are able to portray with fidelity the life of that sex, because they carry within their breast, as it were, a goodly portion of womanhood. *Chamisso* described so wonderfully womanly love, because he himself was largely woman, as his portrait is enough to indicate. Painters may also show the reverse tendency. They paint preferably male scenes or, as sculptors, create statues of men. Their appraisal of esthetic values betrays their hidden homosexuality. Some artists find the male figure much more beautiful than the female, others find the male body repulsive. An overstressed aversion betrays the homosexual trend as clearly as an emotionally overstressed preference.

The choice of a pseudonym may also prove a characteristic sign. Just as the transvestites (wearers of clothes of opposite sex) clearly show their homosexual peculiarities thereby so do men choosing a female pseudonym for their contributions or writings, often betray their homosexuality by the act. Of course, in the case of women, the choice of a male nom de plume is determined partly by the well known common notion that works obtain a wider circulation if attributed to male author-

ship. At any rate, it betrays a desire to be taken
for a man, by the readers, at least. A woman
writer whom I know and who is active under a male
nom de plume has told me, as an objection to this
view, that she is decidedly interested in men. She
confessed herself a Messalina. But back of such
an unsatisfied craving, there stands, as I have already mentioned, homosexuality, the blind instinct,
ungratified. This woman preferred relations with
well known "women killers," typical Cassanovas.
Obviously, the thought of the numerous female conquests must have furnished here the chief attraction.
Such men carry about them the aroma of many
women. They must be proven masters of the art
of love and a woman is disposed to expect of them
special thrills and, possibly, new refinements of the
art; but the heroes, as a rule, when tried fail to
come up to the expectations lodged in them; they in
turn become easily tired of their new conquest. The
unsatisfied homosexual male is incapable of gratifying completely the love hungry homosexual
woman. (That is the tragedy back of many unhappy marriages.) It is also significant that this
woman, who otherwise had allowed herself an unusual degree of freedom about sexual matters, looked
upon homosexuality as Tabu.

I have mentioned only a small number of the
possible masks of homosexuality. Some of the

screens are so transparent they cannot but be noticed even by those who are still novices in psycho-analytic matters. One marries a girl, for instance, after falling in love with that girl's brother; or a girl marries the brother of her homosexual choice, as I have clearly shown in connection with the highly instructive case history No. 93, in my study of Anxiety States.

For this reason a friend's wife may be a very dangerous person and this mediation of homosexuality through a third person has often been the cause of terrific household dramas. I know men who are regularly prone to fall in love with their friends' sweethearts, naturally, without suspecting that back of this proclivity there stands the hidden passion for their friend.

In conclusion I may point out another very significant mask of homosexuality. I refer to psychic impotence, which shows itself particularly during attempted intercourse with respectable women. Men potent with prostitutes but unable to carry out coitus with a 'decent' woman, are latent homosexuals whose libido is sufficiently roused in the presence of the prostitute by the realisation that the woman has been used before by another man. Of course, a relative impotence of this character has many other determinants. But the factor here mentioned is never absent.

The study of this cryptic form of homosexuality alone will enable us to appreciate the inestimable role of bisexuality in the mental life of modern man.

Other forms of masked homosexuality, manifested in phobias and compulsion, I must mention only superficially. There are men who become extremely uneasy if some other man walks directly behind them, men who are unable to remain with another man alone in a room, men who always dream of scenes in which some man points a revolver or knife at them, or who have the uncomfortable feeling that some hard substance, perhaps nothing more than an indurated cylindrical mass of fæces, is pressing within their rectum. With these peculiarities such men betray their homosexuality, just as the paranoiacs do with their delusions of persecution.

Women show similar phobias and more especially morbid anxieties often centering around servant girls. Women who change servant girls continually, who worry themselves over the servant problem or quarrel with the girls, or feel impelled to touch them (acts which really take the place of sexual deeds) are frequently homosexual. Similarly, various forms of fetichism may be a cover for homosexuality.

It is plainly obvious that the study of sexual masks promises to further immensely our knowledge about matters of sex. At the same time it is clear that the opposition of many circles to the new studies must remain a tremendous one. Possibly a great deal of the opposition to the new psychology has its roots in this very peculiarity of human nature. Their basic bisexual predisposition is precisely what men are least disposed to recognise.

These general statements I now propose to prove on the basis of various observations from my practice illustrating the great role played by the homosexual components in the love life of average men and women. This will show clearly why I never use such terms as "contrary," or "inverted" sexual feeling, and why I never speak of "inversion," or of "perversion," when I discuss homosexuality. The very purpose of this work is to bring out the homosexual components in the life of every person and to bring out the normal feature of that state. For normal is everything that is natural; *and from the standpoint of nature we are never monosexual and always bisexual.*

I regret that I must contradict so worthy an investigator as *Hirschfeld.* But I fail to understand the need of setting up, besides the hetero- and homosexuals, a third group, the so-called transvestites.[1] Among the transvestites (personifiers) we find the most pronounced examples of masked homosexuality and stressed bisexuality. This is a designation proposed by *Hirschfeld* for men who—obey-

[1] *Die Transvestiten. Eine Untersuchung ueber den Erotischen Verkleidungstrieb.* Alfred Pulvermacher. Berlin, 1910.

ing an overwhelming inner impulse—wear women's apparel and for women who similarly attire themselves in things belonging to a man's wardrobe. In the course of an extensive review (*Zentrbl. f. Psychoanalyse*, vol. I, p. 55.) I pointed out that it is unnecessary to consider the transvestites as a distinct sexual species, but that they are merely bisexual persons with strong homosexual leanings. *Hirschfeld* lays great emphasis upon the fact that the transvestites experience normal sexual feelings, being subject only to the impulsion to change their clothing for that of the opposite sex. Unfortunately here he takes into consideration only the conscious sexual manifestations. He considers merely the facts as they appear upon the surface neglecting the important mechanisms of repression and masking,—the tendency to play before, and with, one's self. The data obtained upon superficial examination must be subjected to careful analysis; then the results are most surprising. Analysis invariably reveals that there is no such thing as monosexuality and that the transvestites, like the homosexuals, have their repressions. The homosexual represses his heterosexuality, the transvestite his homosexuality. In his phantasy the man is a woman (the woman fancies herself the reverse) and thus he combines the two components of his libido. It were nothing less than doing vio-

lence to facts to attempt to distinguish the transvestites from the homosexuals.

As one reads carefully the cases published by
Hirschfeld, with an eye for signs of homosexuality,
one cannot fail to note characteristic traits of
homosexuality in every one of the cases. For instance, one of them carries out succubus *in coitu*,
which is clearly a symptom of latent homosexuality;
if he appears as a woman, the men who follow him
cause him nausea. Another was able to carry out
the heterosexual act only under the influence of
alchohol, and when going out in women's clothes was
fond of eating in the company of men and coquet-
ting with them. A third is repelled by the thought
of homosexual relations, but dreams of pregnancy,
plays succubus *in coitu*, and fancies that his wife is
a man. The fourth hugs his wife tightly, sinks his
nails into her ears, etc., so as to gain the illusion of
being overpowered through sheer force by some
man.

Then, most interesting of all, case 12: A man
who during four years of married life has carried
out coitus only once. This subject actually betrays an open inclination towards homosexuality,
which *Hirschfeld* declares is only apparent. . . .
How is one to determine between an apparent and
a real homosexual trend? In order to succeed in
that one must purposely overlook the phenomenon

of human bisexuality and be anxious to hold on at all costs to the notion that homosexuality is inborn and irreducible.

The transvestite last mentioned relates concerning his homosexuality: "About homosexuality I learned for the first time through reading the book: *Die Enterbten des Liebesgluecks.* Some passages gripped me powerfully, even more so than the works on masochism, of which I also had read a large number. As I had to renounce my womanly ideal (for reasons mentioned previously), it occurred to me to seek a man as the complement to my yearnings. For even the strongest woman wants to be beneath man during love. But I felt I needed a partner who should overpower and conquer me with some display of force. So I said to myself that such a role can be filled properly only by a man. A great deal of what I read in books about homosexuality confirmed me in this view."

If this is not a tell-tale rationalization of homosexuality—what may we designate as homosexuality?

Comments are hardly needed in this connection. On all sides and from all directions homosexuality is proven in the history of the case. But *Hirschfeld* finds that the tendency to homosexuality is only apparent and that the whole foundation of the subject's libido consists of transvestism. The homosexuality he looks upon as an incidental manifesta-

tion. But there are no 'incidental' manifestations
in our vita sexualis. A dream, which has also been
reported, shows conclusively that M., the subject,
was all along actuated by the thought: I wish I
were a woman. But there are passages in this case
history showing how highly the subject esteems the
male and proving that this wish is an infantile attitude and due to a feeling of inferiority. What else
should we conclude from the statement: "For the
genuine man, who belongs to the proudest specimens of his sex, sexual gratification is merely a
hygienic requirement, a form of physical release;
beyond that his wonderful creative spirit dwells in
higher realms . . . etc."

In the chapter devoted to masochism I explain
the meaning of a case like the above more fully.
The man wants to be a woman and to be overpowered. He is able to have relations with women,
if they assume the aggressive role. His mind insists upon the fictive notion: I am a woman and I
am forced to carry out this part. Naturally he
shifts towards homosexual acts. The male trait in
him tolerates no submissiveness. The female trait
lends itself readily to coercion. The neurosis consists in this suppression of the male components of
the sexual instinct.

A careful reading of the following case history
will show clearly the homosexual roots of the
tendency to personify the opposite sex:

Mrs. H. S. consults me on account of complete sexual frigidity during her marital relations. She is twenty-four years of age and had married at the age of 19. Her marriage was a love affair. She has always been of a loving and sensuous disposition so that from the age of 14 her mind was preoccupied mostly with sexual fancies and thoughts. At the age of 15 she fell in love with an uncle. His kisses roused her passion and she would have readily yielded to him. The father observed what was going on and forbade her uncle the house. She lived in the Country and met no men under circumstances which could have endangered her. She was 19 years of age when she first met her present husband and she fell rapidly in love with him. She withstood her parents' opposition and married the young man in a few months. Already during her engagement she said to her husband: "I don't believe one man will be enough for me. You must watch out for me. . ." During the first few weeks of married life her husband was impotent, and this drove her nearly to distraction. After her husband underwent some medical treatment he succeeded in rupturing her hymen and in a few months she became pregnant. For a short time during that first pregnancy she experienced complete orgasm. After that her feeling for her husband disappeared entirely and she felt very dissatisfied. Her whole character changed completely. Previously she had been happy, joyous, always in good humor. Now she became quiet, lived a retired existence, avoiding men in particular because she was afraid of them.

Deeper investigation of the case shows that, after the death of her father, to whom she felt attached by bonds of deepest affection, she became sexually anesthetic. The father was a very earnest, strong man who adored his pretty wife and he was a model of loyal and dutiful husband. The mother was an artist who, after the death of her husband, lost all interest in life. She could not stay alone and abandoned the country place to live with her daughter in the City. I suspected that the sudden onset of anesthesia probably coincided with the mother's arrival in the house. Might she not hide some special attachment for her mother?

She emphasized that she felt the greatest compassion for her mother, who had lost her support in life. For her mother's sake she would have gladly taken her father's place, if such a thing were possible. And further she declared:

"You would probably find it almost unbelievable, if I told you that I strongly wished I were a man, at the time. I kept thinking of mother all the time! You see—she is so pretty and young yet, so full of life! I also know that she is a very passionate woman. How could she get along without a man? Now, I must confess something, though it is very hard for me to express it. You know already a number of my pet fancies. But there is another which I have persistently kept from you till now. I wanted to put on father's clothes, as I have a few of them in my possession, and to go to mother's bed at night. I acquired a sort of an apparatus . . . for the purpose. But I did not quite have the courage. I put on the clothes but stayed in my room. I kept standing before the looking glass for hours, looking on."

"Did the clothes fit you?"

"To tell you the truth, I had used some of father's old suits for a long time before that. I got hold of them under all sorts of pretexts. I wrote him, for instance, that I wanted to give his unused clothes to a worthy poor man. Then I had them altered for a figure of my size and was glad to wear them while my husband was away. Already as a small girl I remember I was fond of wearing my brother's clothes."

"Do you recollect your thoughts while you were wearing your brother's clothes?"

"Oh, I do. I played I was papa. For a time I felt really dissatisfied because I was a girl. I envied all boys."

"Later, too, after you were married already?"

"Certainly! Do you know, I have never mustered enough courage to do something downright disloyal. But I was thinking, if I were a man, I could never remain true. I have always envied men. In fact, with my soul I felt myself more like a man."

"What were your feelings during the time you were in love with your husband?"

"I had plunged headlong into love and forgot all about my liking of men's clothes. During that time I felt altogether womanly. Especially when I became a mother. Then all my dreams about manliness disappeared."

"That was also the only time when you enjoyed your relations with your husband?"

"I have never thought of the two things together. But you are right. For a short time during that period I was entirely womanly, until father died. . . ."

"And your mother came to live with you!"

"Yes. . . that is so. . . . Do you mean, that then I wanted again to be a man? Now, I can confess to you that I always envied father on account of mama. I used to think that if I were a man, I should certainly be in love with mama."

The further analysis reveals interesting details. Repeatedly she dreams that she is a man and that she has a phallus. She dreams also that she urinates standing after the manner of men. She admits that, already as a child, she loved her mother passionately. She had also overheard a number of times her parents getting together in bed and once she watched them in the act of coitus, peeping through a key hole. She was deeply excited by what she saw and thought that her mother must have suffered great pain and that only the father found pleasure in the act. This infantile conception of male gratification has remained with her to this day. Her favorite expression: "If I should come again into the world I would want to be a man." The homosexual attitude towards the mother deprived her of libido during her marital relations.

I suggested that she should separate from her mother but she resented scornfully this suggestion. She would rather give up her husband. Some time later she actually did so. She now lives with her mother. I was greatly surprised one day, when she called on me clothed in male attire. She requested from me a certificate to the effect that she was an abnormal person and should be permitted to wear man's clothes. She had heard that in Berlin a number of women had been granted such a permit by the police on the strength of such a statement from a physician.

Upon being questioned regarding her sexual life she states that she now maintains relations with a man who, before the sexual embrace, puts on women's clothes. This rouses great orgasm in her. Regarding her relations to her mother her answers are elusive. But I must not think, she adds, that she is a "Urlinde." The thought of such persons only fills her with disgust. Her mother is now merely her dearest friend.

It is plain that this woman has repressed her homosexual love for her mother and is satisfied with the symbol of masculinity, the wearing of trousers. The man whom she meets in embrace, becomes for her a woman, through the wearing of feminine articles. Thus the two partners carry on a comedy in which the heterosexual act replaces the longed-for homosexual embrace.

I am familiar with a number of instances in which a man dressing like a woman, or the reverse, was the means of rousing sexual passion, or, at least, of increasing it enormously. Whenever this happens it is plainly a manifestation of latent homosexuality, —a condition of which *Blueher* appears to have a very poor opinion. Although he seems to agree with my views otherwise ("today it is no longer possible," he says, "to hold that homosexuality or heterosexuality is inborn; instead we must recognize that bisexuality is inborn in every individual, with a special predilection in one direction or the other,"), he makes a distinction between "healthful inversion" and an outbreak of latent homosexuality; one condition he considers aboriginal and in keeping with cultural development, while the other "arises out of the depths of the unconscious, through the removal of the inhibitions. . ." This view is also contrary to facts. *Blueher*, like *Hirschfeld*, is inclined to consider latent homosexuality as 'pseudo,' as something unnatural, and accordingly passes judgment upon it. The practical observations gathered in the course of my practice do not coincide with these theoretical assumptions. I know only one kind of homosexuality, and that is always inborn. Also, I find it always linked intimately with heterosexuality. Awareness of one's own homosexual tendency or lack of it is not a reliable guide. If the number of consciously homosexual persons be estimated at 2 per cent., we may confidently assert that there are 98 per cent. of persons who know nothing of their homosexual traits, or rather that they do not want to know anything about them.

As we become familiar with the various masks of homosexuality, we learn to appreciate surprising homosexual and heterosexual trends. I shall draw attention merely to the manifold significance of "trousers" in human love affairs. How often men fall in love with women only when and because they are seen in tights! I remember a number of classmates in high school, who had fallen in love with a singer, when they saw her in a role which she played wearing tights. *Grillparzer* apparently fell in love once in his life and very passionately. It was with the singer to whom he absent-mindedly sent his famous poem. She had appeared upon the stage as a Cherub in tights. The woman wearing the trousers is a by-word,—a typical compromise.

Through the medium of such compromises it becomes possible for the homosexual suddenly to act like a heterosexual person. *Hirschfeld*, who was the first to point out this fact, relates that a lieutenant of cavalry well known in the circle of Berlin urnings one day surprised his acquaintances with the announcement of his engagement and even more with the statement he had become fully heterosexual. Previous to that time he had loved only boys in girls' clothes but apparently he had found a woman of very youthful type, one who was able to satisfy both components of his libido. Symbols at times disclose tremendous power. The trousers figure as a symbol of masculinity. I remember the storm of popular indignation which arose once when some change in women's fashions threatened man's exclusive prerogative. The skirt and long hair are symbols of feminity. The symbol often furnishes the bridge across which traits, otherwise antagonistic, become fused.

The following case is an illustration:

Mr. E. W. has practiced onanism since he was five years of age and during the act was in the habit of thinking he was touching girls. Later he masturbated jointly with other school boys. They attempted pederastic acts, in the course of which he felt neither aversion nor pleasure. At 14 years of age he was seduced by a servant girl, and he went to her bed every night for a year. A poor scholar up till that time, he became subsequently one of the best in the class. After a time he became tired of her and he sought other opportunities which were easy to find. He maintains that up to his 20th year he has had intercourse with every one of the girls who served in his parents' house, and he estimates them to have been about twenty in number. It struck him that he could not always achieve orgasm. But he was always potent, so much so, sometimes the girls wondered. But he would become indifferent before reaching ejaculation. This happened to him with fat women who excited him tremendously and at the same time failed to satisfy him.

He began early to be interested in painting and made special efforts to experience the feeling of love; for the petty adventures with the servant girls did not involve the heart in the least. As he grew all women only appeared to him to be merely objects for the gratification of lust. He had all sort of love affairs but could be true to none for any length of time and did not always reach orgasm with them. He happened to try once the situs inversus and after that he found it always possible to bring about the orgasm. Coitus a posteriori was also a method which enabled him to attain this aim more easily than the normal position. He was already thirty years of age when he saw at a social affair a girl who appeared as a boy in a "living picture." He felt at once the greatest attraction for her. During the whole evening he kept her in his company, and he felt animated and inspired with the thought that he had found, at last, his soul affinity. A few weeks later he became engaged to her. The picture of her as a boy always floated before his mind. He married soon, experienced tremendous orgasm during coitus and felt himself very happily married. After a few years his potentia began to fail him and this worried him a great deal because he loved his wife tremendously and was ashamed to confess to her the true state of things. He became more frigid and finally his potentia failed him completely.

He came into his wife's room (they had separate rooms) while she was undressing. She was in her tights, the kind in which he had seen her in the role of a boy. At once this roused his passion and he threw himself upon his wife, covering her with kisses, against her protests, for she was very bashful. This happened in day time. His wife had never consented to coitus in day time before. But this time she was taken by surprise and as he pressed her for it, she called out, over and over: "What is the matter with you today!" He did not tell her the reason for his excitement; he was ashamed to request her to dress herself next time in tights.

He called to have this remarkable occurrence explained and to be cured of the peculiarity. Later he achieved potentia again but always he had to think of his wife as dressed in trousers. The man was an out-of-town resident and had come to Vienna only for the day. I was unable to find out much about the psychic roots of this condition. He recalled no infantile memories, but thought that the sight of his little sister in bloomers had already roused him. He was much interested in women's underwear and could have easily turned into a fetichist, one gathering a large assortment of women's underclothes. I advised him to confide in his wife and ask her for his sake to dress herself in the kind of apparel which appealed to him. That was, after all, a harmless desire which he shared with many other men.

A few years later I saw him again. He had followed my advice, and his wife, who loved him devotedly, had finally consented, because he could not attain erection otherwise, and she required the fulfilment of marital relations. Since she "gave in" to her husband's peculiar request, she is able to rouse him to coitus as often as she desires it. She only needs to put on tights. . . . He experiences the greatest satisfaction while his wife wears tights and they assume the situs inversus. Through such a small compromise, by meeting some specific phantasy, it is often possible to turn an incompatible marriage into a happy one.

This is not the only case of its kind of which I know. I know men who, when going to houses of prostitution request the women to retain their drawers when undressing. Others actually demand that the girls should put on male trousers. These latent homosexuals are well known to the prostitutes. They remain passive and expect the woman to be aggressive. This shows they maintain the fiction that they are females and they require relatively but little in the form of overt acts to maintain this fiction in their mind. Many an instance of love at first sight is induced in the same way.

Case. Z. I. A man, 48 years of age, had several light love affairs, was twice unhappily married. After the second separation—some six years previously—he left women severely alone because he had a poor opinon of them. He used to say: all women are worthless decoys and it is a pity to turn a single hair grey on their account. In the circle of women haters he was known for that reason as the decoyman. His physical sexual needs he satisfied with prostitutes or street acquaintances. Beyond that he avoided women and sought only the company of men. It was obvious that he was drifting away from heterosexuality and leaning towards psychic homosexuality. Then it happened that he agreed once to sit as a model for a woman artist. The sculptress was in ordinary clothes and had made

no particular impression on him. She asked him to
wait a few moments and then she stepped out to
put on her working clothes. When she reappeared,
a few moments later, he was astonished. She wore
a long white coat, which covered her whole dress, a
pleasing little cap, under which she had tucked her
hair to protect it against the dust, and a pair of
glasses which she wore only when working. She
appeared so attractive that he fell in love with her
that moment. He did not hide his feelings but immediately hastened to make up on the spot what he
had lost in six years of opportunities to worship at
the shrine of womanhood. She accepted his com-
pliments good-naturedly. He fell in love with her
as he had never been in love before. A few weeks
later he proposed marriage, but she politely refused.
She had made up her mind never to marry. But he
did not give her up; on the contrary he pursued her
with his attentions and tendernesses. His club and
all his cronies he abandoned. He was head over
heels in love, like a frisky boy, and held that now
he knew the meaning of love. One of his friends
proposed to cure him of his infatuation and told him
in confidence that he had heard the sculptress was
a homosexual who maintained relations with a chorus
girl wearing tights. The whole town knew about
it. It was an open secret. This information had
the contrary effect upon him. His passion reached
such a point that life seemed to him worthless with-

out her. He struggled with thoughts of suicide and told the beloved about it. This made a strong impression upon her and she stated frankly: she would agree to be his sweetheart, but his wife, never. For a time he fought against accepting this compromise, desiring nothing short of a union for life. Finally he acquiesced. She was a virgin no longer and told him that she had already been her instructor's sweetheart. That is why she did not want to consider marriage. With her instructor, however, she had never achieved orgasm. His embrace left her cold. She could achieve satisfaction and orgasm only with the aid of *manipulatio cum digito*.

Z. I. remained faithful to her for a few years and during that time tried several times to induce her to consider marriage. He was always most excited when he saw her wearing the apparel which had first roused his love for her. They always met in her studio while she was wearing her working clothes. Finally his love cooled and he returned to the society of his woman-hating companions. An attempt to have intercourse with a girl in his employ failed him and he called for advice.

He believed himself impotent. But it was merely the homosexual trait which comes to the fore at this age in various manifestations which physicians call the climacterium of man.

Analysis disclosed that the woman sculptor was

the cousin of one of his favorite old school mates, whom she resembled closely. This young man also wore, while at work in his laboratory, a white coat, like the sculptress. It was this similarity that roused his libido so tremendously. The young man had become engaged a few weeks previously. He disapproved the young man's step on various grounds. (A young man should not jeopardise his scientific career on account of a woman.) He was in love with the young man without realising it. The transference of the feeling into a heterosexual one was mediated through the fact that the woman looked like her cousin and the costume also helped to transfer some of the homosexual tendencies into the heterosexual channel.

In connection with this case I may make a few remarks about the so-called climacterium of man and about woman's critical period. The psychic process is well known, in so far as it involves a parting from one's youth, and it has been repeatedly outlined and described. The whole love instinct of man rebels against growing old and fosters the utilization to the utmost of the opportunities during the few remaining years. The milder the sexual life in the past, the greater and more stormy becomes the need of making up for lost opportunities "while there is time."

But the significance of homosexuality during this critical period is a matter which most investigators have overlooked. It may be that the involution of the sexual glands brings the opposite sex into stronger relief at this period. One who conceives bisexuality as a chemical process—and there are some data apparently supporting such a view—may speak of the conquest of man's heterosexuality over homosexuality. *Hirschfeld* would say of a man: as he now produces less andrin the gynecin achieves upper hands. Perhaps many cases of so-called late homosexuality (*Krafft-Ebing*) may be explained in this manner. I have known a man who, up to the 50th year of his life, has had no sexual experiences and who was also unaware of his homosexuality. At that age he happened to drift into the company of homosexuals and now he is a confirmed member of the third (intermediate) sex. Possibly the outbreak of homosexuality leading all the way to paranoia—a subject which I shall take up more fully in another chapter—depends on changes in the sexual glands, these changes leading to characteristic psychic expression.

In the last case disappointment after marriage (both women proved unfaithful to the man) induced the breaking forth of the homosexual tendencies.

The behavior of those persons who do not care to acknowledge their homosexuality is characteristic. So passionately do they fall in love, their impulsion to loving is so tremendous that every new passion surpasses all previous experiences.

This peculiarity gives us an insight into the mentality of the Don Juan type, the desolute adventurer, and the Messalina type. . . .

The flight away from homosexuality leads the individual to overstress his heterosexuality (with the formulation of compromises and the adoption of homosexual masks) but that seldom yields the satisfaction craved by the individual. The sexual adventurer is always a person who has failed to find proper gratification. He who has found complete gratification becomes thereby master of his libido and knows the meaning of satiety. When the gratification is only apparent the craving leads soon again to new adventures. Just as the compulsory acts of neurotics cannot be permanently removed, because such acts are only symptomatic and stand for hidden cravings, the unsatisfied homosexual longing which stands masked under an apparently excessive heterosexuality cannot be completely gratified on that path. The sexual instinct,—as *Freud* has pointed out—is of complex character and is seldom brought into play in its full form. Man's unattainable ideal is the whole instinct, undivided and unhampered in any of its component parts; falling in love manifests the expectation of a gratification previously unattained.

During man's critical period—as well as woman's —a number of troublesome compulsion neuroses are likely to break forth and these have been erroneously attributed to excitement, overwork, and other secondary factors. Every compulsion neurosis appearing at this period is a complicated riddle through which the subject aims to hide before his own consciousness no less than before the world at large the true significance of the psychic impulses which reassert their supremacy at the time. Frequently back of the various symptomatic acts it is possible to discern the clear mechanism of defence against homosexuality.

The next case shows an interesting array of symbolisms and of symbolic acts, which are easily understood if one has the key to the psychology of such mental processes.

Mr. B. experiences the outbreak of an acute neurosis at 60 years of age. Suddenly he becomes obsessed with the fear of tuberculosis. He is firmly convinced that he is a victim of the disease and the reassurance of famous specialists quiets him only for a few days. He reads all popular works on tuberculosis as well as the scientific works of Cornet, Koch, and other investigators. He has worked out for himself a systematic method for the cure of tuberculosis. He holds, in the first place, that cold air is the best, and takes long walks out of doors, sleeps with all windows wide open, goes to Davos and generally prefers winter sporting places. He is a confirmed believer in the theory of infection through particles of sputum and therefore avoids the proximity of . . . men.

"Why be afraid specially of men? May not women also carry the infection?"

"No; women do not expectorate so vigorously. Men spit all over, women only close by!"

"How do you know these things?"

"You see, I have given the matter a great deal of thought and I have studied the subject. I thought to myself, coughing and urinating are very much alike. In both operations products of the organism are removed from the body. A woman urinates with a small stream which does not reach far. But many men urinate with force and are able to throw out their stream,—a distance of several feet."

Already this statement showed that back of the fear of consumption there stood some hidden sexual motive. B. carried the analogy still further:

"Men are also able to ejaculate, while women only omit a little moisture which trickles down upon their parts . . . At any rate, I am particularly afraid of infection through some tubercular man."

I inquired into the circumstances under which this fear first showed itself and how long he had it and in reply received the following interesting confession:

"For a long time I lived with a nephew who occupied a separate room in my home. My married daughter came once to pay us a visit because her child had whooping cough and she was advised that a change of air would be beneficial."

(It is characteristic that he was not afraid of catching whooping cough, although he knew of a serious case,—an elderly man who had caught the infection and as a result was seriously ill for months. The fear of tuberculosis thus shows itself to be a misdirected notion.)

"It became necessary for me to share with my nephew the same sleeping room," continued the man. "He had but recently returned from Meran and was considered cured . . . But you know, how these alleged cures turn out upon closer examination. During the night I became uneasy and several times I heard my nephew coughing. I noticed that he did not sleep, and I also could not fall asleep because the thought tormented me that I would surely catch the infection. The first thing I did next morning was to call my physician; he laughed at me but upon my persistent questioning he told me: 'If you are as afraid as all that, you better sleep in a separate room!' I did not wait to be told twice and for a number of weeks after that I slept at a hotel. But here too, I began to think, perhaps some tubercular man has occupied the room before me, and could not sleep! I had night sweats and after that I no longer believed the physicians' reassurances and was convinced that this was a sign of the first stage of consumption. . . ."

We note that the elderly gentleman had become homosexually roused by the presence of his nephew and this craving appeared to his consciousness masked under the form of a fear of tubercular infection.

"I could tear my hairs out by the roots, to think that I had done such a foolish thing!"

"What foolish thing?"

"I mean, sleeping in the same room with my nephew. If I had at least put up a Japanese screen. But, unfortunately, one does foolish things without reflecting upon the consequences. . . ."

B. also displays various compulsory mannerisms, the meaning of which becomes obvious once we appreciate that, in his case, 'tuberculosis' really means 'homosexuality.' As he walks upon the City streets he meets a man coming his way. While still at a distance he steps aside or crosses on the other side; he no longer shakes hands with any man, not even with his friends; one may become infected with tubercle bacilli in that way. All places where men are seen naked or in partial undress, such as gymnasia or bathing resorts, are breeding spots for tubercular infection.

Moreover, B. shows some female traits in his nature. He has shaved his beard because hairs may be nests for tubercle bacilli; he has become emotional, whining and he is unable to arrive at decisions promptly. He finds the fashion of wearing short coats not "dressy" and wears a long coat that has almost the appearance of a jacket. (Similar mannerisms are found in *Jean-Jacques Rousseau; vid.* his *Confessions.*)

This case is one of almost complete outbreak of femininity, closely allied to the paranoiac forms, which will be considered more fully in another chapter. He is also jealous of his wife and thinks he is slighted,—that he is not given the proper degree of attention. He is excitable, sleepless, dissatisfied with life. After a few hours the analysis is given up.

Such persons are tremendously afraid of the truth; they wander from physician to physician and really want but one thing: to preserve their secret and to devote themselves more and more to their hidden homosexuality. If the condition were once disclosed before their eyes they could not continue their indulgence so easily. They always break up the treatment after a few hours under some pretext or other and this justifies the suspicion that, sooner or later, they come to regard the physician also as a man and, transferring their homosexual attachment to the physician they flee from the danger of being together with the object of their love.

This case illustrates, I believe, what remarkable masks the outbreak of the homosexual trait is capable of assuming. Similar masks are the fear of syphilis, the fear of "blood poisoning," and the dread

of physical contact with other persons or objects.
The fear of syphilis covers also other dreads.
Formerly I thought that syphilidophobia was only
a mask for incest craving.   I am now convinced that
it stands for "forbidden love" generally. Syphilis
stands as a symbol either for incest or for homosexuality. 'Becoming infected' means: 'being op-
pressed' by homosexual or incestuous tendencies.
These figures of speech are suggested by the every
day use of language.   One hears, for instance, that
the whole city of Berlin is infected with homosexuality; the opponents of homosexuality fight
against the plague which threatens the whole German
nation; young men are warned against being infected with homosexuality. It is not surprising,
therefore, that the morbid expressions of neuroses
assume similar figurative forms.

The rise of such morbid fear during advanced
age is always suspicious of an outbreak of homosexuality, against which various protective devices
are thus raised. If I should attempt to describe
all these forms of outbreak and all the protective
devices I would have to write a special treatise on
anxiety states. We well know already that all
neuroses have a bisexual basis. But, what is more,
I maintain that homosexuality plays a far greater
role in the development of neurotic traits than any
other suppressed instincts.

I am now turning my attention to a character in whom homosexuality would hardly be suspected as a motive power. I refer to the Don Juan type of personality. The Messalina type I shall describe in connection with my study of sexual anesthesia in woman. But the Don Juan character deserves special attention in this connection.

One would think that a man who devotes his whole life to women, who dreams day and night only of new conquests, who considers every woman worth while when opportunity favors him, a man for whom no woman is too old, or too ugly, if he desires her,—that such a man would be far removed from any homosexual trend. Yet the contrary is the fact and the greater my opportunity to study the 'woman chaser' the stronger my conviction becomes that, back of the ceaseless hunt, stands the longing after the male. Though many explanations have been offered for the Don Juan type,—that prototype of Faust's—none has solved satisfactorily the riddle of his psyche. Only the recognition of latent homosexuality promises to clear for us the meaning of this character.

What are the typical character traits attributed to the Don Juan type? His easily stirred passion; secondly, his indiscriminate taste; thirdly, his sudden cooling off. Of course, there are any number of transitional forms and mixed stages.

I choose for examination the fundamental type, as he is known to me through a number of concrete examples. This triad: "quickly roused, not particular as to choice, just as quickly cooled," admits of numerous variations. Particularly the choice of the sexual object is something that in many woman chasers becomes determined on the basis of particular fetichistic preferences, such as red hair, virginity, a particular figure, a special occupation, etc. The Don Juan collectors of women are differentiated into various distinct classes. I knew one who for his record of adventures specialized in widows. The shorter the period of widowhood the greater was his ambition to make the conquest. Only women in mourning attracted him. But beyond this point he was not particular. It made no difference to him whether the woman was young or old, beautiful or homely, so long as she was a widow in mourning. His greatest pride he took in his conquest of widows on the burial day.

Oskar A. H. Smitz, (in his *Cassanova und Andere erotische Charaktere*, Stuttgart, 1906, quoted after *Bloch*), has attempted to trace a fine distinction between the Don Juan and the Cassanova type: "Don Juan is a deceiving, cunning seducer to whom the sense of possessing the woman, the feeling of danger, and the pleasure of overcoming resistance and of exercising his manly strength are the chief things, but he is not erotic, whereas Cassanova is the erotic type par excellence; he, too, is tricky and remorseless, but he craves the satisfaction of his sensuous needs rather than of his sense of power. Don Juan sees only women, for Cassanova every woman is "the woman." Don Juan is demonic, devilish, he deliberately plans the destruction of the women who yield to him and drives them to perdition, while Cassanova is humane, he is always interested in the happiness of his sweethearts and preserves of them tender memories. Don Juan hates woman, he is a typical misogynist, the satanic type of woman hater, whereas Cassanova is a typical feminist, he has a deep and sympathetic understanding of woman's soul, he is not deceived by his love affairs but needs continual intercourse with women as the condition of his happiness. Don Juan seduces through his demonic character, with the brutal, and wild, attraction exercised by his uncanny power, Cassanova achieves his conquests through the more refined gentle atmosphere generated by his charming presence."

Bloch introduces a third type, the pseudo-Don Juan, or more correctly, the pseudo-Cassanova,— the adventurer perennially disappointed in his conquests, of whom Retif de la Bretonne is the nearest widely known type. He is continually looking for the true love and never finds it. While I admit that the seducer as a type belongs to one of these categories, I must designate all three classes mentioned above, that is, the Don Juan, the Cassanova, and the would-be type of either, as bearers, alike, of a latent homosexuality. None of them finds his ideal. Retif de la Bretonne is the perennially disappointed type, and true love is something he can never find; in his love he displays considerable dependence on woman. He portrays the hopeless flight to woman and away from man. Cassanova feels all the time impelled to prove to himself how seductive a fellow and man he is and every new conquest gives him a new opportunity to do so. Woman is to him but a means to enhance his sense of virility. He must not depreciate his conquest for the glory of his achievement would be lessened in his own eyes if he were to do so.

The Don Juan type is close to the level which leads directly to the well known Marquis de Sade type of character. He scorns woman because she is incapable of yielding to him all the gratification for which he yearns. He is perennially searching for release and in that respect bears some resemblance to the Flying Dutchman who is similarly in quest of love and whom the quest leads eventually to death. But I cannot concur with the idea that these types are so sharply differentiated as *Schmitz* and *Bloch* are inclined to maintain. We meet the finest gradations and the most varied combinations. Moreover individuals change, their character shifting from one type to another by imperceptible degrees in the course of time.

I propose to consider Don Juan as the representative of the type of seducer, irrespective of further variations. In fact it is characteristic of all the types mentioned above that they are alike unable to remain loyal in their love. And, in my view, this is the most important characteristic.

Ready excitability, scorn of womankind, latent cruelty, and perennial readiness for love adventures are traits which show that, in the last analysis, Don Juan represents a type of unsatisfied libido. For him the most important moment is the conquest of the woman. In the joy of this conquest there is betrayed something of the scorn of woman which plays such an important role in the lives of all homosexuals—whether latent or manifest. For the genuine Don Juan the conquest of a woman is a task which apeals to his play lust. Will he succeed with this one, and with that one, and with the third woman? Each new conquest reassures him that he is irresistible, magical in his charm, so that he can say to himself: *thou art a real man!* He must reassure himself over and over that he is fully a man because he fears his femininity too strongly; with the aid of his feminine trait he is the better able to achieve his conquests among women because that trait enables him the better to feel and know what

every woman wants. He is really but a woman in
man's clothes. His narcissistic character (the
morbid self-love) requires continually new proofs
of his irresistible powers. This type of man, one
who practices all sorts of perversions on women and
in this very changing of the manner of his loving
betrays his insatiable quest for new and untried
gratifications, never permits himself any homosexual act, although he is far from particular otherwise and has run the gamut of tasting all ugly and
forbidden fruit. Homosexuality strikes this type
of man as disgusting and unbearable, he must spit
out when meeting a fellow of that kind, he would
have all men and women of that kind in jail, he
would have them rooted out as one would a plague.
Towards homosexuality his attitude is emotionally
overstressed, showing that this negative form of
disgust and neurotic repulsion really covers the
positive trend of longing. But at the same time
he looks for women who are mannish in appearance
and who lack the secondary sexual characteristics,
thin, ephebic women, matrons and girls who are so
young as to look like children and thus represent
really intermediary stages towards manhood.

Certain aversions, which *Hirschfeld* has described
as antifetichistic, sometimes disclose the homosexual
character of their libido and the protective means
adopted against the recognition of homosexuality.
One man dislikes woman with large feet, another is

repelled by women with hair on their bodies. Such
a woman causes him to have distinct nausea. A third
one is repelled by the presence of hair upon the
woman's upper lip, or by a deep voice. There are,
besides, all sorts of transitional types. One seeks
only the completely developed and typical female
figure, another is attracted particularly by the
type of woman resembling the male figure but without disdaining the former type.

His search is endless because he is truly, though
secretly, attracted by the male. His sexual goal is
man. Through each new woman he expects to experience, at last, the completely satisfactory gratification which he craves. But he turns away from
each one equally disappointed because his libido
cannot be fully gratified by any of them. In the
manner of his conquering and abandoning each
woman he shows his scorn of the sex. The true
woman lover is really no Don Juan because he
distributes his sexual libido among a few women at
the most and the emotional overvaluation of these
women furnishes the key to his attitude towards the
whole sex. Don Juan makes love in a manner apparently as if he respected womankind. But the
cold manner in which he dismisses his victims betrays
his complete contempt for the sex. He admires only
the women who withstand him and whom he cannot
subdue. Such resistance may lead eventually to the
marriage of a Don Juan, a marriage which neces-

sarily proves unhappy and he continues his former
life. For the step has not furnished him what he
is really seeking, man has eluded him again.

Closer examination reveals the characteristic fact
that frequently the choice of lovers is determined
by homosexual traits of one kind or another. The
Don Juan who runs after married women may be
goaded on by the fact that he likes the physical appearance of their husbands. Naturally the thought
heightens his feeling of self-esteem because it must
be a harder task to induce the wife of a handsome
man to deceive her husband than it would be to bring
to one's feet the wife of an ugly man. A Don Juan
told me once: "I have possessed all sorts of women,
but never cared for the wife of a simpleton. I have
always considered it beneath me and not worth while
to deceive a fool." Here we have a type of man
desirous to measure his wit against that of a sharp
rival. (If you are so very sharp, why don't you
look out better for your wife!) The emphasis here
is really upon the fact that he likes the husband,
admires him, and considers him a bright man. Before he makes up his mind to get a woman he must
like her husband, and he can be attracted only by
intelligent men. That condition is imperative before he engages in any love adventure. *Maupassant*
describes this type of man in one of his stories. The
hero is interested only in married women whose husbands attract him and are among his friends. I

give the history of an extreme case of this type in my chapter on jealousy in the present work.

H. O., 49 years of age, is undergoing a severe mental crisis. He relates that he was happily married, until an actress crossed his path. He fell so deeply in love he could not leave her, he neglected his home, was unable to follow his calling and was on the point of committing suicide. It was not his custom to cling for long to any one woman. Usually he changed sweethearts every few weeks.

"Did you say that your married life was happy?"

"Yes; that has never troubled me. I cannot be true to any woman. I must change all the time. I am a polygamous being. This woman is the first to whom I feel loyal and true right along, I did not feel so towards my wife and only a few weeks after marriage I preferred the embrace of other women, but this sweetheart of mine,—she has taken me off my balance entirely, to her I am loyal. Think of it! I stand for her going with other men, who support her. Who could have told me that I would come to this! Every little while I decide to break with her and never see her again. I have sworn it to my wife, who is heartbroken over the affair. But I am too weak . . . Save me! Free me from this terrible plight! Restore me to my family."

. . . . This man's life history is typical of the neurotic. He understood sexual matters and

masturbated at a very early age. He began to
masturbate as early as the sixth year at school and
thinks that he can even trace the beginning of the
habit to an earlier date. He had many play mates
with whom he carried on the "usual childish games."
These "usual childish games" turned out to be fellatio, pederasty, manual onanism, and zoophily.
The children pressed into service a dog who by lick-
ing the parts produced the highest orgasm in them.
The last homosexual love he carried on at 14 years
of age. He and a colleague performed mutual
masturbation. Once the two were warned against
the dangers of masturbation and they went together
to a house of prostitution. This they kept up for
a long time because it increased their satisfaction.
Often they exchanged their sexual partners. (This
is not an uncommon practice through which latent
homosexuals achieve a heightening of their orgasm
and cryptically reach after their male companion.
In houses of prostitution this practice is common
among friends.)

In a short time he developed into a genuine Don
Juan. At 16 years of age he had already become
a full-fledged woman hunter and succeeded in at-
tracting his high school professor's wife as his
sweetheart. He went after every woman, young
or old, pretty or plain. He claims that old women
have yielded the highest pleasures and shows me a
letter in which *Franklin* advises young men to cling

to old women. But this pronounced gerontophiliac tendency does not prevent him from having relations with girls below age, almost children. His whole thought, night and day, was concentrated upon women. His first thought upon rising in the morning usually was: "What adventures await me today?" If he finds himself in a room with a woman alone invariably he thinks: "How can I get her?" Every woman he gets hold of he looks upon merely as a means for gratification and soon tires of her. With the exception of one elderly woman whom he occasionally visits he has not kept up with any woman longer than a few weeks. Often after the first intercourse he feels disgust for his new sexual partner and thinks to himself: "You are not any different than the others!" Since his 16th year he has had intercourse almost daily and often several times a day. He was 32 years of age when he first met his present wife. Her father was his superior at the office, a man for whom he had the very highest respect. ("There are not many such men as he.") He married the man's daughter, whom he held high in esteem high above all others of her sex, and it was a very happy marriage. His only fear was that his wife would find out about his amorous escapades. For no woman was safe near him and even during the early part of their married life he kept up sexual relations with their cook. Finally he managed to control himself at least to the extent of avoiding any escapades under his own roof so as to be more sure of keeping his wife in ignorance of his amorous proclivities. But he always kept on the string a lot of women and girls who were at his disposal whenever he wanted any of them.

He became acquainted with a young man whom he liked a great deal. But there was one thing about that young man which repelled him: he was homosexual and proud of it. This was something he could not understand and he endeavored very zealously to rouse in his friend a love for women. He failed completely; on the other hand his new friend introduced him to the local homosexual circle, in which he became interested merely as a "cultural problem." He frequented a café where homosexuals were in the habit of congregating and noticed that many among them were of pronounced intellectual caliber. He was particularly impressed by the fact that their common peculiarity levelled so completely persons of different social standing. A Count met a waiter or post office clerk as cordially as he would a most intimate friend. A few weeks later he met the sister of his new friend and fell deeply in love with her at first sight. That was his tremendous attachment.

It was plain that contact with the homosexuals had released some of the inhibitions which had kept back his own latent homosexuality and the latter trait now threatened to overpower him. There was but one safeguard against that, namely: flight into love. The attachment to his friend became now a passionate love for his friend's sister, who resembled her brother very closely. During coitus with his new sweetheart it occurred to him early to give up succubus, and to try the anal form of gratification, and this produced in him tremendous orgasm such as he had never before experienced.

His wife was informed through anonymous letters of the state of affairs. Moreover he had become very weak in his sexual relations with her and was able to carry on his marital duties only with greatest difficulty.

Psychoanalysis brought wonderful results in this case. He learned quickly to recognise his emotional fixations and only wondered that he was too blind not to have seen for himself that he really loved the brother through that woman. He broke with the actress in a dignified manner. He proposed that if she should give up her intimate relations with all other men he would keep his word and marry her. He still loved her but he was no longer in the dark. She laughed in his face. Did he really think that he could meet the cost of her wardrobe and other needs? That put an end to the attachment. He was ashamed afterwards to think that he should have

preferred such a woman to his wife. The analysis
of a remarkable dream brought about the complete
severing of his infantile fixations.

The dream: *I am with Otto*—that was his friend's
name—*in a room. He walks up to me and says:
"Don't you see that I love you and want you!" I
try to avoid his love pats and draw a revolver out of
my pocket. I hold it high and am ready to shoot
my friend. But instead of my friend I see standing
before me my son, and my boy's sincere blue eyes
look up at me imploringly: 'Protect me!' I throw
down the revolver and run out of the room.*

His young friend resembled somewhat his boy to
whom he was specially devoted just before the unfortunate love affair. . . .

This case shows that sometimes a great and passionate love arises to save the lover from himself.
There are times when it becomes necessary to love
and then the object of one's love, though falling
short of the actual yearnings of one's soul, becomes
emotionally overvalued so that the intoxication of
love leads to forgetfulness (like every other intoxication). Any love affair which breaks out during
later life rouses the suspicion that it is an attempt
to save one's self with all one's might from homosexuality. The characteristic signs of such a love
are its exaggerated and compulsory character. The
lovesick man is unable to keep away from his sweetheart; he wants to have her by his side all the time;

she must accompany him everywhere; even in sleep he puts his hand out to his sweetheart as if to protect him from every temptation. And I have seen cases in which the curious infatuation was able to withstand all opposition when it must be looked upon as a successful healing process.

In the course of analysis it not infrequently happens that those who call for advice transfer their attachment to their consultant, feel tremendously attached to him and in this state of emotional readiness the first woman who happens along becomes the object of their most intense love emotion as the shortest way out of a sexual danger. The sexual danger in question is homosexuality.

Don Juan, Cassanova, Retif de la Bretonne,—all flee from man and seek salvation in woman. Retif is a foot fetichist. The choice of this fetich, typically bisexual, already indicates latent homosexuality. Insatiable woman hunters often end their flight away from homosexuality by falling into the deepest neuroses.

The next case history illustrated this fact:

G. K., a prominent inventor, 32 years of age, consults me for a number of *remarkable* compulsory acts which he must always carry out before retiring for the night. He must prove about twenty times to make sure that the doors are all locked. Then he goes through the house and submits every foot of the place to the most painfully detailed and careful search to make sure that no burglar is hidden anywhere. He looks not only under the beds but into every box and drawer and closet, opening and closing each one in turn, and very carefully. One can never tell where a burglar may hide himself! By the time he has concluded this search it is nearly midnight. The terribly arduous procedure fatigues him for he has to look everywhere, emptying even the book cases in the course of his search for fear that the burglar may be hidden back of the books, and it is midnight when he crawls into bed, although he begins his preparations around ten o'clock. Then he is usually tormented with doubt whether he has done everything. It occurs to him that he did not go into the nursery at all, where his three children are asleep. The boy's room, too, has not been searched. Jumping out of bed he lights a candle and in his night toilette makes his way to the children's rooms, unable to rest any longer. The girls are already accustomed to seeing him that way, nevertheless they jump out of their sleep scared. In his white nightgown, like a shadow, he moves from place to place with lighted candle in hand, looks under the children's bed, under the servant girl's bed and incidentally makes sure that no man lies by her side in bed. During these rounds every door and every window is tried whether it is safely locked. It is now long past midnight. Exhausted he returns to his bed. Again various doubts begin to torture him: did or did he not try this, or that, or the other particular door, is the gasometer safely turned off, and again in his thoughts he rehearses every detail. His logical faculty tells him: you have done everything, you need not have any further concern, it is high time you went to sleep! But logic is powerless when his doubts overpower him. Again he rises and takes a few additional precautions which I need not detail here. Thus it may be three or four o'clock in the morning and even later before he is finally through. Then he lies down in his wife's bed and wakes her up. Only after coitus, which he carries out regularly every night, he falls asleep. But by that time the night is over and the dawn is just breaking. He remains in bed exhausted, often sleeping till past the noon hour, much to his wife's disgust. The whole house is in uproar. The children wake up but are taken to another wing of the house because "papa is asleep and must not be waked up!" As he is very wealthy, he has his way. The servants are paid extra well so that they are willing to put up with "that queer household." Afternoons he is at work in his chemical laboratory. His researches have made him famous. He is a very capable chemist, possessing wonderful ideas and his patents have brought him a great fortune.

In addition to all that he is obsessed by another compulsory thought, which seems very extraordinary. Continually he wants to know how everybody

likes his wife and whether she is still considered a
pretty woman. Regard for her appearance is his
greatest concern. Many afternoons he spends with
her in the fitting rooms of modistes and tailors. He
reproaches her for not knowing how to dress tastily,
and scolds her because she does not take proper
care of herself. On the other hand he is entirely
indifferent regarding the manner of her appearance
in the house. He is greatly concerned only with
the impression his wife makes upon other men. It
also disturbs him if other women do not find his wife
beautiful but he worries more if men fail to notice
her. As he dreads evenings he spends the time in
the company of friends. (Thus the ceremonial on
retiring is delayed and he sleeps to a late hour into
the day.)

His chief thought is his wife's appearance. If a
man says to him: "Your wife is charming today!"
or if some stranger says to him: "Who is that beautiful woman?" as has actually happened at balls and
entertainments he feels supremely happy. Or, if he
introduces his wife to some man who gallantly remarks later: "I did not know that you had such a
charming wife!" his happiness knows no bounds
and his wife has a good time in consequence. The
very next day he buys her a costly gem, he is tender
with her and bestows upon her pleasant flatteries.

But, on the other hand, if he sees that his wife
passes unobserved in a crowd, or if there is some

other pretty woman in the room, he feels unhappy.
Then he meets his wife with severest reproaches because she does not know how to dress attractively,
he growls, and raves, and is angry for several days
until another event takes place and his wife is
again noticed by men and women when he quiets
down. He cannot endure to hear that some other
man also has a pretty wife. He does not rest until
he meets that woman and is happy if some one says
to him: "Your wife is really prettier." But if he
hears that another woman is praised and his wife
is not mentioned at same time he feels again very
depressed and his wife pays unpleasantly for it. His
uncles—he has no brothers—all have pretty women.
His chief concern is to find out whether his wife
is really the prettiest. He asks this question frequently of his acquaintances, in an offhand manner
of course, for he would not have them suspect his
feelings for anything in the world and the opinion
of a man towards whom he is otherwise completely
indifferent often determines his disposition for the
whole day. He is happy if he notices that some
one is making love to his wife. On the other hand it
troubles him if he sees there are young men around
and they fail to gather around his wife. He is not
jealous because he knows his wife well, can trust her
and, besides, she is never alone. She is either with
him or in her mother's company. That is why he
is very happy to see men gather around her. He

goes with her wherever any beauty contests are on and spends a great deal of money to make sure that his wife will win the prize. If another woman is the winner it makes him unhappy and he genuinely envies the man who possesses or will possess such a woman.

In spite of all that, the man is a Don Juan and was never true to his marital vows. He maintains a second house where he receives girls and also such of his friends' wives as find favor in his eyes and are willing to accept his attentions. As he is a well preserved, stately man of most attractive appearance he is very lucky with women.

Besides that he receives a number of girls in his laboratory where he has fitted out a room for this purpose. Not a day passes in which he does not possess some woman—any woman—in addition to his wife. He looks well, though occasionally a little pale, feels physically very fresh and energetic. He works really but two or three hours a day. In this brief time he accomplishes more than other men in a day's grind.

The character of his sexual gratification is noteworthy. While carrying out normal coitus with his wife, with the girls and other women he indulges in the kind of practices which furnish him the greatest orgasm. He gives them his phallus which they take hold of, and kisses them, *dum puella membrum erectum tenet et premit*. He carries out coitus if the partner requests it. But the act is interrupted and again exchanged for hand manipulation. As he is a very potent man, he is able to satisfy the woman and still has time to withdraw his penis before ejaculation and put it in the woman's hand to be manipulated by her. There have been also various other indulgences. He has tried everything. The form of gratification just mentioned he prefers to all others. A certain feeling of shame has prevented him from asking his wife to do it for him.

His anamnesis is very fragmentary. He remembers no particular incidents of childhood or early youth. He began to masturbate very early and up to the time of his marriage masturbated regularly every night before falling asleep. Already before marriage he had had such compulsory habits, but usually he was through his bed time searching in about one half hour. At any rate he masturbated daily even when he had intercourse with women. He never took women to his house. They always came to his laboratory. He is greatly attached to his mother who is yet a very attractive woman and shows great veneration for his father who brought him up with strict but just discipline and who showed some light neurotic peculiarities.

He recalls no homosexual episodes. He masturbated excessively and began intercourse with women at 18 years of age; after that he rapidly became a confirmed woman hunter but he developed a very

particular taste. All his women had to be very fair,
have a pretty, round, strongly feminine figure, a
delicate tint and be, above all, very beautiful. Yet
a very white and smooth skin would make up for the
lack of other points of beauty in his eyes. With
the perfectly white face he required dark, fiery eyes.
This type of beauty seems to coincide with his
mother's who was a remarkably attractive woman
and who to this day carries with great dignity the
obvious signs of her former great beauty.

He had also certain antifetichistic peculiarities.
If he notices hair on a woman's body, for instance,
at once she loses all attractiveness in his eyes. Such
a woman he finds as disgusting as a woman with a
mustache. Equally disgusting to him are all
women with sharp figures and no breasts such as
remind one of a man. "A woman should be a
woman," is his favorite remark. He despises all
"blue stockings" and emancipated women and has
requested his wife to drop the acquaintanceship of
a friend of hers who had taken an interest in various women's movements.

In the course of the analysis he refers continually
first of all to his wife. According to him he has
married an angel of patience. It takes great love
to endure this man's moods and whims. But the
wife loves him devotedly and has learned to stand
everything from him because she knew that he loved
her and she said to herself: every man has his

peculiarities. She was contented and the house
vibrated with her happy laughter. If he troubled
her with his foolish reproaches she did not pout for
long. On the contrary she soon smiled forgiveness
so that their married life was really a model.

He insists that his wife is an ideal person. When
early in the course of analysis one confesses such a
deep affection, the opposite feeling, scorn, is sure to
become disclosed before long. First the advantages,
—then the disadvantages. But this woman seemed
to have no unpleasant component in her nature. He
could tell only favorable things about her and about
his concern regarding her beauty.

But before long—in the course of a few weeks—
the tone of his talk changed. There was another
trauma about which he felt he must tell me, something of tremendous significance which had shattered
his whole married life. At the time of his marriage
he had resolved nothing less than to give up his Don
Juan adventures and to be true to his wife. Just
before marriage he had been carrying on with six
different girls at the same time and it kept him on
the jump to keep each woman from finding out about
the others. He wanted to live quietly after marriage and be true to his wife. He had also resolved
solemnly to give up masturbation after marriage.
As a married man this would be easy,—instead of
masturbating before going to sleep he would have
intercourse with his wife.

Before the marriage ceremony he became obsessed with the thought that his bride might have hair growing on her breasts. That would be unbearable. He was on the point of demanding that his bride should be examined by a physician but, as a man of high standing, he was ashamed to make such a suggestion. During the bridal night he discovered a few light hairs on her breast and a light soft down on her abdomen. He was so shocked that he would have wanted to send her back to her parents. For months after that he was very unhappy and every night he wept over his misfortune. His great hope, to find a woman who would take the place of all other women in his life, was gone.

This notion about his wife's hairs made him most unhappy and prevented his moral resurrection. He had planned to turn a new leaf. But he continued to feel himself irresistibly attracted to beautiful white women with marble-like smooth skin and no hair to remind one of a man's body.

The most remarkable feature, characteristic of the whole case is the fact last mentioned.

The man is avowedly bisexual with a strong leaning towards homosexuality. This homosexual trend was gratified up till that time through masturbation —as he has pointed out. He sought contact with fully developed women, to forget man. He wanted a very beautiful wife because he imagined her beauty would serve to drive away from him all thought of man and to focus his libido exclusively upon her. He wanted to have the prettiest woman in the world: Helen. If his wife's appearance pleased other men, this so roused the homosexual component of his libido that he enjoyed sexual intercourse with her more keenly. Above all he wanted to avoid the thought of man. The anxiety on account of man came over him particularly before retiring at night and it was a morbid anxiety over masturbation at the same time. In his head, within his brain, man was a living thought, something that threatened him and demanded release. But this was also something his consciousness refused to recognize and therefore the thought of man tortured him and he could not fall asleep. He projected this intruder into his room and it led him to search his empty closets for a non-existent man, as if saying to himself: I have no trace of any homosexual leaning whatever! That is what he actually told me when I referred to the homosexual significance of his compulsory acts: such a Don Juan as I! I have devoted myself completely to woman. The thought of man is repulsive to me.

I explained to him that disgust is but a hidden form of longing. If he were indifferent to the thought of man it would be more convincing.

"Well then, I am indifferent to the thought."

Thus he tried to convince me that he was not homosexual. But we conceive that the hairs he discovered upon his wife's body reminded him of the fatal homosexuality. He felt so unhappy over it he was considering a separation on that account. Whatever reminded him of man was painfully unpleasant to him. He threw himself into love adventures to forget man. He gave up his clubs and male companions because he wanted to be all the time in the company of his wife.

I pass over for the present the further significance of his neurosis as disclosed by the analysis of his dreams. I shall only give an example illustrating how untrustworthy are the statements of those who attempt to give an account of their lives and insist that they remember everything accurately. This or that particular kind of incident, they are sure, has never occured in their life. Regarding sexual matters all men lie consciously, unconsciously and half-consciously.

After further, continuously progressive analysis the subject himself came to the conclusion that he must have been struggling against homosexuality. Now he understood his sudden decision to get married, after having maintained right along that he would remain a bachelor. He was interested at the time in a laboratory assistant, a young man with pretty rosy cheeks. He showered gifts upon that young man and planned to give him an education so as to have a friend always close to him. The first compulsory acts appeared at the time. He married,

felt unhappy for a time but for a few years he lived
at least a relatively quiet life. Then another man
came into his life destroying his peace of mind, a
man who had lived for some time in foreign countries
and now returned to his fatherland. This was an
uncle.

Now he recalls something of which he had not
thought for many years—for he was going to keep
this from me,—namely, that he had maintained certain intimacy with this uncle for about a year. They
lived in a boarding house where they occupied a room
together. The uncle always came to lie in his bed
and they played with each other before falling
asleep.

His uncle carried out the kind of manipulations
which he now required of his women lovers: manual
gratification. During his relations with his wife,
however, he wanted to avoid all thought of homosexuality; she should not practice this form of gratification for him nor should her body remind him of
homosexuality. She must save him of the burden of
homosexuality which still plagued him under the
form of onanism.

After resurrecting this memory a mass of other
homosexual data came trooping forth out of his
past.

This man was strongly bisexual from childhood
with particular predisposition towards the male sex.
As a child he did crocheting and showed various fe-

male characteristics. After the onset of puberty his homosexuality was strongly repressed, persisting chiefly under the guise of onanism. For the act of masturbation takes place just before falling asleep in a half dreamy state during which he thinks, though indistinctly, of his uncle and of other men. The latent homosexuality was the most important factor in his neurosis.

The result of the analysis was most gratifying in this case. The subject soon abandoned his compulsory acts and was able to sleep quietly. His life became regular; he ceased being a Don Juan. He allowed his wife to carry out those manipulations which seemed essential for his orgasm and for his peace of mind. Occasionally I see him.

These observations show that in the dynamics of the "polygamic neurosis," homosexuality plays a tremendous role. The observation that every love is really self-love receives new confirmation. Don Juan seeks himself in woman and finds in her that femininity which has turned him into a Don Juan.

In his book (*Don Juan, Cassanova and other Erotic Characters*) already mentioned (Stuttgart, 1906), *Oskar A. H. Schmitz* states:

"Cassanova would not begrudge woman the possession of all those traits which are called 'male,' through ignorance, just as he himself has been described as possessing many female traits. The division of mankind in men and women is a great convenience. But he who undertakes to investigate erotic problems to their bottom must bear in mind that there are no absolute male and female persons any more than there are persons who are purely quick tempered, good-natured, envious, Germans or Semites. All these designations, like Theophrast's characters, represent so many psychic elements which must have a name. But they are met only in various combinations which may be compared and contrasted with chemical combinations. I believe it is noticeable that men of over-stressed virility do not necessarily appeal to women, who find them, instead, partly repulsive, partly amusing. On the other hand it is certainly true that all female tempters were remarkable for their intellect and wit—some of them were veritable amazons intellectually—and we note in our own day with great reason the disappearance of the *"crampon"* together with the leaning instinct of Epheus. Even the disappearance of Don Juan may be due partly to his overstressed virile characteristics. The erotic temperament includes a number of female traits; such peculiarities as tenderness, vanity, talkativeness need not interfere with his amorous adventures."

III

Diagnosis of Satyriasis—Priapism—A case of
    Satyriasis—A second case of Satyriasis—A
    case of Nymphomania—Proof that the cravings
    represented by this condition are traceable to
    the ungratified homosexual instinct.

Wenn man die letzten Funken einer Leidenschaft
im Herzen trägt, wird man sich eher einer neuen
hingeben, als wenn man gänzlich geheilt ist.

La Rochefoucauld.

III

So long as the last ember of a passion still glows in the heart it is easier to rouse a new passion than if the cure is complete.

La Rochefoucauld.

The last case has shown us that cryptic sexual goals which remain hidden make for unrest and in spite of frequent sexual experiences bring about a state of sexual insatiety, endless hunger, longing and unrest. Man's unsatisfied instinct drives him like a motor to all sorts of symbolic acts; it induces him to taste all gratifications which are not under the sway of inhibition, robbing him of sleep and rest.

All the symptomatic acts we have mentioned, trying the doors,—looking under the bed, etc.—were due to the subject's fear of homosexuality. The doors of his soul must be hermetically sealed so that the terrible enemy should find no entry.

The subject also displayed a number of other symptomatic acts which richly symbolized his inversion. He turned around certain objects from the left to the right. He felt more satisfied after doing

so. Why did he do it? Because in consciousness
the right side always stands for what is permitted,
while the left symbolizes the forbidden. Some things
he turned around and upside down to see whether
they would keep their balance. If they tumbled it
filled him with uneasiness, if they stood up, he felt
satisfied. Occasionally he found a vessel that kept
its balance when turned upside down. But he was
satisfied if it did not break.

His phantasy played with the possibility of turning sexuality upside down. If the change involved no
mishap it carried to him the meaning: even if you are
homosexual, you need not lose your balance, you
can keep up and stand on your feet. After such
a symbolic act he experienced promptly erection and
ran to his wife who only disappointed him because
she did not gratify him enough. These men have a
strong yearning for great heterosexual passion
which shall make them forget their homosexuality.
Usually imagination comes to their aid and they find
women who give them so much spiritually, that they
overlook the absence of physical attractiveness.
They sublimate their homosexuality, heighten the
meaning of sexuality by endowing it with spiritual
erotism, and by means of spiritual ecstacy they make
up for the lack of physical lure.

If this transposition does not take place, if the
flame blazes only upon the physical sphere, a permanent love hunger becomes established known as

satyriasis. This condition must be differentiated
from priapism which is caused solely by organic conditions and consists of a more or less continuous
state of erection.

Priapism is often brought about by diseases of
the *corpora cavernosa,* by diabetes and diseases of
the spinal cord, and is a condition very unpleasant
to the sufferer. Here the instinct is not brought
into play, the excited organ requires nothing,—it
is merely unwell. The psychic impulse is entirely
lacking. The subjects feel their condition as something painfully unpleasant, they cohabit merely to
get rid of the troublesome erection. On the other
hand, the victim of satyriasis is continually impelled
to seek gratification and it often happens that he
is unable to carry on intercourse because erection
fails him. The impulse is psychic rather than physical. Satyriasis is an attempt to exhaust a psychic
impulse through the physical channel. A transference of priapism into the psychical sphere, that is,
the establishment of a disposition along this path
on the basis of a priapistic excitation, is something
I have not encountered.

Satyriasis may be produced in a number of ways.
We have seen already that persons with sadistic
fancies, necrophiliac tendencies and with all sorts
of infantile misophilias may be addicted to masturbation. In all these cases, if onanism is given up, a
condition develops resembling satyriasis. What

these persons seek is a transference of their libido upon the normal path. At the same time my observations enable me to declare that the various conditions mentioned are overshadowed by the significance of latent homosexuality. The most important as well as the most powerful driving force is homosexuality. But I also know of a homosexual in whom the latent heterosexuality has broken forth as a satyriasis directed along homosexual channels.

We shall now turn our attention to a case which illustrates many of these points:

Mr. Alfred V., clerk, 26 years of age, complains of a long array of nervous symptoms. In the first place there is his inability to attend to his work. He is without employment, because he is unable to hold on to any place. He cannot concentrate his thoughts as his mind turns all the time to women.

In the morning, as soon as he wakes up, his first thought is: I could enjoy a woman now! He thinks this over and finds that, after all, it is too early in the day. He goes to the restaurant and there looks over the morning papers. It is almost too much for him to do even that. Usually he only glances over the news of the day and then turns to the want ads, particularly those marriage offers and "personals" with more or less pointed allusions. Several hours pass that way and meanwhile he looks at the women passing by the window. Then he takes a walk and tries to talk to the girls he meets and to strike up acquaintance with them. If he finds that they are after money he breaks up his talk with them. He would rather take a real prostitute than pay a half-prostitute. Occasionally he finds a girl who meets his wishes. Then he goes with her to a hotel, although it is still forenoon. For a short time after that he is more quiet and he even feels that he could work an hour or two. But soon his restlessness seizes him again which is always at first a purely psychic urge. It is not erections that trouble him, but craving and unrest. He attains erection only when he is with the *puella*. His *potentia* varies. Sometimes he is through very rapidly, sometimes he requires a half hour before he accomplishes erection and orgasm. Again he may indulge in coitus several times in succession, although he feels quieted down after the first.

This condition he naturally describes as painful and unpleasant. He tries to interest himself in art and science, as other men do; he would also like to carry on intellectual conversations. But he can only think of "obscenities" to talk about. The more foolish and cynical the better he likes them. He feels impelled to use the grossest expressions, especially before prostitutes and doing so brings him great pleasure.

He also has fits of anger during which he is almost beside himself. If something is not to his liking it makes him raving mad. At such times he is likely to break out with violence, for instance, destroy a chair, or hurl things through the window regardless of the danger of striking some passer-by, and he may say the most awful things to his landlady. He has had many quarrels and violent scenes have been caused on account of his uncontrollable temper.

For some months he kept a fairly good job but had to quit because he talked back to his office chief, using bad language. It always made him mad to have worked piled up on him. Work is a red rag to him. He found on his desk twenty letters which had to be done. Instead of settling down to work he began swearing. What did the folks think anyway? How did they expect one man to do it all? The very impertinence! etc. After several hours of fuming that way he fell to his work. Then everything was all right and he got through fast enough for he always finished his work before all others in the office.

He wondered that he was not dismissed from that office long before. His chief had the patience of an angel. Finally even that man's patience was exhausted and he was discharged. After that he could find no permanent employment. He kept a job a few days at a time; then the chip on his shoulder would cause him to be discharged.

He related his sexual life in great detail; of particular importance is his statement that he never had anything to do with homosexuals; though he well knew there are homosexuals. Such folks were "beasts" who inspired him only with disgust. . . .

We allow here Alfred to speak for himself. In the account of his life there are a number of observations which are characteristic of the whole man:

"I remember nothing of my early childhood. What happened during that time I cannot recollect; my earliest memories date from the time when I was already in school. I only know that both parents were nervous. I lost one brother early, I know nothing of the circumstances. There were a number of insanities in our family, especially on father's side.

"My sexual feelings asserted themselves at a very early age. I remember that when I was seven years old I played with myself before father, without any feeling of shame, because I did not know that it was wrong. Father scolded me and forbade me doing this. But his threats only had the effect of forcing me to continue under cover what I tried to do openly before him. I believe that my power of concentration and my ability to work were impaired already at that time. From playing I merged quickly into systematic masturbation, a habit in which I indulged excessively. At ten years of age we had at school a regular ring of masturbators and we carried on all sorts of things jointly. Nor did we limit ourselves to manual handling. . . .

"At about that time I had terrible nightmares. I saw wild animals, was overcome or bitten by them, thieves wanted to kidnap me, and in my dreams I often saw my father coming after me with a great long stick. These nightly dreams tortured me considerably, every night I was feverish and bathed in sweat.

"In the morning I had an 'all gone' feeling. I gazed blankly before me at school always holding my hand on the penis,—in fact, I often masturbated during class. I became less and less able to concentrate on the work or to carry on my school tasks. In various ways I attempted first to keep up with the work and then I tried all sorts of makeshifts to avoid my school duties. As early as at that age it was characteristic of me that what interested me I had no difficulty in doing. I learned easily but only subjects which I was not taught in school. Thus, for instance, as a boy I became interested in mineralogy, astronomy and botany, and I acquired quite a fund of information on these topics. I should have never learned a hundredth part of what I knew about the subjects if they had been drilled into me at school. . . . Everything that was a duty seemed unbearable to me. Work was a hard duty and always unpleasant. Therefore I got along rather poorly in school. I reached the status of a one-yearling (the privilege to do but one year military duty) only with the aid of home coaching and by the use of influence. And I attained that privilege only at the last moment, during my twentieth year, when I faced the danger of having to serve three years. In a few weeks I prepared and crammed, so as to pass my examinations because I knew that, unless I did, I would be in trouble. I always went to extremes that way, the midway never appealed to me. I would pour over my astronomical books for five hours at a stretch or devote myself uninterruptedly to my plants and my collection of stones, but if I spent a half hour upon my school lessons it made me mad and in my fury I tore the note book.

"My memory for past events is poor. But some incidents, here and there, I recall very vividly. For instance, I remember nothing of a journey through Thuringen which I made with my uncle when I was ten years of age. I was like in a trance during that journey. I made that same journey a second time and then I recalled of one spot that I had already been there. There was a stone there where I had tripped and fallen during the first journey.

"As a boy I was often punished for my laziness and I was even strapped for my obstinacy. I thought I was treated unjustly for I considered my lack of concentration as something I could not help. I was always restless, perennially moody, sometimes very joyous and again very depressed.

"Masturbation I carried on excessively. I masturbated daily—seldom a day passed,—sometimes several times daily, up to the 21st year, when I first had intercourse. Then I decided to give up onanism. At first I had only normal intercourse and felt great satisfaction. But I had to do it very often or my nerves would be all to pieces. During my military service I felt excellently well. I endured easily all sorts of physical exertion and I was very proud of my uniform. As I am very tall and well built I attracted attention in my uniform and the girls looked at me and this made me very proud. But I continued masturbating at the time and avoided intercourse. During the service I was often nervous when I had to carry out an order or if I was kept at one station for any length of time. I pressed myself forward wherever I could, and finally a horse kicked me and I used that accident as a chance to be freed of the service and received for some time the accident pay granted under the circumstances.

"If I am able to get the best of some one, especially of some one in authority, it pleases me beyond measure.

"After the military service I took a position. As I had intercourse daily with women I was in good condition to keep up my work. But I could not endure to have two tasks piled up on me at the same time. I could do only one thing at a time. I was not easy to get along with and had to change positions because I quarreled with my chiefs and because I always avoided hard work. Then I came to Vienna and got a place which I kept for some time. The business interested me, because it dealt with an article which appealed to me. Here I began to grow restless and my uneasiness increased when we removed to Berlin. Normal intercourse no longer satisfied me. I became acquainted with a French woman who became my sweetheart and with whom I practiced all sorts of perversities. I became more and more unstable in my work, often neglecting it for hours at a stretch. I do not know whether that was on account of the Berlin air, which did not agree with me, or because of an accident I met with on the railway. I gave up my position, that is, my chief advised me to do so, although it was a responsible position of great trust, of which I was very proud, especially as my father had bonded me heavily. But I grew more and more restless, it drove me continually to women. I had nothing else on my mind and I wracked my brain to think of new, unheard of perversities to try out. I even tried *podicem lambere* and for a time this brought me great satisfaction, but it quieted me only for a few hours. Then I turned again to Friedrichstrasse looking for the other girls I kept on string besides my regular sweetheart. These adventures required a great deal of money, only a part of which I was able to earn at the time. It was to me always a

pleasant thought that father had to pay for my
indulgences.

"My unrest reached its highest point when my
father came to Berlin to see me and I lived in
Charlottenburg. I had a formidable anxiety about
meeting him and so it happened that he was mostly
alone and saw me but seldom. He did prevail upon
me to see a specialist who promptly put me in a
sanitarium. While there I was much more quiet,
but only outwardly. Within me the old struggle
kept on as usual. The physician ordered me to give
up women for a time because I was super-excitable
and indulgence would harm me. I was abstinent for
a few weeks but thoughts troubled me every night
and I was plainly afraid of losing my mind. Then
I turned to my old remedy, onanism. I did this in
spite of the fact that the physician and the specialist both declared that my condition was due to
excessive masturbation. I was torn between con-
flicting thoughts at the time but noticed that I became more quiet after masturbating. At any rate
after three months of sanitarium treatment I was
still in no condition to work. I am depressed and
life loses its zest the moment I turn to work. After
the first few minutes my mind turns to women and I
must interrupt whatever I am doing and run into the
street. Leaving the sanitarium I returned to Vienna
where the old vicious cycle began once more. I made
the round of physicians and was given any quantity

of bromides. Neither the medicines nor the various hydrotherapic courses helped me in any way. Only if I have intercourse about three times during the night do I feel a little quieted down in the morning. Then I am a little more alert and can work for a short while. But already on the following day, usually the first thing in the morning, the old trouble reasserts itself. I am irritable and depressed. After a coitus which does not gratify me I feel worse than ever. Then I am tremendously excited and want right away another woman who might satisfy me better. Sometimes I long for true love and for the companionship of a lovely being. I then feel the terror of loneliness fastening upon me. I literally pant for air and again rush to the street where temptations meet me. I feel as if something within me has taken possession of my soul driving me on from one adventure to another. Personally I am inwardly inclined towards everything that is noble; but something within me compels me to act as a bad and evil person.

"I believe I am like a man who is the victim of an insatiable hunger. I have often thought of poor Prometheus, condemned always to linger in hunger and thirst. In the same way I feel within me an unquenchable thirst for love and its pleasures and I have no other thought than to satisfy this thirst in some way. I feel like a mechanism destined only to serve the penis in its demand for gratification.

"I have often resolved to change. But I am unable to carry out any resolution, I cannot undertake a thing. I can only hunt after women. *Ich kann nur coitieren,* (I can only ————,) every other activity about me is in a state of suspension. I am uncertain and vaccilating about everything. Today I feel a little religious twinge, tomorrow I poke fun at church and priest. Today I decide to learn something new or to find a job, tomorrow I think something else entirely. I want to buy a new hat. I decide today to go to a certain store. I go to the place but linger before the windows, unable to make up my mind to step in. "No," I say to myself, "I don't want to buy a hat just yet." And meanwhile I also think about women for that is a subject which never leaves my mind for a moment. I stroll up and down the street watching the hundreds of women before I make up my mind to speak to one.

"I draw no distinction between old and young, pretty or plain ones. I weigh the matter over considerably but in the end I pick up the first one that comes along. If it only quieted me! But it lasts only an hour, sometimes, at best, a whole day, then I must rush out again to the street and hunt. Sometimes I cohabit with three women in a day.

"My worst time was when I had gonorrhea (not yet completely healed). I was forbidden to have intercourse for a time. But I could not listen to

the doctor, because I was afraid that I would go
literally to pieces. I kept up intercourse right along
and was inwardly glad to think that so many others
will also have to suffer what I suffered. Then I
felt remorse over my meanness, I felt myself a repro-
bate, a criminal, and resolved that I must change
my ways. I fell into a deep depression and for a
few hours I was free of my usual erotic thoughts.
Then they started again and the same thoughts now
plague me night and day as before." . . .

We have listened to the poor man's terrible confession. His hunt after gratification has that
tragical quality which the poet has so fittingly expressed: *"Und im Genuss verschmacht' ich nach
Begierde."*—"And I starved with yearning even
while I tasted." The deep depressions indicate that
this trouble is approaching a crisis. For the depressions occur at closer intervals and satisfying experiences are more rare. That is also the reason why
he seeks professional advice. He feels that this
cannot go on. He cannot and does not want to
endure life under such conditions. He wants to work
like other men and to be capable of turning his mind
to other matters than sexual.

Two things stand out in the patient's account.
First, his complete amnesia regarding his first journey through Thuringen, as pointed out by himself—
except for the slight accident of tripping—and

next, the fact that his condition became so much more serious during his stay in Berlin, when he was already on the way to get well. He had given up masturbation of his own initiative, substituting for it intercourse with women, he was working, he held a responsible position, and kept up his work, according to the statement of his superiors in office, in spite of disturbances . . . then suddenly his condition made a turn for the worse. Some strong impression or unusual experience in Berlin must have brought on this sudden change.

It is noteworthy that the subject denies having ever carried on any homosexual act. He claims such men only fill him with extreme disgust. The childhood experiences, of course, do not count. All children did the same things; one would conclude that all boys were homosexual. As a matter of fact they are married and happy, most of them heads of happy families. "I have a frightful passion," he says, "exclusively for women. Men do not exist for me."

At night he dreams:

I see a turbulent ocean before me. The waves are in continuous agitation. I think to myself: it were a pity if the waves ceased their agitation. A ship passes by, and the boat carries everything that I love. I believe my mother is also upon that ship. There is an orchestra playing on board: "Oh, how could I possibly leave you!" I awake feeling sad and depressed.

Such a dream is a resistance dream and indicates that the subject does not want to get well. His soul is an ocean, continuously in a state of agitation. "I think it a pity that the waves should cease," means: *I do not want to become quiet at all!* The boat symbolizes the illness, the neurosis. His neurosis covers everything he loves, including his mother; and should he give up all that? Impossible! He cannot renounce his infantile sexuality. He wants to remain a child and be ill.

The analysis is carried out under very great resistance but satisfactory progress is made. I want to outline the results limiting myself to the most important points.

His sexual life comes more and more to light. It appears that in his free account he covered under silence a important form of pleasurable gratification because he was ashamed of it. He indulges in a very curious form of infantile sexuality. The habit must be widespread but in this form I have met it only twice.

Every two weeks he does as follows: he lies down in bed dressed in his underclothes and defecates. Then he lies in his stools for several hours. After that he takes great pains to remove every trace. He washes the drawers and the shirt or he burns them up. At the baths, where he is always very excited sexually he does the same thing. He does that there more readily because the means are at hand for cleaning himself afterwards. He usually takes along a package of clean linen. At the public baths every cabin has a couch. He lies down and allows his bowels to move. There he lies feeling very satisfied and masturbates or has a spontaneous ejaculation. Then he bathes to clean himself and the package of soiled linen he throws into a river or anywhere where it disappears quickly.

In these scenes he reproduces the infant in swaddling clothes. He even presses the covers tightly around him so that he cannot move, to give himself the illusion of being tied down. He repeats the infantile scenes of cleaning by the mother, during which in his fancy he plays the double role of mother and child.

He struggles with greatest anxiety against this remarkable paraphila but always submits to it in the end. The longest interval up to the time of the psychoanalysis was four weeks. After that "orgy of filth,"—as he calls it—he feels depressed and is ashamed of himself. He has not mentioned this to a living soul and even the physician at the sanitarium knew nothing about it. He went through this act several times not at the sanitarium, but in his room because the baths were not private. When discussing sexual infantilism we shall learn of several similar cases. His attitude towards his mother is very changeable but not so emotionally tense as his relations with his father. He carries on a quiet and

occasionally affectionate exchange of letters with
his mother, but with his father, never. He is to a
certain extent fond of his mother. As he tried masturbation in front of his father as a child so now
he keeps nothing of his sexual life secret before me.
He relates frankly everything. As a child he loved
his mother very much and often wished to be with
her. His mother is now an old woman, partially
paralysed. Nevertheless he noticed during his last
visit home that she is still a pretty woman and repeatedly felt impelled to approach her. . . . At
such times he treats her very roughly and scornfully, and is inclined to make fun of her and her age.
He has had repeatedly affairs with old women. At
his last lodging place there was an elderly woman,
whose face was badly wrinkled, with whom he became intimate but after a short time he sought a
quarrel with her and moved out. That is the way
he behaves with everybody. He quarrels over some
trifle, becomes very excited and makes a terrible
scene. Then he is through with that person for
good.

We shall see that this is his way of protecting
himself against temptation. He quarrels only with
persons with whom he has pleasant relations and
who play some role in his sexual fancies. That is
also how he parts from his mother, for he usually
leaves her after a bitter quarrel. This is also why
his parents let him dwell among strangers, although

they think a great deal of him. His letters are sufficiently irritating but easier to endure than the
scenes he creates when at home.

His attitude towards his father is worse. He is
easily moved to anger when speaking of him. He
makes copious use of vile terms when referring to
him. Such expressions as "the old rascal," the
"miserable thief," are customary with him when
speaking of his father. He knows no reason why he
should feel so bitter towards his father. That is,
he gives a thousand reasons but all trivial and hardly
relevant. The father brought him up badly; the
father is responsible for his condition; the father is
wealthy, nevertheless complains always that he has
nothing; the father lives only for his mother and
cares nothing for *him*. He wants to make himself
independent and wants to get money from his father
for that purpose. The very thought that his father
may deny him the money makes him angry: "I shall
go to him and kill him and shoot myself." Such
murder fancies are not infrequent about his father.

How close the neurotic is to the criminal! Against
his father he raises all sorts of complaints, equally
unreasonable. One day he called on me to say that,
having passed a sleepless night he has figured out at
last the reason for his illness: the father has mur-
dered his brother! The brother was incurably ill
and a burden to his father. He knew it well and had
decided to go home and confront his father with

the truth, then demand his share of the inheritance.
Even as a boy it was clear to him that the father
had deliberately put his brother out of the way.
The father always felt uncomfortable when the talk
turned to the boy and always tried to avoid the
subject.

He judges his father according to his own inner
self. He carries within himself the soul of a murderer, as the pathologic strength of his instinctive
cravings already indicates. The suspicion directed
against his father is determined psychically by the
fact that during his own youth he wished his
brother's death because he did not want to have any
competitor for household favors and he knew well
that the fortune would have to de divided between
them. But he was not the kind of man who would
consent to dividing anything. He wanted everything for himself exclusively. He wanted his brother
out of the way and had actually indulged in various fanciful dreams how to go about it. Now he
shifted his fancies over to his father, while for himself he conjured up an attitude of sympathy and
regret whenever his brother was mentioned. He is
most unhappy because he has no brother, his father
has robbed him of what was most precious in his
life. Had his brother lived he would not be ill, only
the realization of his father's deed is what brought
him to such a state. The father passes for a prominent person and enjoys a high position in his com-

munity, he has been mayor of the town, but should he start proceedings against him, the father would land in jail. He is filled with jealousy because his father has done so well; his own incapacity he explains away chiefly on the score of his illness.

It takes a long time for the original love of the father to come to the surface, back of this thick cover of hatred and jealousy. But the masking layer melts, surely though slowly, and meanwhile explanations for which the subject is as yet unprepared would do more harm than good. The art of analysis consists in showing up only so much as reveals itself from time to time. Our subject is not yet prepared to see that he is in love with his father. Nevertheless he begins to talk about his father's preëminence and other favorable sides, the man's knowledge, his great library, etc.

Gradually the father's picture looms up in terms more and more favorable. The subject relates pleasant episodes from youth, when he botanized along with his father who introduced him to the science; he withdraws his murder notion, admitting at last that it was only part of his over-heated fancy. At this stage when he takes me for the *locum tenens* of his father, he assumes an aggressive attitude towards me and uses an expression which amounts to an insult. I had already made clear to him that he sees his father in me. Now he undertakes to treat me as he would his father. At once I break up the

analysis. Three days later he returns remorsefully
and begs forgiveness. It will not happen again, I
must not leave him in the lurch, he cannot stand this
condition any longer, and I must save him. That
was the only conflict I ever had with him; after that
he behaved well and to this day he shows himself
appreciative and filled with gratitude. He was ready
to recognize how strongly his homosexuality determined his attitude towards his superiors, towards
his father, as well as towards me. He now sees it
clearly. He admits he practically fell in love with
his last chief and that is why he had to quit the
place. He relates a dream which he had kept to
himself till then, and which shows his homosexual
attitude towards me, and admits that during childhood he had idealized his father and loved him
deeply.

We learn more than that. We find out what
brought on his turn for the worse at Berlin. At
his lodging house there was a young boy 14 years
of age, very attractive, whom he coached evenings.
He began to play with that boy. He masturbated
him and was masturbated by the boy in turn. The
relationship kept up for about three months. These
were the first three months of his stay in Berlin.
Then he felt remorse, sought a quarrel with the landlady and moved out. From that moment began his
insatiable craving for women. It was his last homosexual period. He had led astray other boys before

that one and always gladly introduced them to the habit. A court case in which the defendant was sentenced for a similar offence decided him to give up the homosexual practices. He never repeated them after that Berlin episode.

His satyriasis developed on account of the repression of his homosexual tendencies. Back of his morbid passion for woman stood his ungratified longing for man.

The subject now sees clearly that he carried on with the boy the act which he expected of his father. His hatred of the father is reversed love. In the chapter devoted to sadism we will describe more fully this relationship between father and son.

Our subject expected his father to do with him what he did with the boy. It shows how little credence we should lend a patient's first statements. Presently numerous similar episodes come to the forefront and soon we learn that his greatest desire at one time was to procure a pretty boy for himself and that boys roused him more than girls. He seeks the company of women to forget all about his inclination towards boys and hopes to overcome his homosexual tendencies through excessive heterosexual experiences. His craving for women his obsessive thinking about them, serves only as a means to prevent his mind from reverting to the other sex. Compulsory thoughts often serve the purpose of preventing other thoughts from intruding. This is

the law of resistance which plays such a tremendous
role in the mental life of neurotics. In the course
of treatment he transfers upon me all his passion
—as was to be expected. He has some dreams,—
which he relates with great difficulty,—during which
he sees me naked and handles my penis or even carries out *fellatio*. He now recalls passionately watching his father, also how happy he was to go bathing
with him, and how he liked to hide in order to see
his father's phallus. The dissolution of this transference and reference back to his father he does not
like at first, but it becomes more and more pronounced as we proceed. He is now abstinent for a
week at a stretch and no longer chases after women
although I gave him no particular advice on this
point. The consciously acknowledged homosexual
leaning has no need for this cover. As leaning
comes to surface openly it is openly overcome. He
again experiences anxieties. His landlady tells that
he is heard tossing and groaning and even crying
out in his sleep. He is now sentimental and soft,
becoming greatly changed in character, to his advantage. Again he goes to the theatre and reads
books,— things he had not done for years. His
letters to his father are more quiet in tone and
sympathetic. He becomes economical and spends
less than his father sends him.

Then something happens which promises to mark
a new epoch in his life. It is a typical experience

of these men during treatment. As the infantile ties are loosened in the course of the analysis they fall in love.[1]

Our subject is in a state of highest preparedness towards love. His homosexuality, which had been completely repressed—he no longer took any interest in boys—was again manifest. He now played his trump card. He fell in love with a girl who was to replace for him all other women as well as all thought of man. This happened in so remarkable and typical a manner that it is worth while to report fully the occurrence.

He was still in the habit of accosting girls on the street, even if for no other object than sheer amusement. One evening he came across a demure little girl who looked rather like a young boy, boldly spoke to her and fell deeply in love with her on the spot. In three days he declared himself her beau and six days later they became engaged. He thought of nothing else but his sweetheart. As if bent on revenging himself on me and on his father he spoke of nothing else but his love and his new found happiness. The satyriasis was replaced by a psychic intoxication even more powerful. He picked up a girl belonging to an ordinary family to punish his parents. He chose that girl although she was no longer *virgo intacta* (because this did not interest

[1] (Cf. *Angstzustaende*, p. 417. An English translation of this work is now in course of preparation and will appear shortly.)

him). He told that to his parents and it was, he
felt, the strongest revenge and punishment he could
bring upon them. They thought a great deal of
their social position; and now, their son was marry-
ing the daughter of a motorman, a girl without any
education and who served as clerk in some store.
And he threatened his parents that he would take his
life unless he could marry the girl. He would marry
her without their consent. His love was so great,—
such a love never had its equal in the world! The
very thought that his father might try to prevent
the marriage made him raving mad and he talked of
violence and murder.

I advised the father to disarm the son by placing
no opposition in his path. He should make but one
condition: the son must support himself and his
wife. Only a man capable of maintaining a wife
has the right to marry. I took the same attitude
explaining to the young man that he must make
himself independent of his father through his own
labor. He perceived plainly that the idea of maintaining himself through his own labor did not appeal
to him. His greatest pleasure was the thought that
his father had to pay every time he went out with
a woman and that he was squandering his father's
money.

At this time he confesses to me that he was about
to get married once before. It was in Berlin, shortly
after the homosexual relations with the young boy.

He became acquainted with a girl who kept up intercourse with him. This girl he wanted to marry and his father went through the same trial with him. He could not think of a greater revenge. Such subjects show this trait again and again. It is not the only case of the kind that I have met. The occurrence is common and every experienced nerve specialist is called in consultation over similar problems several times in the course of a year. That girl was the Frenchwoman who introduced him to all forms of paraphiliac practices. The father, naturally indignant, threatened to disinherit the son. That was precisely what our patient was looking for. He was afraid only of a soft-hearted father and he managed always to rouse his anger as a sort of protective screen between himself and his father. The patient also felt that his father scorned him. During the Berlin episode he clung to his Frenchwoman, did not rest until his father met her, wanted always to keep in her company and was afraid of being alone with his father.

At this point the subject's journey to Thuringen with his father came up through numerous associations. He accompanied on that journey not his uncle, but his father, and he now recalls that during the trip he frequently occupied one bed with his father, and that it made him happy to think that his father took him along instead of his mother.

It will be recalled that previously he remembered

only the incident of slipping on a stone. That is really a "Deckerrinerung." The fall covers other incidents. It stands for a fall into sin. I must point out that the subject also links the return of the trouble and its aggravation to an alleged fall. The accident happened in a merry go round. He fell unconscious but after a short time came fully to himself and returned to the sport. The accident could hardly have been a serious one. At any rate the riddle of a fall belonged to the fancies with which he had beclouded his journey to Thuringen. The fiction established itself in his mind through his occupying one bed with his father in the course of that journey and his substituting the father for the mother. His dreamy mind conceived the companion as a woman, as the mother, and added the fiction of a fall into sin, symbolically represented by the trivial incident of an actual fall.

He now finds himself in a new homosexual danger. I see him daily and he tries by various tricks to induce me to give him a physical examination and to show me his penis. He thinks he has again gonorrhea, perhaps he has phthiriasis, I ought to examine him, it would be foolish for him to go to another physician for that. I explain these symptoms and the man confesses that he has indulged also openly in fancies in which I played a role. And now he takes revenge by telling me about his bride and dwelling on her tenderness for hours. He has no other theme for talk. He must always have her near him to feel quiet. She must not leave him for a moment. Day and night he wants to hold her hand . . . thus he insures himself against homosexuality.

Finally I tell him I shall give up the psychoanalysis if there is nothing else to come up. Then, lo! his talk turns to other matters. He knows now that his engagement is a defence measure against his homosexuality and his filthy onanistic acts. But he also sees that in his bride he has found a surrogate for his mother. He surrounds her with tenderness like a man who truly loves, and presently his psychic intoxication turns into a deep and true affection. He still has serious quarrels with his bride. He still storms against his father and against all authority. He is an anarchist at war with all authority and assumes an obstinate attitude towards everybody. But his father, apprised by me of the true situation, keeps his temper and thus disarms his son. Thus the engagement no longer serves the object of worrying the parents. His parents apparently let him have his own way, insisting only that he should go to work. I doubt his ability to get to work and express to him my sympathy. He wants to show me that he can work. At every opportunity I sympathize with his bride, a quiet, brave little woman. He will surely abandon her. He cannot keep true. Not so! he declares. He is going to show me that he can be true.

In a few weeks he finds a position and does his work so carefully and diligently that his condition is greatly improved. Then he marries and in every sense of the word becomes a new man.

But there was a great deal more to do. His paranoiac notions of grandeur, his feeling that he could do anything which others may not, his obstinacy and his rebellion against all authority were gradually replaced by social tendencies. He became modest and agreeable. . . .

His complete recovery, he learned early, depended on his keeping away from his parents. A short stay in the old home roused all the old antagonisms and he resolved to stay away so as to keep on friendly terms with his parents.

At first all his affection was centered on his bride and he did not wait for the marriage ceremony. . . . He attained unbelievable accomplishments. . . . But this did not continue for long and soon he quieted down and had intercourse with his wife at regular intervals. . . . Pregnancy and childbirth made it necessary for him to keep away from her for a time and he did so easily enough, without being untrue to her.

I do not know how long this improvement will last. He has kept his place for the past three years with dignity and honor, and is today a quiet, brave man who shudders when he thinks of his past. His parents have reconciled themselves to his marriage and the birth of two grandchildren has ratified in their eyes the inevitable fact.

The character of satyriasis is richly illustrated by this case. We see also why the Berlin air did not agree with the subject. There he was in danger of becoming overtly homosexual. In one Berlin office where he worked there was a homosexual who wanted to introduce him to his circle. He took a sudden liking for his chief of whom he grew daily more fond. The other men in the office made him jealous and he resorted to quarreling, using vile talk. Finally he broke with his chief as a defence against the pent-up feelings within himself.

It is interesting to note that during his relations with the young boy he identified himself with his father. He carried out the act of seduction which he vainly expected to be acted out by his father. His identification with the father went so far that he felt himself aged, tired, played out and he thought he might not live long. During his coprophiliac acts he played the role of a suckling.

It is interesting to observe what role he assumes now while in love with his wife. A few remarks on that point may not be out of place here:

During the first stage of his infatuation the subject identified himself with his mother, while the young woman stood for a boy, mostly himself. He

acted out the love scenes between mother and son
and he was surprised to find himself capable of such
motherly feelings.   He emphasized his strong
femininity.   He had, he thought, womanly hips, scant
beard growth, gynecomasty (full breasts).   Or-
ganically he was of that bisexual type which careful
examination of the neurotic never fails to disclose.
He was also attentive, gallant, dainty and man-
nerly.   Sometimes the bride was the mother and he
played the role of the child.   He snuggled up in her
arms saying: "I should like to crawl in and lie like
a child in its mother's bosom!   That would be bliss."
During coitus he preferred succubus and once there
occurred a strange incident.   A fancy seemed to
dawn on him that he was having intercourse with
his mother.   This was not a phantasy that I had
in any way suggested.   I let the subject relate
everything that comes to his mind without influencing him in one direction or another.

As he improved the identification with his mother
disappeared.   He made up with his parents, exchanged friendly letters with his father, and felt he
was making satisfactory progress.   For the first
time in his life he was himself.

He became aware of his own personality.   Now
he loved his wife as a husband, and felt that he was
a father who had a mother of his own.

That may seem self-evident and an irrelevant remark.   But the whole task which I aimed to achieve

was to break up his identification with his parents, destroy his projection upon the old home. Previously the leading motive in all his conduct was the thought: *what will my parents say?* The knowledge that his father would be troubled made him happy. He wanted to punish the man whom he held responsible for his sufferings on account of his lack of proper responsiveness and to keep the father always in trouble. Now he abandoned his infantilism. He was a child no longer, he was a man. Overcoming all disguises and masks he came to himself.

His homosexuality persisted as formerly. But he saw this clearly before his eyes and recognized it openly in his relations with his superiors, his friends and his psychoanalytic adviser. He could meet the issue and overcome it. Perhaps he shifted a part of it over to his son. One thing is certain: he is through with the homosexual longing and so completely that it no longer troubles him. He is alert and active. Such result would not be attained without the art of analysis and without the physician's educational skill. This man, in the absence of analysis, would have probably ended his misery in suicide.

I must also point out that his genuine affection for his wife developed out of an impulsive infatuation. He met the woman, spoke to her, and fell in love with her at once. Yet the marriage is happier as time passes. Trifling storms do occur—where do they not—but they blow lightly over and his home life is one of quiet happiness. The dream about his great historic mission is gone. He who had once the ambition to become a Napoleon or a Herostratos, a Satan or a Don Juan, a bomb-thrower, is now a reliable, efficient and satisfied book-keeper; he now sits at his desk in the office dutifully adding long columns of figures, brings home little presents for his wife and children, and if his old folks send him a sum of money he is pleasantly sur-prised and puts it in the bank for his little daughter. This case illustrates also the relations of homo-sexuality to the family and to the problem of incest. More about that later. . . .

Nymphomania shows the same homosexual basis as satyriasis. In the study of Sexual Frigidity in Women [1] we shall have occasion to point out types of women who are undoubtedly nymphomaniac in character, Messalinas. These women are usually anesthetic, a condition in itself of considerable significance and one which is often seen also in ordi-nary prostitutes. They have a hunger for man similar to Don Juan's longing for woman. It is characteristic of them, too, that they never find satisfaction. These persons in perpetual quest, Ahasuerus, the Flying Dutchman, Faust and Don Juan, who are condemned to wander and search and

[1] English translation by James S. Van Teslaar.

who never find rest, portray the libido which does
not find its proper sexual goal.[1]

There are also among women endless seekers continually dreaming of man,—some man who shall completely and lastingly gratify them. The conditions
are even more complex in women than in men. For
the present I want to report briefly one case, pointing out merely what may serve as an illustration of
our present theme. We shall take up the whole subject more fully in connection with our discussion of
dyspareunia.

A woman, strikingly beautiful,—we shall call her
Adele—comes to me with a most unusual complaint.
She is married to an excellent man with whom she
had fallen in love and she still loves him. She has
no inclination whatever to remain true to him. She
lacks completely any resistance to temptation. She
is easily the victim of any man who comes near her.
She is a woman who does not know how to say "no."
Her husband who has no inkling of her doings wor-
ships her. Sometimes she is conscience stricken, as

[1] Faust finds this temporarily in his Graetchen. But it is
only an episode and presently he is again restlessly searching
until he finds Helena, the most beautiful of all women. The
Flying Dutchman is released by a woman who remains true to
the last in her love of him. That is the projection of a sub-
jective feeling upon the woman. He wishes he could find a
woman for whom he would feel a love so dear that it would
relieve him. In Ahasuerus the same problem is glossed over
with religious terms as the problem seen in the Don Juan
story as the requital of the all-highest father. All four must be
faithless, they cannot remain true to one woman.

now, and wishes to find something that would quiet her so that she would not have to think from morning till night only of sexual matters. But, what I shall find unbelievable, she adds, is that she remains cold during a man's embrace and must always follow it up with onanism. Only cunnilingus produces an adequate orgasm in her. She thinks that if a man satisfied her regularly in that way perhaps she could remain true to him.

From her life history I quote the following data. Already as a child Adele had gathered certain experiences on the subject of sex. She was about eight years of age when her brother began to carry out coitus with her. She was very sensual even at that time and claims that she experienced great pleasure in the act. The brother was two years older. All the children in the apartment building where they lived were introduced early to sexual acts. Often there took place regular orgies. She was loaned by her brother to other boys when he received their sisters in exchange. She remembers having been used once by four boys in succession. These doings went on for over a year. Then another girl's mother discovered what was going on and matters came very near being aired in court. There were scenes and investigations but all the children lied themselves out of it.

From that time on she masturbated and to this day she cannot give up the habit. Even as a "flap-

per" she had no other thought than to attract men.
She was very coquettish and easy going, improved
for a time, becoming very devout as well as retired
in her disposition and even thought of joining a
nunnery and taking the vows of chastity.

But this pious attitude did not last long. Soon
she flirted again and turned to all kinds of erotic
books, the reading of which so excited her that she
masturbated several times during the night. At 17
years of age, a pupil of her father's who was teacher
of piano at the musical high school, took advantage
of her. She was alone with the young man for a few
minutes. He kissed her and she accepted this without resistance. Then he dragged her on top of
himself—there was no couch in that study room—
and she lost her virginity. She did not know how it
happened. It was over in a few minutes. She kept
away from the young man after that, although he
pursued her, and for a few weeks lived in terror,
afraid that she might be pregnant. But fortunately
that was not the case. She soon noticed that all
men were interested in her. Young and old pursued
her. The mother to whom, with tears in her eyes,
she related the incident with the young man and
who kept it from the father (fearing that he would
murder the boy) kept careful watch over her, never
left her alone, always saying to her: "Child, you
must marry soon! Your blood is too hot."

At 19 years of age she found her man, with whom

she fell in love so desperately that she became the laughing stock of the town. During the very first days of courtship she fell into his arms and offered no resistance when he tried to possess her completely. He was so excited that he failed to observe that she was not a virgin. She enjoyed the experience but little, although she was tremendously excited at the time.

From the very beginning she was untrue to him. She carried on with a friend of his, going even to that man's house. She was unhappy and wanted to do away with herself. But she soon got over that and again began flirting.

After the marriage ceremony—three days later—she recalled having heard that Dr. X., an attractive young single man, was a great Don Juan. She decided to look him up at once and seduce him. She complained to him of a red spot upon her privates, claiming it troubled her. Was that not a sign of some illness? In short, she attained her purpose, was his sweetheart for a time, and learned then of cunnilingus for the first time. That she regarded as the highest achievement in the art of love. Another man required of her the anal form of copulation. All such things amused her, although she never experienced the orgasm as satisfactorily as during masturbation.

Before long she felt painful remorse. She had the best of men for a husband. She tortured herself

with the most severe reproaches, daily saying to
herself: "This must be the last time; I must not
do it again." But the very next day she felt impelled again to go into the street or to telephone
to one of the many men who were at her disposal.
It is interesting to note that on her list of lovers
there were physicians, lawyers, army officers, clerks,
nobles and commoners. She never took payment and
never accepted presents. That would put her in a
class with the prostitutes. She also tried coachmen
and chauffeurs, but her disgust afterwards was so
great that she gave this up, although she always
felt the temptation.

She acquired a gonorrheal infection and this compelled her to claim "female trouble" as an excuse to
keep her husband away from her for a time. She
was so provoked with the man who had infected her
that she wanted to revenge herself on all men and
in her anger thought of transferring the infection
to every man in her circle. She did not carry out
this plan because the gynecologist who treated her
forbade all sexual congress. Nevertheless twice she
could not control herself and she infected two
men. . . .

She wanted me to hypnotize her. There was no
other thought in her mind than men and again men!
Her mind revolved continually around sexual scenes;
she has even thought of going for a time to a house
of prostitution, and, like Agrippina, allow any num-

ber of men to use her until she shall have had enough.
Perhaps then she would quiet down! If she meets
a stranger that night she dreams of intercourse with
him!

I ask her about the dreams; whether they lay stress
on some special form of intercourse or portray
merely the normal act.

Hesitatingly she answers: "Always the normal.
Only I am regularly on top. . . . Why is that? I
have often thought of it."

"Did you have such a dream last night?"

"Let me see. Certainly; a foolish dream,
though. . . ."

"Please, let me hear it."

"I am in bed with my brother-in-law. A man of
whom I would not even dream."

"But you did dream of him."

"I cannot understand it. I have never given him
one minute's thought."

"And never anything happened between you?"

"No . . . with him, never. Although he is attentive to me and I know he likes me. I love my sister
too dearly to treat her that way, although my sister
is not faithful either, and things like that don't matter with her. It seems to be in the family. Still, I
would rather have nothing to do with my brother-
in-law. The dream is nonsense, I have forgotten the
most of it. It was much longer."

Observing that she tries to avoid the dream I

insist that she should try and recall it as nearly as possible. "Well, then," she continues her narrative, "the dream was as follows:

"*I am in bed with my brother-in-law. It seems I am the man and he the woman. He has no mustache and lies under me. Suddenly he changes and it is my sister and I kiss her passionately. 'You see,' she says to me, 'you should have done this long ago and you would be well.'*"

I inquire about her relations to the sister and learn that she has not been in touch with her for the past few months and that during this time she has grown more nervous and her craving for men also grew worse than ever. "When I am with my sister I seem to forget men more easily. She is a very spiritual person and extremely charming. If you should ever meet her you would fall in love with her."

When one hears such talk, and one hears it rather often, the diagnosis is easy: the narrator is in love with that person and therefore thinks it natural that everybody should fall in love with the person in question.[1]

---

[1] Once I treated a man who had separated from his wife, wanted to marry another woman with whom he had fallen in love and to divorce his wife. In the course of our interviews during that time this man said repeatedly: "I would not introduce you to my first wife; you would fall in love with her if I did; no man can help that." At once I recognized that the man's neurotic disorder reached back to a suppressed love for his wife. In his mind there rumbled continually sounds

Further inquiries disclose that she was preoccupied with but one thought: her sister. She always
looks upon her sister as the best dressed, most
spirited and most charming person she had ever
known.

Why was the woman no longer on friendly terms
with her sister?

Because, she claims, her sister is egotistical and
cares nothing for her. She was lying ill for a few
weeks and her sister let her lie there and took no
more notice of her than if she were a dog; she wanted
her sister's company when she went out, she could
not do her shopping alone but she could not get her
sister to go along. So she had to go around with a
woman friend who was a disgusting and vulgar person. She ought to be ashamed to show herself in

which he could not reproduce. He recalled scraps of melodies
which he could not place at all. But once I was able to get
at one such melody. It was a song of which he did not know
the words. When the matter was ferreted out it was found
that the words bore distinctly a reference to his first wife.
The vague melodies permitted his mind to dwell on her and
at the same time to cover from his consciousness the fact that
he could not keep her out of his mind. Here is a characteristic passage from *Eichendorff's* poem:

> Ich kam von Walde hernieder,
> Da stand noch das alte Haus;
> Mein Liebchen schaute wieder
> Wie einst zum Fenster hinaus—
>
> Sie hat einen andern genommen—
> Ich war draussen in Schlacht und Krieg—
> Nun ist alles anders gekommen:—
> Ich wollt es war wieder Krieg. . . .

These verses represent a summary of his great conflict.

such company; if she were in her husband's place, she would not tolerate it. . . . After all, it would not be so very sinful if she did become intimate with her brother-in-law; her sister was not true to him and kept up relations with an army lieutenant but the poor fool does not see it and thinks the army officer is his best friend. . . .

She keeps up an incessant flow of talk. She wakes up thinking of her sister, she thinks of her all day and she dreams of her every night. I have studied her dreams over a period of weeks. There is not a dream in which her sister fails to figure and none but portrays her erotic attitude towards the sister.

In the course of the analysis her childhood experiences come to light and she recalls that for a long time she slept in one bed with her sister and they performed cunnilingus on one another. That was so long ago, she had forgotten all about it. That experience discloses her true nature. She is continually looking for woman; specifically she is looking for one woman, her sister. She wants to forget her, the traumatic experience with her she wants to drive out of memory, by covering it with new experiences.

We see that her latent homosexuality drives her into the arms of every man she meets. We also note the role of family relations in homosexuality, a subject which we shall take up specifically later and illustrate with proper data.

IV

Description of Don Juan Types who are satisfied
with conquest and forego physical possession—
An unlucky Hero, whose love adventures are in-
terfered with by Gastric Derangements—A
would-be Messalina who hesitates on account of
vomiting spells—Influence of Religion on Neurosis.

Ich wüsste kaum noch etwas Anderes geltend zu machen, das dermassen zerstörrisch der Gesundheit und Rassenkräftigkeit, namentlich der Europäer zugesetzt hat als das asketische Ideal; man darf es ohne Übertreibung das eigentliche Verhängniss in der Gesundheitsgeschichte des europäischen Menschen nennen.

Nietzsche.

IV

I know hardly what other factor could be held so harmful to the health and racial vigor of European peoples, as the ascetic ideal; without exaggeration this must be looked upon as the striking fatality in the health history of the European.

Nietzsche.

We have spoken thus far of the active Don Juan and of Messalina types and we have attempted to prove that homosexuality is responsible. Along the extreme types we find endless varieties of transitional types. Nature nowhere confounds us through the richness of her varieties and combinations so much as in the manifestations of human sexuality.

The would-be Don Juan and would-be Messalina are most interesting types. They behave precisely like the true type. They manifest the same uncontrollable and restless craving. But somewhere in their development the capacity to carry out heterosexual adventures fails them. I am not now speaking of the man who plays Don Juan in his mind's fancy or of the Messalina who does not truly possess

175

the courage to try to live up to her instinctive cravings.   There are numberless such cases and a bit
of the type lurks in the breast of every person, a
fact we recognize as the polygamic tendency.

The type which I wish to describe approaches the
ascetic.   It is plain that the ascetic ideal would
not arise if a strong homosexual tendency did not
depreciate heterosexuality.   For every action is the
product of instinct and repression.   An overpowerful
instinct may overcome even the strongest inhibitions.
But if a portion of the individual's sexual energy is
anchored homosexually the aggressive sexual acts
are endowed only with a portion of the energy they
require.   If the energy is shunted off its proper track
entirely we have the ascetic person; and if the
energy is but partially side-tracked and is insuffi-
cient for the accomplishment of the sexual aim, we
have the would-be Don Juan type.

There are any number of men who daily dream
only of their possible conquests, begin adventures,
and carry them along for a time only to drop the
affairs suddenly . . . because they "get cold feet."
They envy men who are able to pursue their adventures to the end, men fortunate enough actually to
make conquests and they bewail the fate which brings
them so close to the most tempting fruit only to
prove elusive just when the fruit seems ready to fall
into their lap,—and to be gone forever.   Better than

all generalizations may serve the account of an
actual case, like the following:

Mr. Xaver Z., would like to be a "lively fellow,"
like most of his companions. He claims that his
shyness spoils his success. He is 29 years old and
has never yet had a "real" affair. When he wakes
up in the morning he thinks: "Will you have luck today to talk up to a girl and get her?" The whole
day he thinks of this so that he is continually distracted and unable to work. He is also dissatisfied
with his business accomplishments. Others work so
easily and accomplish everything without friction,
he is slow and not energetic enough. He thinks that
somehow he lacks initiative. He is always tired and
depressed, and he has already been in sanitaria several times vainly trying to get well. He can hardly
wait for evening to arrive so he may go into the
street in search of adventure. He speaks to a number of girls but nothing comes of it. He has also
tried a "personal" in the newspaper and corresponds
with several women. But they are only platonic relations. He either lacks the courage to become
more intimate with the women or finds himself
repulsed when making a suggestion of the kind. He
thinks he is unlike other men and it discourages him.
He always feels lonely and Sundays are a torture to
him. He tries to meet poor people and pays them

occasionally to partake of an evening meal with them so as not to feel quite so lonely.

He is a travelling salesman. He fears that he is not an efficient salesman. He lacks the power of influencing his prospective customers, he seems unable to talk as convincingly to them as other men in his calling. He acts indifferent and if he sees that the customer does not intend to buy he goes right off. He is employed by an older brother. He is lucky. Another employer would have dismissed him long ago. While his brother does not reproach him in words he can read it in the brother's eyes.

Regarding his sexual life he is able to state that sexual matters began early to interest him. He does not remember the beginning of it. He does remember that he masturbated at 10 years of age and he continued the practice till he was 20 years old. Then he heard about the evil consequences and gradually gave it up. But even after that he masturbated every two months or so and always felt very worried after doing it.

He began going to women at twenty years of age. Since that time he has intercourse about once every two weeks with prostitutes, or occasionally with some girl whom he picks up on the street and who usually expects pay; he is strongly potent. He has no particular pleasure with prostitutes. He goes to them out of a sense of duty because all his colleagues have intercourse with women and he wants to be like them. It is a hygienic measure rather than an inner compulsion with him. But he always fancies that, under the right conditions, when the girl gives herself out of love, it must be different. He felt so dissatisfied because he was never lucky enough to have a real sweetheart. For the girls he picked up on the street were really nothing more than ordinary prostitutes since they, too, expect some present if not regular pay.

He was distinctly unlucky. Other young men were always lucky but he, quite the contrary. There must be something about him that makes persons keep away when they get to know him more intimately.

If these complaints are looked upon as true facts one would really think that the young man was unlucky. But as a matter of fact he himself lays the foundation for his lack of luck, he alone spreads the bed in which he is to lie. He is a Don Juan who carries on flawlessly the first part of his adventures; it is only when he tries to bring the adventures to a head that his luck fails him and then the expected conquest turns into a deception.[1]

It appears that he has actually brought many of his adventures to a crisis only to withdraw at the supreme moment on the score of some triviality or other. These occurrences are all alike except that

[1] Cf. chapter entitled, *Der Pechvogel*, in: *Das Liebe Ich.* Verlag Otto Salle, Berlin.

the alleged motives for breaking up the adventure differ in every case. Perhaps it will be best to mention his last adventure as an example, for it is particularly typical:

It was Sunday. Xaver felt again very lonely and neglected and went out looking for a girl. An old friend whom he was to meet at a certain place he neglected to look up. Today he must succeed. He is tired of loneliness and neglect. Today he will get a girl. He makes a few attempts but in each case he find the girl expects pay and that does not suit him. Finally he sees passing by a fine, sinewy, supple figure. He hurries after it—she is an elegant, attractive woman. He speaks up, telling her in one breath that she must not be angry, his intentions are "entirely honorable." He merely feels lonely and would like to spend the evening in pleasant company. The woman is not prudish, she permits him to accompany her and confesses that she, too, is lonely and feels terribly depressed. He now worries because he promised her "an honorable acquaintance" and during the walk tries to make up his mind whether he ought not to change his tactics. It begins to rain. They enter a Café where they listen to some music; then they go to a restaurant for dinner. He shows himself very gallant, pays all expenses and conducts her home. The woman tells him she has a telephone, as she conducts a little business and suggests that he may call her up. They agree to meet the following Sunday and spend their time together. During the weeks he plans a line of attack and decides to put an end to his shyness and come with her to the real object. . . . He calls her up, they decide to go to the Opera together and then to a late supper. On Sunday forenoon he purchases the tickets and intends to put them at her disposal. Suddenly the thought strikes him, he ought to give up the relationship. He sends the spare ticket to a friend and telephones the woman that some of his relatives having arrived unexpectedly he cannot go to the Opera. Afterwards he is unhappy over it, etc.

The friend was otherwise engaged, he remained alone, the ticket was wasted. He worried considerably over the matter and returned home feeling sad. When I pointed out to him next day that he really fled from the girl, he shook his head and said his sister was really responsible because "I told her everything and asked her what I should do. Sister said: 'she is pulling your leg, it will cost you money and nothing will come of it.' "

"Do you tell your sister these things?"

"Certainly. We speak very frankly about all sexual matters. Sister has started the custom and I find it natural. Why should I not advise with sister?"

I explain to him that he expected her to turn him against the adventure, that he was really afraid of the relationship and its possible consequences. I show that the friend was more to him than the woman and that the sending of the ticket to him meant: *my friend is more important to me than a woman!*

I have occasion to prove again and again that he paves the way for his failures very adroitly and sometimes tactlessly because while acting the role of a "lively" man he wants at the same time to preserve his inner attitude. The initial stage of conquest satisfies him and thereafter he voluntarily renounces to its consummation.

That he vehemently denies,—he knows absolutely nothing about any homosexual leaning! He declares he would be right if he could only have the right kind of a love affair. He is continually looking for it. It was really unbelievable to hear how many adventures he was able to start in the course of a week. He was a handsome interesting man and found no trouble conquering women's hearts. But he always managed affairs so as to break them up before they went too far. At the last moment he always thought of something or other which prevented consummation of the adventure.

This was shown typically one New Year's day. A woman from a distance, with whom he was in correspondence—they had also exchanged their photographs—invited herself for that evening. He was to meet her at the train and they were to celebrate the New Year's together. He went to the

station but missed her because he "waited at the
wrong place." Next day he succeeded in tracing her.
Naturally she was angry by that time; then, thinking to make up with her he proposed on the spot to
take the woman to a hotel with him. Naturally she
resented the insult and made him scurry out of her
presence. He had provoked this precipitate dismissal by his sudden proposal. He managed things
so that every promising victory turned into a defeat
in the end.

He was late at his appointments or showed himself overanxious and even coarse at the last moment,
when the situation was most delicate, or made some
uncalled-for remark. Thus, to one girl who was
already on the way to a hotel with him he said:
"Ah, all women are alike, they all run after men
and when they catch one they are happy!" She
looked at him with lifted brows: "Is that what you
think of a girl who goes with you? Then I want to
have nothing to do with you . . ." and turning
around she walked off.

That does not prevent him from running again
after girls; he even accosts married women on the
street but he always complains about his poor luck.
At the same time his sexual desire is not excessive.
His physical requirements never cause him any uneasiness. It is a psychic urge that drives him to
seek women. At the same time he longs for friends
but then, such friends as he seeks are also not to be

found.   Only the last friend was such a one because
"he understood him."   They went to brothels together.   That was the first time he experienced a
really strong orgasm.   We know this custom on the
part of men to be a convenient mask for homosexuality.

The motives of his conduct are revealed in a dream
which throws considerable light on the significance
of homosexuality.

We have recognized for some times that this is a
case of latent homosexuality, repressed on the negative principle of aversion.

Xaver speaks incessantly of women, thinks of
them all day long, so as to avoid thinking of men.
He tries to lean on women, but never becomes intimate with them because the negative force that
drives him is not powerful enough.   The better
woman is for him a "noli me tangere," he suffers from
an inhibition which keeps him from every woman who
is not paid.   The prostitute is not considered a
woman and, besides, her charm is increased by the
fact that she has intercourse with other men.
Through her it is therefore possible to give an outlet to a portion of the homosexual tendency.

We shall now turn our attention to his dream.
Naecke [1] justly remarks that the dream is the best
reagent for homosexuality.   Unfortunately he was

[1] *Der Traum als feinstes Reagens fuer die Art des Sexuellen
Empfindens.   Monatschr. f. Kriminalpsychologie,* 1905, and
other contributions.

not familiar at the time with the revelations of dream
analysis and he paid attention only to the manifest
content. How much richer in meaning the dream
shows itself when we learn to read it and to interpret
its hidden symbolism.

The Dream:

*I am pursued by men and fear they are about to
do something to me. One man in particular, bran-
dishing a big sword, is very hotly on my trail and
already he touches me from behind with the tip edge
of his sword, a curved thing like the Yatagan used
by Turks. I run to the cemetery to mother's grave.
I find there my cousin (female) who is also afraid of
the robbers. First we try to hide, then we look
around carefully and see that the coast is clear. We
leave the cemetery together in a carriage and we
drive upon an endless dark road. I snuggle up to
her, as if for protection against the robbers and I
am ashamed of my unmanly attitude.*

Of course it is not proper to conclude that a
dreamer is homosexual merely because the dream carries a homosexual meaning. For, as I have shown in
my *Language of Dreams*, every dream is bisexual,
consequently homosexual traits may be found in
every dream. The dream only portrays once more
man's bisexual nature and even the dreams of homosexuals are, without exception, bisexual. We see
through them merely the degree of the repressed
homosexuality and the dreams enable us to recog-

nize more easily the motives which impell the subjects to adopt a monosexual path. . . .[1]

This dream begins with a typical portrayal of a
homosexual pursuit. The subject is really pursued
by his homosexual thoughts. The great curved
sword is a well-known phallic symbol. That the
sword touches him from behind is something easily
interpreted. Equally obvious is the reason why the
sword appears curved when we learn that his brother
has a hypospadia and a phallus of that shape so
that medical advice was even sought on the matter.
The pursuer had a big heavy beard exactly like his
brother and the same figure. Thus we see that the
brother, who stands out of the mass of pursuing
males, in a certain measure typifies the homosexual
pursuit.

He flies to his mother's grave in the cemetery.
His mother shall save him from homosexuality. She,
she representative of femininity, is the one to whom

[1] If homosexuals had only homosexual dreams, as *Naecke*
maintains, the fact would stand as a strong proof against my
conception that all men, including the homosexuals, are bisexual.
But as a matter of fact genuine homosexuals often have
heterosexual dreams if one cares to look into the subject
carefully. *Hirschfeld,* through a questionnaire, found that
among 100 homosexuals, 13 per cent. dreamed all sorts of
heterosexual situations. Analytical investigation of their
dream life would lift the 13 per cent. fully to one hundred
per cent. The heterosexual dreams are associated with anxiety
feelings in many cases. They dream that they are married
and find themselves impotent, so that they are confronted with
the compulsion of carrying out heterosexual intercourse. We
find here one more confirmation of the fact that the dream
releases all the excitations repressed from consciousness through
the day.

he flies, when pursued by men. The cousin is the wife of another brother. She represents the typical incest compromise. Many neurotics who are emotionally fixed upon their family, finally marry a cousin. The cousin, whom he finds at the grave, is his savior and he starts with her upon the dark path of life, a half man. . .

He tells that he was to marry the woman but she became instead his brother's wife because he kept hesitating and would not make up his mind. But he had the fancy that he could be her sweetheart. He is specially fond of his brother's wives and his sisters. . . He has numberless phantasies revolving around incestuous deeds. His two sisters also figure in these day dreams. . . . He grew accustomed to talk over sexual matter with his sisters not without reason. He tells her all his adventures with pre-conceived watchfulness. Thus he told her also of the late acquaintance, as mentioned above, and was advised, as she had previously advised him in a number of similar instances, to keep away. Unconsciously he was awaiting from her the reply: *Why go out of your way?* *Why seek in other women what you can find in me?* . . .

We understand now the inhibition which stands between him and women of "the better class." The latter stand for the sister and the mother. The incest taboo is what stands in his way. He looks for a true adventure but cannot find it. He looks

for his sister and he looks for the man. His brother's
wives are the objects of his jealousy and his yearning
at the same time. With his questions and problems he
goes to his sisters-in-law, never to his brothers. His
conscience is uneasy with regard to his brothers.
In their presence he is always timid and ill at ease.
He is in love with his older brother though he does
not acknowledge the fact to himself. His brother's
strength and energy rouse his admiration. Occas-
sionally his brother sang. The voice lingers in his
ears so sweetly that he declares his brother to be
the best singer in the world. He feels that his
brother neglects him. The brother does not seem to
notice how ill he is or how much he suffers. Once
he was quite a jolly fellow but now (since giving up
masturbation) he is mostly depressed. But the
brother takes no notice of it and never asks him how
he feels or how it goes with his health. If he only
could quit his brother's business! He belittles himself in order to cling to the brother more lovingly.
He could not endure being away from his brother.
He does poorly during his business trips because it
is against his wish to travel at all and because he is
jealous of his brother's large business.

His attitude towards the second brother, who was
his playmate in childhood, is even more tense. He
never visits that brother and when he cannot avoid
meeting him has but little to say. He shows that
peculiar uneasiness towards the brother which

persons manifest when they try to cover a certain erotic attitude.

The following characteristic dream may be instructive at this point:

I am in my brother's store....He puts before me an assortment of underwear to mark up. I refuse to do it and step out of the store saying: "Brother can kiss me. . ."

His brother advised him to get married. This is the incentive to the dream language "underwear to be marked." But he loves only his brother. The remark, *"er kann mich gern haben,"* (equivalent to the colloquialism, "he can kiss me," and its more vulgar variants) plainly embodies a reference to a sexual act.

Incidentally anal irritation is one of his strongest paraphilias. He suffers more or less continually of "anal itching," which is at times so unbearable that he cannot sleep. He consulted for this complaint a physician who found no local trouble and who declared that it was merely a "nervous" itching.

The fact is this subject is now on the point of becoming a homosexual. Some precipitating occasion and his homosexuality is bound to become manifest. His last friend is dearer to him than all the girls. . . This is shown clearly by the fact that he sent him the ticket which he had bought for his lady friend. A portion of the hidden impulse had broken forth on that occasion. Usually he covers his homosexual leanings very cleverly. His friends and colleagues at the office think he is a lucky Don Juan and have no idea that he never enjoys the ultimate advantage of the role he plays. They see him always in the company of girls, always going around with pretty women; he runs after them on the street, he goes to public places with them; at the office he speaks of nothing else but his conquests and new adventures.

But not to his brothers. He never mentions any sexual matters especially in the presence of his younger brother, the one who was his playmate in childhood.

The analysis did not last long. But during the very first few weeks there came to light experiences with this brother which explained the subject's reticence.

Considering the remarkable fact that Xaver was animated by the desire to be a regular Don Juan we have something with which to contrast the extent of his moral qualms. For a long time he was very pious and then all of a sudden he turned into a free thinker. Analysis discloses that his religious piety still persists undiminished. Don Juan stands to his mind only for the unreachable ideal of a free man, a man undisturbed in his actions by any inhibitory feelings. But he invariably hears an inner voice calling to him, at the last, supreme moment of action: *Don't! It is sinful.*

It is the voice of his mother, who never failed to dwell on moral themes, who warned him against the dangers of the big City, his mother whom he so loved and honored. How often his dreams lead him to the cemetery where his mother lies buried, as if to conjure up before his eyes the dear image and to remind him to avoid all evil and to follow in the Lord's righteous path!

This case illustrates the significant role of family environment in the genesis of that homosexuality which *Hirschfeld* calls genuine. We find a fixation upon the sisters, also a fixation upon the mother, and the passionate love for the brothers, particularly for the older one, with whose wife he sees himself driving off in a dream. That cousin really stands for his brother. Through her union with his brother she had acquired a new attraction for him. Before her marriage he was rather indifferent towards her. The homosexual experiences with his younger brother date back to his 16th year.

His craving for love affairs, the impulsion to women, was but a flight away from the pursuit of man.

The next patient shows an entirely different constellation. Whereas Xaver was clever enough to free himself from the terrible women through his peculiar tactlessness, the following subject reassured himself by conjuring up an ailment which be-

came very troublesome, it is true, but which proved
an effective means of defence.

Mr. Christoph—we shall designate the subject by
that name—is a victim of chronic stomach trouble
which, according to the opinion of various physicians, is of a nervous origin. He has attacks of
sharp gastric pains, and loss of appetite so that he
has grown very thin and looks like an advanced
victim of consumption. (Lungs and all other organs are in excellent condition.) He cannot digest
any meat, any attempt to do so produces intense
pain, and if he swallows so much as a mouthful he is
likely to vomit. He denies that he ever masturbated,
and claims that his sexual life is entirely normal.
Formerly he was in the habit of going around with
girls, but it gave him no pleasure, probably because
prostitutes are disgusting to him, and with other
girls he did not care to become too intimate for
ethical reasons. He would like to be hypnotized so
that he should be cured of his aversion to food. I
decline hypnosis and advise, instead, a complete
analysis. Only in that way may he learn the way
to a complete cure. He insists he has not withheld
anything in his talk with me. He has told me
everything and wants hypnosis by all means but
this I refuse.

He says he will think it over. My questions took
him by surprise. He was unprepared. He is one
of those men who have to think matters over and

don't make up their mind in a hurry. One of his rules through which he learned to protect himself against life's sudden perplexities is: "Don't lose your head. Think it over."

He calls a few times continually talking about his pains. One day he states that he has about made up his mind to quit. But next day he returns and brings me a lengthy written document: "You have asked me repeatedly about my dreams. I have written down my last night's dreams. I always dream a lot and my dreams are always lively and about like those of last night. I have also brought along my true confessions to let you know what I really am. You will see from the confession of my life history what brought about my illness. I see I cannot get along any more trying to keep it all to myself. Let the truth come out."

I am now giving this life history as it was presented to me in writing, following it up with the dream report.

The Story of My Illness and My Biography

I lived in the parental home up to my 4th year and then I was taken in charge by my mother's people. My father's business compelled him to be away from home for months, sometimes for a whole year at a stretch. My grandparents brought me up with much tenderness, and as they were very re-

ligious, my education was also based on piety. They
lived in a very prettily situated village, an old,
lovely resort place. The river flowing near-by was
naturally the meeting place for us children. On
account of the danger of drowning I was an object
of great concern to my grandparents, so that they
tried to keep me close to them as much as possible.
I went with them to church daily, visited with them,
usually at the homes of elderly people where the conversation was almost exclusively about religious
matters, and on every occasion it was drilled into
me under the most terrible threats and admonitions
to pray and be good.

I heard numerous stories of deeds and miracles
attributed to the Holy Mother and I was shown
the places where some of these took place in the
neighborhood.

Then I returned to mother. Soon afterwards I
went to school. Sister taught me the primer and
soon I was able to go through my favorite book,
an old large copy of the Bible, whereas formerly I
depended on questioning others.

Frequently I gave up all games preferring to sit
in a corner poring over my Bible. It is customary
in the country to undergo a public examination in
the church every half year. My sister two and one
half years older than I prepared herself for that
event for some time because she did not learn easily.

I followed her study carefully and was able to recite everything as well as she.

The examination came up at the church and no one could answer a certain question. But I knew the answer, because it was part of sister's lesson, made signs, the vicar asked me and I surprised everybody by giving the correct answer. It was the prayer, "Our Father." My folks admired me for it, gave me presents and said: "Boy, you will grow up to be a fine man." This praise touched me very deeply.

I was about seven and a half when a girl of twelve induced me to join her in forbidden games, we played with each other's genitals, etc. This occurred very often. I liked it very much and the experience became deeply imprinted on my mind. Then I felt a strong desire to repeat the same games with other girls. My mother's sister visited us about a year later and while she caressed me she roused in me a new feeling and I could hardly refrain myself from asking her to play with me the games that the first girl had taught me.

Beginning with the third year of school we had a new teacher. He took notice of me early because I was a good scholar and soon I became one of his favorite pupils. This teacher had the horrible habit of calling me to his desk where he held me by the member until it became stiff, while talking to me. I wondered a great deal what it meant; but I did not dare mention it to any one.

At the end of that school year we removed to Vienna permanently. I was tremendonusly homesick for the old place; the coolness and indifference of the new surroundings at Vienna affected me and secretly I resolved that I would rather starve than stay there. I was threatened that I would not be allowed to visit the old home if I did not make progress and I would be sent to a sanitarium; the last threat in particular scared me especially as I was shown some (false) papers to indicate that the first steps had already been taken to have me interned. That and the perpetual anxiety at school where we had a queer teacher who mistreated horribly the pupils (and I did not know a word of German at the time), had a serious effect upon me; my physical condition was impaired, I grew thin and lived in a sort of dream state. During my solitude I often sought relief in tears.

I lived through the period. In two years, here too, I reached one of the first places as a scholar. I had a colleague at school, whose sixteen-year-old brother was compelled to stay at home for a year on account of illness and we played with him. The two initiated me into all sorts of nasty practices. The brothers slept together in one bed, underneath their parents, and had frequent opportunity to see their parents lying together. They always told me about it and showed me their mother's stained shirt. This impressed me very much and I also began to watch my parents. Till my twelfth year I slept in one bed with my sister. Then I slept near mother in bed, as father was mostly away.

My fancies grew to such unhealthy dimensions, that I began to think my uncle, mother's brother, who was living with us at the time, was guilty of criminal intimacy with her. Slowly my suspicions were allayed, as I could observe nothing out of the ordinary, despite watchfulness.

Around thirteen a school boy taught me to masturbate. I did not do it often because I feared it was sinful and it kept me in continuous anxiety. Then a book fell into my hands describing the terrible consequences of the habit. That scared me off completely, and as a positive protection, when I was about fourteen and a half I swore over grandfather's grave that I would have nothing to do with sexual matters till my twentieth year. I suffered a great deal in consequence on account of my pent-up desires. But I was fairly faithful to my oath.

At fourteen I joined a higher institution. My preparation was far below that of my colleagues and one of the teachers warned me that I might not be able to keep up with the course at that institution. That worried me a great deal. It affected me considerably to think that in this way I might be hampered in the free choice of a vocation.

At the first examination it turned out that only I and one other student passed successfully and I looked upon that as a divine favor, the more so because my very affectionate grandmother prayed for me continually.

I was permitted to take the course on condition that I should earn for myself remission of the school fees, which amounted to a considerable sum. Only the best scholars received free tuition. I plunged zealously into the subjects on which my preliminary preparation was weak.

My thrifty zeal was not flawless. I was always confident that God was with me and I thought that I owed to his intervention, rather than to my constant application the position of a scholar of the first rank which I had attained in two years' time.

During that period I came again into contact with that girl who was the first to initiate me into sexual matters. Her presence continually disturbed me.

When I was about seventeen and a half I had some innocent love affairs with some other girls, but although opportunities for coitus were frequent, I never took advantage of them. Reason: my fear of immoral deeds.

I slept with my sister and a girl cousin in one room. I concentrated my attention upon the girl cousin. The frequent allurements kept me in a continuous state of agitation the more so because I could see that the cousin, too, had to struggle hard to suppress her inclinations and desires. I withstood all temptation and remained innocent.

Towards the end of the school years I came into closer contact with a girl who had already previously attracted my attention. We became deeply interested in one another, but we could meet only occasionally and that under very strict conditions. We had to part in the end; as I really loved the girl it made me suffer a great deal. During the occasions when we did steal away to our secret trysting place I felt a peculiar excitation which settled on my stomach; if I ate it caused me nausea.

After completing my course of study I entered the employ of a local business house. I became acquainted with another girl, and strange enough, we two also had to overcome considerable difficulties when we tried to meet. After about a year we could meet freely and shortly after there were no more difficulties in our way. But I lost interest in her by that time, and decided that I would have nothing to do with any such foolish love affairs.

Whereas formerly I was kept back from any thought of coitus with a decent girl because I considered it an unworthy and dishonorable act, now whenever I was about to meet a girl I was seized with a gastric discomfort and even vomiting. Once in the girl's company that would disappear.

I gave up all affairs of heart, but my condition became gradually worse. I vomited several times daily, I could not even tolerate a mouthful of bread on my stomach, even clear soup was hard for me to take. Every time I swallowed I felt like vomiting and I could not even drink. Besides that I suffered of sleeplessness and of strong neurasthenic pains.

Finally I had to give up work for a year and I spent four months of that time in the country but my condition did not improve very much.

It caused me a great deal of tension to suppress my strong sexual impulses. Contact with a public woman seemed shameful to me, and with a good girl I could not enter into any intimate relations partly for moral reasons and partly on account of lack of favorable opportunity.

I felt inhibited from the moment my illness began. I decided to resort to public women upon the express advice of a physician.

This remarkable case is as clear as a school problem and richly illustrates the various factors which determine a person's attitude regarding sexual matters. The subject is a simple man who has not yet mastered completely the German language and he has repressed but little. His youth and his sexual struggles apparently stretch before his memory like an open book. He has had many dreams and remembers them well. We note the genuine religious background. He is no longer pious and does not care to go to church service. Nevertheless it ought not to be difficult to perceive that back of his fear of immoral acts stands the fear of divine punishment,—a consequence of his early moral training. This man has been brought up with fear in his heart. This breeding of the germ of fear in his soul was responsible for his anxiety neurosis. Witches appeared to admonish him, in the school he was spurred on by dire threats to do his best. Then there was his powerful sexual craving which he, nevertheless, found possible to withstand. Whence did he acquire the strength to keep away from his girl cousin, although she so warmly attracted him and even encouraged him? Was it the proximity of his sister who occupied the same room? Some occurrences between him and that sister he had overlooked in his voluntary account of his life, otherwise fairly accurate. He avoided incest, but besides the moral and religious inhibitions, there must have been something more to keep him so effectively away from women. His trouble which asserts itself before keeping a secret appointment is nausea. Dislike and fear are protective defences against sinning. We recognize readily this disgust for woman, so strongly emphasized by most genuine homosexuals. We know that this aversion covers a repressed craving, a craving which is unbearable to consciousness

for one reason or another and therefore breaks out
in the negative form as disgust. The latter serves
as defence and protection against the very tendencies
which generate the powerful cravings.

The disturbance is a cover for the incest motive.
He cannot approach a woman because he sees in her
the grandmother, the mother, or the sister, a fact of
which he was often fully aware. *Quo me vertam?*
There is open before him the homosexual path, since
the road to woman is closed. The episode with the
teacher, the "vile doings" with his school companions
were a sort of initiation . . . Here repression sets
in. He knows nothing about his homosexuality.
But the dream betrays and tells more than the
subject is prepared to see as yet. We shall therefore begin the analysis with an analysis of the dream.

That Night's Dream.

I stand before the door of a dwelling in my home
town and gaze upon the surrounding landscape.

While I am immersed in thought, my uncle comes
along; he had helped through the day working in
the field and on his way home stopped near me in
front of the big door; he throws out some jocular
allusions; among other remarks saying: "it would
be healthier for you if you plowed up a few acres
instead of idling away."

I point to the team of horses hitched to the har-
row, jocularly saying: "oh, yes, certainly, but not

with so poor a team. These two animals should have been dumped on the scrap heap long ago, specially this left one bearing himself so proudly when he is only an old nag."

I hardly finished my words, when the horse started and broke his traces madly to jump at me.

I started to run, fled up the first stairway and ran into the kitchen shutting the door after me. Then I ran into the next room and barricaded the door with every furniture article I found handy. The horse was already at the door kicking until he broke through and made his way into the room.

Meanwhile I ran to another room, again shutting the door but even as I did so I knew that it wouldn't be an effective barrier. I looked around the room for some other means of escape and to my surprise saw my sister standing behind me.

The horse had broken down the door enough to be able to stretch his head through into the room and his dilated nostrils snorted angrily.

Sister handed me a small round stove calling out to defend myself with the stove lids, they will prove an effective weapon.

The horse was ready to jump inside the room so I hurled at him first the covers then the whole stove as powerfully as I could. At the last critical moment I caught sight of another door, hurried out ran to the stairway and woke up.

I went over the whole dream in my mind to make

sure that I will remember to tell it to my psycho-analyst. Shortly after that I fell again into a light slumber and dreamed that I had gone to the analyst who treats me:

He occupied a commodious residence with broad stairways. I found myself face to face with him; he was doing something in a closet. I stood by and told him the foregoing dream.

He went away for a while to attend to some important matters, as he had to drive off in about one half hour. Then he called me down to him and asked me to continue my story while he was lacing his shoes.

When I finished I moved off and through a side door and there I met my mother. I exchanged a few words with her, opened the door, which led to a glass-covered veranda and saw a locomotive and open fire.

The engineer moved various levers in vain, he could not start the engine. Meanwhile the physician arrived, looked at his watch, and remarked impatiently that it is already late. Suddenly a servant girl comes running down the steps bringing three carefully tied up paper packages (or bundles).

In order to raise the required steam pressure it was necessary to feed the fire lively. The physician decided to help and threw one of the bundles into the fire. It burned up quickly but produced no effect.

Then mother spoke up from the other side saying,

there it must be all right, took another package and threw it in at that spot without accomplishing anything, any more than the physician did.

Saying: "That is not the way, look here," I took hold of the third package, jumped on a protruding piece of machinery in the midst of the flame which surrounded it and threw the bundle into the center of the burning mass. The flames broke forth, the safety valve began to whizz, a whistling was heard and the engine began ponderously to move.

The physician jumped on, reached out his hand to me as he was moving off and I barely had time to ask him where he was going. He said he was going to Brünn. I wondered at that and—woke up again.

After I fell asleep once more I had another dream like the first. I found myself in an elegantly furnished residence.

The door opened and a young pretty woman came in. She looked at me for a while, then smiled wickedly but I did not lose my poise and said something to her. She became more irritable, raised her hand, in which she held a weapon and threatened me.

I looked on quietly, confident that she could not do a thing to me. Then she jumped at me. I ran to another room, she pursued me, and thus the chase continued through several rooms.

I was about to open another door when I felt she was directly behind me holding in her hands some instrument that looked like a perolin sprayer. It squirted a white soapy fluid. She gave a few squirts without touching me, although a few drops fell on my clothes. I thought it was some caustic fluid and wanted to escape.

While she was preparing for a new attack I quickly shut the door and the nozzle of the sprayer caught between the door and the frame.

I grasped the nozzle, twisted the sprayer out of her hand, threw it aside, caught the woman by the throat, and was going to throw her down. But she caught me also by the throat, kissed me passionately and staggered towards a sofa, dragging me along. I held her with my left arm around her body while I pushed my right hand between her legs. I felt a pleasant sensation; as we looked in each other's eyes we slid down together. . . .

She was saying she meant no harm, laughed heartily, pressed me to her bosom, her face began suddenly to change,—I now saw my sister smiling at me.

Overcome with affection for her I wanted to press her closely to me—suddenly the door opened and an elderly woman came storming in. It scared me and I awoke—pollution.

His first dream carries him to his home town and birthplace. Our previous analyses have shown us the meaning of this and no Freudian student will fail to recognize that the birthplace is a symbol for

the mother. We learn that the father's brother
resembles the father and conclude that the uncle
stands for the father in that dream. The conversation between himself and the uncle is a repetition of
old reproaches. For a long time he was unable to
work and at the present time he is unable to help in
his father's business. He finds a ready excuse in
his illness. The incestuous relation to his mother
is fairly obvious. The inhibitions which developed
so that he is unable to make himself useful in his
father's business, are due partly to his hatred of
the father as a rival. The day before the dream he
had a small controversy with his father, because
the latter had made an error in one of his calcula-
tions and was unwilling to acknowledge it. In the
dream he revenges himself for the reproach implied
in his unwillingness to plow (plowing here stands
for coitus) by a slurring reference to his father's
age. He was no longer fit for marital duties. The
parental couple are too old, they have already lived
too long ("the pair belong on the scrap heap") and
the one at the left (the father) is but an old jade.
(In German, *Mähre*, jade, old horse, here is also a
play upon the old home, *Mähren*). This is followed
by the revenge of the scorned father in the form of
pursuit by the horse.

The dreamer relates that he was fully aware of
his incestuous thoughts with reference to his mother
and sister, only he thought that he had outgrown

them. But he finds that occasionally he still dreams of contact with his mother and more often with his sister. On the other hand he did not think the dreams signified anything, believing that they were but the echoes of a past stage. He does not remember having ever dreamed of his father in an overt sexual connection.

But we recognize the bipolar attitude towards his father. His trouble must be intimately linked with an unconquered homosexuality. The account of his illness now brings up a childhood occurrence which had made a strong impression on him. There was a teacher in that home town who had a most peculiar and extraordinary way of recompensing his worthy pupils. If one did something praiseworthy and the teacher was pleased, he said: "very well, my boy! You shall be honored for this,"—and gave the boy his erect penis to hold until ejaculation followed. This was done openly before the whole class. The teacher carried on this sort of thing until five years ago without any trouble and then left the place suddenly, to avoid court trouble as the result of a complaint. Christoph, who was a special pet of that teacher, was probably chosen for that honor more often than any other boy. He was also the prettiest boy in the class.

Beginning with that experience various episodes of homosexual character are disclosed extending up to the time when he was seventeen years of age, when

they suddenly ceased. But he does not know that
these were homosexual acts and still insists that he
always felt only the most terrible aversion towards
"all these homosexual things." The subject maintains unconsciously the wish to do with his father
what he had done with his teacher.

He is pursued by homosexual thoughts (the *left*
horse). We are now turning our attention to the
functional significance of the dream. It represents
a pursuit. The attitude displayed towards the
physician is clear. The physician pursues him
through all his memories (the flight through the
rooms). This flight through rooms has been interpreted by *Freud* as a flight from women
(brothel). I have repeatedly pointed out that
rooms represent the compartments of the soul, that
the pursuit is really through all the parts of the
brain (the upper story stands for brain; compare
the colloquialism, there is something the matter with
some one's "upper story"). We see that a certain
thought pursues him past all obstacles and
hindrances, and he is unable to elude that searching
thought. His sister is the one who comes to his aid.
She hands him a miniature stove with which to defend himself against the horse. The stove and the
lids represent the sister's sex. . . . The dream
means: *only your sister, only a woman can save you
from your homosexual inclination towards your
father*. The dream also indicates a prospective

tendency: he throws the sister upon the father and saves himself through another door. He means to overcome his complexes. The attitude towards the physician is also clear: he expects to put me off his trail by confessing to me his incest fancies about his sister, when I had not asked him about it. The dream indicates his intention of telling me about his fancies and episodes in which his sister figures. But he expects to escape thereby any further inquiry into his wish phantasies and to avoid telling me about his attitude towards his parents.

Then the patient falls asleep again and repeats the dream so as to be able to tell it. We may presume that the dream was distorted and changed somewhat in the course of its first rendition. We really get but an extract, the chief parts omitted. . . In the next dream he tells me the first dream. Such dreams are seldom remembered. When a woman dreams that she has told her physician the dream, it means that she is through with the unpleasant task and the dream vanishes from memory as in the cases when the patients declare: Today I dreamed something important; I said to myself in my half slumber: "This is something I must tell the doctor! I don't remember what it was. But it was something really significant." Thus is the physician thwarted; the resistance is vicariously overcome in the dream, the wish to tell the dream is fulfilled but the wish to keep it from the physician is stronger; during his dream experience both tendencies are given expression by the subject.

The next dream: Again, an exposition of analysis. I am upstairs busy with a closet, which represents the brain or his shut-up soul. But the analysis will not last long. The wild hunting after his secrets and treasures will cease soon. The physician has to leave (die?). Here the physician substitutes the father. The dream shows plainly the transference from the father to the physician. The first dream dramatizes the pursuit of the father, in the second and third the father no longer figures. His name is not mentioned at all in the dream, he is the secret, the unspeakable theme. . . The physician laces his shoes; that is commonly known as a death symbol and shows the clear wish to be through with the analysis.

An engine has to be started. He is a machinist and has daily to do with machines. Engine is symbol for his soul which functions so poorly, a symbol for himself, for all the impulses and energies within him. He accomplishes through his own powers what his physician and his mother are unable to bring about. First I try to put the engine in motion. I take the mysterious paper package and throw it on; the mother attends to the other side of the fire. But he gets up and takes care of the fire from above.[1] He is above, he triumphs over me and

[1] Correction of detail after first report of the dream.

surpasses me in the ability to cure him. He recalls a pupil of his who had to commute to Brünn. It brings to his mind an occasion when he was the teacher. Thus I am his pupil, I am learning from him how to start an engine. Though I may know something about sick souls, I don't understand a thing about his specialty (he is a machinist), there he is the master and I am ignorant. This consoling thought serves to strengthen his feeling of self-regard and prevents a feeling of inferiority from developing in his relations to me. There are a number of scornful references to the impotent father and to the equally unskilful physician. He is with me one half hour daily. He had noticed that I looked at the watch, to see whether his time was up. The half hour and the looking at the watch appear in the dream. The day before he showed his father how a technical problem was solved. In this dream he also shows me that something must be done a particular way.

We observe that this attitude towards the physician, as representative of the father, pervades the whole dream. But this does not exhaust the meaning of the dream. It is a pollution dream (gratification without responsibility). It is interesting to see how the onanistic act, represented as pollution, is dramatized in the dreams. In the first dream he flees from homosexuality and there the relationship between homosexuality and the

hidden mother complex is clearly shown. In the
second dream the mechanism of sexuality is represented in action. Neither the father (the engineer
working around the engine), the mother nor the
physician can do it. He alone is able to accomplish
it. This shows the secret pride of the masturbator,
the self-sufficiency of the autoerotic personality.
(The engine's flame covered running board, a phallic
symbol; later note.) Onanism is shown as a protection against all sexual perils. The safety valve
hisses and relieves itself—an intimation of the subsequent pollution.

But the fear of onanism, the strong effects, the
dread of homosexuality and incest wake him from
his sleep. Consciousness (the engine conductor)
attempts to control the thoughts and to banish the
nocturnal ghosts. The thoughts about a man and
about his sister are interrupted and he falls asleep
once more. Three times he dreams of various situations before the anxiety in him is transformed into
wish. First he fled from the horse and from his
sister, then he fled from his mother and the physician and finally there came his release. He was
strong enough to withstand his homosexuality,
strong to overcome the heterosexual longings. Now
the instinct throws forward its highest and strongest
card to overcome the last inhibitions: bisexuality.
The girl with the phallus, his sister, appears . . .
and pursues him. He is frankly preoccupied with

the thought: give in and masturbate. The thought itself he avoids, he tries to push out of his mind. He sees himself in the dream. He sees the womanly side of himself, the woman with the phallus, and this thought troubles him during the nightly hours when he should be resting. He jumps at the female person to strangle her: that is how he fights with his instinct, how he tries to thwart his autoerotism. The instinct recognizes the weakness of his defence and suggests that it seeks only his welfare. With the right hand he seizes his genitals while with the left he carries out an embrace. He has an orgasm (the sister smiles at him) but it does not last long; for an old woman appears upon the scene. The door opens, that is, the door of conscience (the threshold symbolism of *Silberer*), and remorse seizes his soul. He rouses from his sleep and the pollution worries him. The old woman may also be a symbol for his mother (further significance of the old woman as symbol will be shown later). But I have no proof of that inasmuch as the subject describes her otherwise.

What is the sense of the dream with reference to its central theme? Is it a wish-fulfillment, a warning, or a prophecy? Undoubtedly many wishes are fulfilled in this dream. The subject resists many temptations, he embraces his sister, he triumphs over his father and over his physician as well. But the most important feature that the dream portrays is

the pollution as a defence against all sexual dangers
and as successful cover for all inner inhibitions.

Another meaning of the dream should be pointed
out. His neurosis must be represented by some person or object in the dream. Asked what the engine
suggests to his mind the subject answers: my illness.
The glass-covered porch: the transparency of his
trouble; the engine: his neurosis. The subject
habitually compares his body to a steam engine, especially his stomach. He shows various effects of
starvation: unable to eat, he loses weight, and
looks like a skeleton because he wants to starve out
his sexual longing and punish himself for his sinful
passions. This man had built for himself a mar-
velous safety valve in his neurosis. When he thinks
of going to meet a girl, he gets such a severe attack
of gastric pain that he must give up the appointment. The gastric discomfort is induced before-
hand through excitement and inability to eat. The
clever staging of his gastric trouble is noteworthy.
Nausea and vomiting are first induced to prevent the
taking of food. Then hunger supervenes and that
gnawing sense of hunger, spoken of as gastric
cramps, becoming so strong as to overshadow the
heart affair. The craving for food becomes more
obsessive than the desire for woman. These episodes are followed by a ravenous appetite.

He recalls that after the first dream he woke up
with a terrible hunger. This hunger was even

stronger after the second dream but disappeared after the pollution.

I have already maintained in my work on *Morbid Anxiety* that hunger may stand as a substitute for sexual libido and here this is clearly shown and illustrated.

Now we understand the firing of the engine with the paper packages. The caloric value of paper is as small as that of nutrition, when the latter is substituted for sexual desire. Thus he makes use of his stomach as a remarkable safety valve. He starves himself out because the gratification of food serves as a substitute for sexual gratification. He relates a number of incidents showing how cleverly his neurosis serves him. Every woman he meets excites him but even when he goes so far as to arrange an appointment with one and she agrees to call at his residence or to go to a hotel he stops short of actual intimacy.

From the standpoint of the analysis the prognosis is unfavorable. He does not want to give up the neurosis, his safety valve, he wants to keep up his own way of "firing the engine" and wishes the physician were out of the way. Indeed, he continues to have recourse to masturbation, he endures the consequent regrets and self reproaches, rather than give up his defence.

We observe inwardly a strong "will to power" and

formally a decidedly feminine attitude; the orgasm occurs while he plays the role of woman; but the highest gratification always depends on the most powerful inner forces. He does not avoid women because he fears defeat, for he has repeatedly proven his *potentia* through intercourse with prostitutes and feels supremely confident that he could master any situation involving no moral scruples. What hinders him seems to be the association of his sister with all decent girls, and of his mother with all married women. His homosexuality is inhibited by his fixation on the father. And back of all inhibitions there stands his overstressed religiosity, which he had cultivated for years although he had apparently outgrown it. He intended to embrace a religious career but gave up the idea when he was 14 years of age. It is very likely that most of his troubles will disappear after marriage, if he should break away from the parental circle.

I believe that even one who is inexperienced in dream analysis will readily recognize a phallic symbol in the perolin sprayer which gives forth a soapy fluid. It was natural that at 16 years of age he should fall in love with a colleague who resembled a sister. The obvious incest thoughts kept him from the girl. All girls of good family were sisters; he treated them like sisters. The prostitutes were not in the same class with his sister and he could be potent with them. The homosexual path was closed to him also on account of his sister. In all young men he saw his sister with a phallus.

It is significant that further analysis discloses a fixation upon the father to an extent I had not quite suspected before. Back of the apparent scorn of his father, underneath his tendency to speak lightly of him there was an unquenchable love which nothing could quite gratify. The ugly example given by his teacher suggested intimacies possible only in the realm of phantasy. (His subsequent dreams placed him with me in a similar situation.) Thus he vacillated between homosexuality and Don Juanism.

Why do these men hesitate in the end and why do they not become genuine Don Juans? In large measure this is due to the inner religious scruples. These rudimentary types are weighted down by an excess of morality. They like to play at immorality but very carefully see to it that morality wins in the end.

I wish to add a few remarks about the religious significance of the dream. It is remarkable that all dream interpreters have overlooked the obvious import of dreams, from the religious standpoint, in spite of the fact that they are aware of the great role which religion plays in man's mental life and must appreciate that such a force necessarily finds expression through the dream.

The subject has been for years a very pious young man. Witches and devils filled his fancies as real tempters. The dream also shows the fear of the devil who misleads the weak to drink, whoredom, shortly, into sin. The homosexual tendency is often felt as the work of the devil.

Our subject who was so very pious for a long time, declaring himself now an atheist and free thinker. He promised his mother, under oath, that he would attend church services regularly on Sundays but he gave this up when he reached the 20th year. At first his mother objected, and was very angry over it, and desisted only after her son convinced her that he had no faith. But she said repeatedly: "I feel certain that the Lord will enlighten you and that some day you will come back to the faith." He only smiled at that for on his part he felt certain that he would never again be a believer. His greatmother, whom he visited every summer, was even more pious. Two weeks after the dream we analyzed he had the following dream:

I am with my grandmother. She goes early in the morning to church and asks me to go along. I hesitate. Next morning she repeats the request. I have a strong attack of gastric pains and tell her. I will take a sunbath, it is the same thing. . .

We see that, under the grandmother's request, the dream portrays the subject's childhood disposition. We note a connection between the hesitation to go to church and the gastric pains and we hear of sun-baths as a substitute for religion,—a fact which I have repeatedly observed in other cases as well.

Further inquiry reveals that every evening the patient struggles with the impulse to recite "Our Father"; he resents the inclination,—"it is nonsense. I don't believe any such folly as that." Nevertheless sometimes he murmurs portions of the prayer, while in a half dreamy state, when he has the illusion of being again a child. He carries around in his pocket a couple of small "holy mother medallions" which he bought at a fair: "it is really a superstition; I always carry them in my coin purse, because I have an idea it is good luck." He has presented his prayer book to his younger sister and so the book is always accessible. He goes to churches because he is "interested in the church music." . . .

How does the dream show this? The devil appears to him in the shape of a horse (horse's hoof is a characteristic sign of the devil) and tries to seduce him. The horse breaks down doors and all obstacles. At one time he believed in a personal devil. He attended once a church where the minister preached considerably about the devil and who said that there were living witnesses to testify that they had seen the devil. His grandfather was angry because the minister told believers such far-fetched stories, and forbade him going to that church. But the fear of a personal devil had been deeply implanted in him at home. If he misbehaved, he was threatened with the evil one. If he refused to pray some one knocked in the next room and he was told that it was the devil that was after him. He was brought up the same way to believe in witches. An ugly old woman once came to his room dressed as a witch to scare him and the other children into better behavior and it affected him so horribly that he remembered the scare for years. In his dream the devil pursues him and he eludes the pursuit. In the second part of the dream he himself is the devil and can do charms. To do magic was his highest ambition in his youth and he would have gladly given himself up to the devil for the privilege of learning magic. He starts the engine by means of a charm. In his childhood his great wish was to build a magic locomotive with which he could travel wherever he wanted.

The servant girl who brings down three bales of paper (play on trinity?), (his love letters?), is a symbol of the Holy Virgin, as it is in all dreams, a fact which I could easily prove. He was a confirmed admirer of the Holy Mother. He must give this up if he is to learn magic. But the dream is a compromise between the two tendencies and expresses a bipolar attitude; he fires the engine with divine fuel, with faith, which upholds his life along the right path and protects it. He wishes me to the devil that he may continue secretly to cling to his religion. But the infantile wish to be a magician comes foremost to the surface. (The dream does not portray one wish, but a number of wishes which cris-cross the soul.) The supplementary portion of the lengthy dream also illustrates the power of magic. The religious meaning of spraying (with holy water. . . Perolin cleanses and disinfects the air) is readily obvious and so is also the admixture of religious and sexual motives which play such a tremendous role in the neuroses and the psychoses.[1] He yields to the temptation, a she-devil seduces him. The old woman, after all, is the witch of his childhood, coming to punish him for his sins. (He admits also a strong gerontophilia and once he fell in love with a 60-year-old woman).

The old and the new testament, his prayer books, his confession slips, are in the paper packages which he must burn up to free himself of all religious inhibitions.

The dream thus portrays a prospective tendency, —the overcoming religious inhibitions, subduing the dread of hell and devil as well as the fear of witches so as to give himself up to his cravings. He takes his life in his own hands, fires his own engine,—he will take unto himself any woman who looks like his sister.

[1] Cf. Hans Freimark, *Das Sexuelle Moment in der religiosen Exstase, Zeitschf. f. Religionsphilosophie*, vol. II, No. 17; also, *Das Hexenproblem, Die Neue Generation*, vol. VIII; and *Sexuelle Besessenheit*, ibid., vol. IX.

The dream expresses clearly also that his homosexual fixation is due to the mother and sister Imago
which he finds in all women. Finding himself upon a
sexual path which leads away from women and in
the direction of man, he wants to leave that path and
become a normal man by overcoming all inhibitions.
He no longer requires the protection of his neurosis,
he is master of himself, scorns the religious im-
peratives, becoming magician and God in his own
right.

Through the history of this subject we obtain
a glimpse into the mechanism which eventually leads
to homosexuality. This subject might have become
a homosexual and would have then presented the
usual homosexual life history: Very tender for a
time, girl-like, played with dolls at his grandmother's
house, liked to be busy in the kitchen and preferred
the company of girls. Such experiences are commonly shared also by the heterosexual persons but
the latter forget them. Later, if the course of development favors the outbreak of homosexuality,
these recollections, emphasized and fixed through
repetition are pointed out as proof that the condition is inborn.

One episode in our subject's life might have led
him to overt homosexuality: his experience with the
teacher,—the more so as it took place openly. But
what amounts to an inciting factor in one case may
act as a deterrent in another. Every influence may

assert itself either on the negative or positive side. Childhood dreams as carried out by adults, may generate either a gerontophilia, or a similar inclination towards children, depending on whether the subject assumes the role of the adult or of the younger person. Fixation on the mother may drive a man entirely to homosexuality as I have clearly learned through the history of a certain case. The homosexuals frequently have a morbid mother, a woman who suffers of depression and is unwise in her actions. Unfortunately my observations indicate that the fancies are generated by parents as often as they are incited by guilty servants and that such occurrences are far from rare.

In the case under consideration the experience with the teacher and the latter's revolting openness about it acted as an inhibition to homosexuality. The thought, "You may get to be like that teacher," acted as a deterrent against the outbreak of a so-called genuine homosexuality, though all conditions were otherwise favorable. Even the characteristic dislike of women was there as well as the incestuous fixation upon the female members of the family.

And although much of his sexual life was perfectly clear to this subject's mind, including things which to others appear only in the dim light of day dreaming or upon the lowered state of threshold consciousness, there was one thing about which he was entirely ignorant: his true attitude towards, and relationship to, his father. He was continually more irritated with his father and avoided to be alone with him because he knew how easily they break into a quarrel and how misunderstanding would arise between them on the slightest provocation. This hypersensitiveness in his relations with his father, shows that there were feelings at work over which he was not master. What he demanded and expected of his father I have already indicated. He wanted to be treated by him as he had been treated by his teacher. In the course of the analysis he also had a dream during which I was the one assuming that role. He is homosexually fixed on his father and heterosexually fixed upon the female members of his family.

It is interesting to see that the homosexual inclination, despite all childhood experiences, is repressed and masked under the feeling of disgust. We understand in this light the meaning of the gastric pains. He thinks only of women and is a typical instance of a would-be Don Juan. He begins numerous adventures but always meets difficulties. That is, he starts relations which from the beginning present these difficulties and in that way there is no danger for him. If the difficulties (symbol of the unattainable, that is of the incestuous goal) are overcome, the attraction disappears or else his protective defence comes to his aid: the gastric attacks. He goes so far as to take a girl to a room but at the last moment he can do nothing on account of his gastric pain. The nausea is a sign of disgust. It is brought about by the homosexual tendency pressing forward as much as by the subject's inhibition against heterosexual relationship. At the most critical time before meeting the girl he is restless, and a voice within seems to say to him: "you do not really want this woman, you want a man, like that teacher, or that friend of yours!" As a protection against these homosexual notions his nausea comes up and this also acts as a defence against women. For woman, as such, he feels no dislike, he is able to have intercourse with prostitutes, without aversion. But homosexual acts are repulsive to him. Thus he remains hanging midway between homosexuality and heterosexuality. On account of his religious scruples both pathways are closed to him and the result is— his ascetic behavior at the end.

His asceticism is back of the rudimentary Don Juan role which he plays but cannot carry out in accordance with his instinctive promptings on account of his inhibitions. One step nearer and we have the Don Juan of day-dreams and ascetic in fact,—if the adventures with women are not even begun. A step further advanced is represented by the complete repression of all sexual inclinations. We may define the ascete as a person who remains

in the narcissistic stage of fixation because both
paths of allerotism (that is, homo-, and heterosexuality) are equally closed to him. An exclusive
monosexual goal is incapable of rousing the instinctive excitation necessary for carrying out a
sexual act, because the religious scruples are oppressive. His perennially unattainable ideal is a bisexual being, he longs for a passion so strong that
it should be capable of overcoming all obstacles. His
asceticism is not voluntary, but a state induced by
his sexual constellation.

Our subject has found his sexual ideal in the dream
world. That is a sister who has a phallus. He, the
valiant warrior, struggles against his instinctive
promptings and masturbates. This act acquires in
his conscious mind, as pollution, the character of
an involuntary act, an accidental occurrence which
cannot be helped, thus being robbed of its significance.

Freud points out rightly that the psychologist is
particularly interested in cases showing a late development of homosexuality,—a condition which
Krafft-Ebing has described as *"tardive,"* or Late
Homosexuality. In such cases homosexuality develops after a period of hetero-, or bisexuality.
We will describe a number of cases of late homosexuality elsewhere and then we shall also attempt
to trace the reasons for the occurrence.

The next case also represents a transitional stage showing us a woman in the throes of a struggle between the two tendencies. We have here a rudimentary, a would-be Messalina, an interesting female counterpart to the case described above.

Miss Wanda K. complains of an unfortunate split in her mental make-up which prevents her from enjoying life as she should. She suffers of strong and uncontrollable vomiting but the trouble arises only when she is about to keep an appointment. She holds the most liberal views that "a modern girl can and should have." She meets gladly men who interest her and even those who rouse her sexually. She knows she will never marry. She is 29 years old and although still very pretty and attractive,—how long will this last? She wants to enjoy life, she would not care to die without having tasted the supreme gift and prize of life, love. But she has a "delicate" stomach which interferes at the most critical moment. Here is an example:

"Last Sunday I was to take an excursion with a gentleman whom I met in an unconventional way. I am not at all prudish and do not mind being spoken to on the street. As I walk downtown often I think to myself: will someone talk to me this time? I try to attract attention, just a little, and return home disappointed if no one notices me. A few weeks ago a very elegant elderly gentleman addressed me on such an occasion. He is a very intel-

lectual man, which is the chief consideration with
me. I like intercourse only with intellectual persons.
Persons lacking culture are a trial to me. We entertained ourselves very pleasantly and since then
we meet daily. When the store where I am employed
closes at the end of the day, I find him already waiting for me at the street corner. Then we go for a
walk and we talk about all sorts of things. He has
never dared yet mention anything erotic in our conversation. I have no reason, therefore, to fear him.
Nevertheless I am watching and waiting eagerly for
the opportunity to show him that I am a modern
girl, unafraid of anything when she finds a man
sympathetic and to her liking, if he should ever
begin. I do not expect anything more. One cannot fall in love all of a sudden! Now, we promise
ourselves an excursion around Vienna for Sunday.
Saturday I feel very excited, and I picture to myself
how he is going to bring up sexual matters, how he
will kiss me in the woods, I already plan what I shall
say to him, how I will resist him, just a little, and
finally give in. You will excuse me. It is high time
that I quit being an old maid. Is that not a pity,
at twenty-nine? At the office where I am employed
all the girls have a sweetheart and some have several
at once. That keeps going through my mind. I
am very excited and I even whistle a tune. But at
the evening meal I am unable to swallow a morsel of
foods. My stomach seems shut tight. Nothing will

go down. I hope it will be over in the morning. I get up early, put on my excursion suit and want to have my breakfast. I struggle with nausea, try to eat some breakfast, only to vomit promptly every particle of the food. Then the terrible nausea continues and keeps up so that I must stay home while the gentleman waits in vain for me at the appointed spot. Naturally when this happens a second time he drops me . . . unfortunately it ends just that way every time."

She relates numberless occurrences of this character which always end in uncontrollable nausea and vomiting. She has a long list of admirers, young and old, rich and poor, educated and some less so, every one thinking he can conquer her as she is very free and open in her talk and does not avoid sexual topics in her conversations with them. She is a member of various women's orgaanizations, like *Mutterschutz,* which is devoted to the protection of the unmarried mother, she is a champion for women's sexual freedom and also a Shannaist. But every one of the men she dangles on her string who tries to pass from theory to cold fact discovers, much to his astonishment, that there is quite a difference between this woman's views and her practical conduct. She circumvents all occasions which might prove embarrassing to her. An office colleague invites her to his home. He is an art collector, she is interested in painting, and he would like to show her his collection. She finds all sorts of excuses to postpone accepting his invitation and finally appears at his house . . . accompanied by a girl friend . . . She had dwelt so much on all the possible consequences of a visit of this kind that at the last moment she lost her courage.

It is interesting that her mental state developed first after an engagement. Until the age of 23 she was fairly normal, very much like any other girl. At that age she made the acquaintance of a man of good standing in whom she became much interested. She became engaged to him and this made her happy for she was in love as much as any girl could be who thought she had found her ideal.

The man had but one serious fault. He was tremendously jealous. He tortured her with questions about her whole past life and she had to relate to him with particularity everything that she had experienced as a girl. She frankly told him that once she was in love with her piano teacher and also with her school teacher, a girl, but that there was nothing else of any significance in her life. Nevertheless he kept torturing her with further questionings insisting that she must tell everything before marriage and he will forgive her absolutely everything, but he did not want to be deceived, he wanted perfect candor and truth between them.

One night she woke from a dream in which her brother and she had figured in a rather intimate

role. This brought to her mind an occurrence she
had entirely forgotten. She was visiting her married brother in the country. His wife had gone to
some relatives and he suggested that she should sleep
in his wife's bed. She did so without having any
particular erotic notions, since this was her brother
with whom she had always been frank, not as she
was with her other brothers, for she had four others.
During the night she felt her brother's hand touching her. He crawled in to her bed and kissed her.
She was sleepy and thought she was dreaming. He
kissed her again and sleepy as she was, she re-
sponded. They embraced warmly. She knows that
she took hold of his *membrum.* She thinks her
brother must have exercised wonderful control over
himself after that and that he crawled back in his
own bed. The whole experience of that night is
rather unclear. That much she is certain, no coitus
took place.

This remembrance awed her for she knew then
that she had lied to her man. It happened only
once for next day she left the place and her own
brother advised her to do it. She went to visit a
friend of hers in the neighborhood and returned
only after her sister-in-law was back home. But
since her young man had such complete faith in her,
she felt that she must tell him the whole truth. She
told him of the occurrence relating how it took place

as in a dream. He began to investigate and to question until it drove her to distraction and there were times when she herself wavered in her recollection as to what really occurred. But she could only repeat the one thing: she knew positively that they kissed and touched each other that night, but could not say that between her brother and herself matters had gone beyond that.

Her bridegroom stayed away a few days. Then she received from him a note stating that he does not feel that he can take her to the altar after her confession and he considers himself therefore a free man. He sent her back the engagement ring and demanded the return of all his gifts and letters.

This was like a physical blow to her. That was the thanks she received for her complete candor! She had taken at his word the man whom she dearly loved. How could she help thinking that he merely sought an excuse in her eyes, and in his own, a pretext to declare himself free?

For a time after that she hated all men. She made no exception, including in her hatred even that brother who was responsible for her misfortune, in the first place.

Then she arrived at a second deduction: "it is not worth while to be honorable! Better be easy going, like all your women friends!"

Shortly after that she apparently ceased hating

all men and her great yearning began causing her to think continually of nothing but men. At the same time there began also her uncontrollable vomiting.

It seemed that her tremendous inclination to love was struggling with an equally powerful antagonism. During that difficult period her only consolation was a woman friend and her sister to whom she felt herself very closely attached.

But her dreams show that back of her running after men there was something else: the homosexual instinct which was struggling powerfully to come to surface and which she tried to hold back by her love affairs with men. She showed a number of unmistakable signs. She dressed simply and rather mannishly; she cut her hair short, and began smoking cigarettes; her appearance and gait assumed more and more a mannish form; she lost her mildness and soft nature becoming hardened and strong. Her whole nature expressed one supreme wish: *I want to be a man, he has a better life!* And, strange enough! Now she does attract men and they dangle after her by the dozen. But she only played and when it came to a serious issue in the course of any of her adventures,—for some of the men had earnest intentions,—she deliberately turned the whole thing into a huge joke.

She was no longer lured by men alone. She was on the point of becoming overtly homosexual passing through the last phase of the struggle. The nausea stood more and more clearly as a protection and defence against the homosexual inclination. Her dreams were filled with homosexual episodes. She herself was astonished when she began to observe her dreams. The very first dream she related concerned her sister and her friend:

I am with my friend on the Gaensehäufel (*a popular promenade on the Danube embankment in Vienna*) *and we are naked; I say: How beautiful you are! You are more beautiful than any man. She embraces me and kisses me on the breast, on the spot where I am so sensitive. I wake up with dread,—palpitation of the heart and nausea.*

Other dreams represent endless variants of this theme. Men figure in them but seldom. Occasionally she is pursued by them and flees to her sister or her friend. Thus her conflict is also shown in her dreams as a flight away from men, an escape through homosexuality.

This young woman also imagined herself to be a radical although inwardly she was pious. Sundays she visited the church, to hear the music, she was not a believer, but occasionally she prayed, because it was an old habit, she was fond of reading the Bible and she had to suppress a small inner voice which impelled her to go to confession. One day she said to me: "Do you know, yesterday it occurred to me that if I were again a believer and could go to confession, everything would be all right. . . ."

Here we see a young woman who was at first on the proper path to become a normal, heterosexual woman. She experiences a serious trauma and begins to despise all men. She turns away from them. This aversion is favored by the fact that all men remind her of the love for her brother, which was repressed and forgotten but which flared up again on the occasion of her unfortunate experience. That was the reason why she was able to entertain herself best with elderly gentlemen and go on excursions with them, etc., without being overcome with nausea. The danger was not so great and these men were less typical of her brother. . . . She turns away from men and her sexuality flows into another channel. We have therefore a regression back to a childhood phase, apparently past and gone, in *Freud's* sense. She also becomes more agreeable at home, where during the past years she had been accustomed to pay no attention to her mother. She again becomes fixed upon her family and turns once more to her childhood piety. The period of her nausea represents the last stage in her struggle against homosexuality.

As we glance over the three cases just analyzed we are impressed in the first place by the powerful rôle of the inner religiosity, which often passes unrecognized. Both men stood upon that emotional level which leads to polygamy as a defence against homosexuality. But they were unable to overcome their religious scruples. Too weak openly to embrace asceticism, they wandered through complicated neurotic by-paths in the attempt to circumvent all the dangers that threatened hem. One of them played very cleverly the rôle of '*Pechvogel*,'—a man who would gladly be a libertine but who was not lucky enough to succeed,—the other was prevented by his stomach trouble from abandoning the path of virtue.

The counterpart is the "modern girl" who dreams about free love and mother-rights and at the same time generates a nervous nausea as a defence against any danger to her virtue. Here again we must admire the subtlety of the neurotic who finds such clever means to assume a certain rôle in the eyes of the world no less than before himself, in order to cover up his true nature. All men who really lack inner freedom are over-anxious to act as if they were free. They apparently adopt some modern liberal principle while as a matter of fact secretly they adhere to the religious scruples of their ancestors.

As a great sin and "unnatural" act, it is plain that homosexuality was out of question in these cases. Religion acts here as protection and outlet at the same time. But it is also clear that under an other educational régime these men would have found open to them two paths neither of which they were able to choose under the existing inhibitions.

The woman may become overtly homosexual and some late episodes indicate that her resistance to the homosexual longings may yet be overcome. In this case the traumatic incident which turned her against all men did not occur during early childhood. It is a great error to assume that traumas of late occurrence lose their pathogenic rôle.

There are periods in our life when we are impervious to traumas. But there are also times during which we are hypersensitive to any influences which play upon us. Every decennium of our life has its crises and morbid periods during which we show a peculiar sensitiveness.

Die Kranken sind die grösste Gefahr fur die Gesunden; nicht von den Stärksten kommt das Unheil fur die Starken, sondern von den Schwächsten.

Nietzsche.

V

*The sick are the greatest danger to the healthy;
the mischief done to the strong comes not from the
stronger, but from the weakest.*

Nietzsche.

Experience in the course of psychoanalysis has
shown us that the recollections as told by the subjects are partial and incomplete.

The repressed memories and all those images which
the subjects are unwilling at first to see come to
surface only after weeks of analysis. Then the subjects are astonished to discover that they did not
really know themselves. The solution of our problem appears to depend on the successful analysis
of a large number of homosexuals. Meanwhile there
are a number of striking facts which every psycho-
analyst can verify and which those who uphold the
theory that homosexuality is inborn look upon as
proof of their contention that homosexuality is truly
hereditary: most homosexuals are apparently well
satisfied with their condition and do not particularly
care to be cured of it. They call on the analyst only
after they come into conflict with the law or if they

241

fear such a conflict. They do not want to have
heterosexual feelings, they are proud of their condition and they always insist that social ostracism
alone is what makes their status an unhappy one.
They belong to those remarkable persons who refuse
to appreciate their plight. Hence the customary
statement: since I began homosexual relations I am
happy. I desire nothing else! Only a small number retain any desire for "wife and child" and for
normal relations, but even those fear it as much as
the "manly hero," proud of his homosexuality.

We must not forget that exclusive homosexuality
is the end result of a long and tortuous psychic
process, a sort of self-healing process in the midst
of a quasi-insoluble conflict. The dangerous heterosexual path is apparently blocked altogether, because certain inhibitions stand actively in the way.
The removal of the inhibitions renews the acute
character of the conflict,—it means changing a state
of truce for a state of active warfare. The homosexual finds in his condition a makeshift for peace
and quiet. It is a poor peace, to be sure, for the
heterosexual inclinations are still powerful enough
to generate neurotic symptoms. But it is a safety
outlet and anxiety prevents its abandon. Just as
the woman seized with fear of open spaces (agora-
phobia) finally refuses to leave the house and thus
avoids her anxiety only to experience the attacks
of anxiety again the moment she endeavors to step

out of the circumscribed area of peace,—the moment she endeavors to go beyond the sphere within which her inner voice keeps quiet,—so the homosexual feels once more the full strength of his revulsion whenever he attempts heterosexual activity. His customary attitude towards woman is one of dislike or disgust, she may leave him indifferent, but never will he admit that—he is afraid of woman. He would rather assume the mask of indifference; he may be willing to approach woman but only upon intellectual grounds, he may even appreciate her as a friend, but he flees from her as a possible lover.

The homosexual resembles the fetichist in this regard: he has found his compromise, he has become accustomed to his limitation and willingly puts up with his limitation as being something organic, final, inherited. That is why we usually hear that the homosexual felt his peculiarity already in his childhood, that he was from the first unlike the other children, that he was always "different."

The pride over his condition, the continually repeated and stressed notion that he is exceptional, the attitude of contrariness towards what is normal, all these things render difficult a subsequent correction of the trouble.[1]

[1] The following statement of *Hans Freimark* on the *Zuchtbarkeit der Homosexualitat* displays excellent insight into human nature: "It does not require much psychology to note that some persons are particularly impressed by and interested in whatever popular belief ascribes as particularly characteristic of homosexuality. Repression against homosexual deeds

How may the homosexual be cured? If he is made
heterosexual he represses his homosexuality and becomes neurotic for that reason; the endeavor to turn
him bisexual meets the course of social development.
The proper therapic course would be to remove the
inhibitions which stand between him and woman, to
make him de facto again bisexual and heterosexual
for all practical purposes. That is certainly possible and it may be attained through analysis pro-
vided the subjects have the patience and perseverance
to carry it out. Where the will is lacking no therap-
ist can accomplish anything. Unfortunately in most
instances the will is absent.

Analysis has taught us how misleading the first
accounts are as obtained from the subjects, how
much they recollect their past in a spirit of partizan-

is in itself almost invincible. But that which is considered the very essence of homosexuality acts apart and frequently does so in a sense far from proper. It is enough to
induce young men who have no other claim to distinctions to
try to imitate these 'singular doings' and they become finally
interested in the acts. . . . Once the pose is assumed, it becomes
part of reality, and then contact with the homosexual circle
contributes not a little towards strengthening the attitude.
Such an influence, naturally, is possible only among young people. But the young are the ones who generally raise the problem at all. It has been assumed that in view of the constancy
of the instinct, such a complete shifting from one sex to the
opposite is most unlikely. But since all investigators admit a
certain period of indifference, and since it is admitted further
that during that period the individual may abandon himself
to an eroticism contrary to the form adopted finally, the possibility cannot be excluded that weak characters may be turned
away from their original developmental goal."

ship. Every person carries out a one-sided choice
of remembrances recalling merely what suits a particular occasion. This came to me as a great surprise when I first undertook the analysis of a homosexual especially as at the time my experience was
limited and my knowledge of the technique and my
understanding of resistance very imperfect. At the
time I still believed that the patient wills to get
well; I am convinced today that the will to be ill is
the strongest force which we must fight against.
That first homosexual gave me the usual history,—
the development from early childhood of feelings
exclusively homosexual. My surprise was great
when the subject recalled a large number of heterosexual experiences in the course of the following
three weeks, all dating from his childhood. I learned
then in one lesson that homosexuality is *developmental* and not something *inborn; an acquired, not
an inherited character.* I was much impressed with
Hirschfeld's theory of the intermediary stage
(*Zwischenstuffentheorie*) but placed no credence in
this theory and awaited further proofs. At the
First Psychoanalytic Congress, *Sadger* reported
similar experiences based on psychoanalysis. To be
sure, *Sadger* conceived the psychogenesis of homosexuality in rather narrow terms and for a time, I
must confess, I too looked upon the repression of
the mother Imago, which every woman is alleged

to reproduce, as the sole cause of homosexuality.[1]

But my diligent researches extending over a period of years have since convinced me that this problem is very complicated and that there are clearly a number of genetic factors, and that several of them must and do cooperate in every instance to bring about the thwarting of the heterosexual and the enlargement of the homosexual craving.

It occurred to me at first that in many cases the inhibitions may disappear also in the homosexual leading him to become again a heterosexual person. Every one who has had any experience with the homosexual knows that occasionally a genuine homosexual may change and fall in love unexpectedly with a woman or he even marries and after that continues as a normal person. Thus, for instance, *Tarnovsky*, in his work, "*The Morbid Manifestations of the Sexual Instinct*," states: [2] " I know a pederast who maintained relations almost exclusively with young boys; at a relatively advanced age he fell passionately in love with a young girl, whom he married and with whom he had children. He was able to carry out sexual relations with his wife only because her face resembled that of a young man

[1] "The flight to homosexuality is the result of repulsing the incest phantasy." *Nervose Angstzustande,* 1st ed., 1908, p. 311. A translation of the latest edition of this work is in preparation and will appear shortly.

[2] Berlin, 1886. Verl. Aug. Hirschwald.

whom he once loved." A rationalisation of that
kind, such a transformation, may be seen here
and there. It is quite likely that the young man,
whom *Tarnovsky's* patient once loved, in turn resembled the homosexual's sister or some other beloved female person and that the subject took that
step to return at last to his first heterosexual ideal.
Only a few days ago there called on me a "confirmed"
homosexual who had suddenly fallen in love with a
cabaret singer whom he wanted to marry. She was
the exact image of a sister of his who had died long
ago. Before this he did not want to hear of contact with women. Cases of this kind—without any
treatment, of course,—are discussed very heatedly
in homosexual circles and the news is rapidly spread.
The deserter is spoken of as traitor to the holy
cause, he is counted out and banished from the
circle. Anathema sit! Such cases are not infrequent.
But they do not come to the attention of the physician and if they attract the specialist's attention,
the latter invariably declares them instances of
"pseudo-homosexuality." No "genuine" homosexual
would do such a thing! Homosexual physicians, unfortunately, only add to the confusion on this subject. They constitute themselves judge and jury at
the same time, but claim to be objective in their
judgment,—they have tried the experiment in their
own case, etc.—Oh, those wonderful psychologists
who know all about their own soul! What have I

not endured from those enthusiasts who imagine that they have really penetrated the depths of their own psyche! But any one who has opportunity to analyze a psychoanalyst is invariably amazed at the degree of blindness possible where one's own attitude is concerned. The practice of psychoanalysis on others does not prevent ignorance where self is concerned. I have analyzed dozens of psychoanalysts and found "analytic scotoma" an appropriate designation for their mental state. Every one is blind about those complexes which he has not yet conquered, whether he meets them in himself or in others. The homosexual physician is also blind about his own condition and should never undertake to furnish testimony on the question whether homosexuality is inherited or acquired.

There are occasions when the cover which screens from view our inner attitude, the repressions and transferences, the metamorphoses and changes, is torn aside by more powerful forces and then we obtain a view of the forces which act behind the setting of consciousness. These occasions are the intervals during which our inhibitions are lifted. *Insanity permits us occasionally to see truths which reason timidly keeps under cover. But alcohol also tears aside the screen which covers the inner man.* Many physicians know of persons apparently heterosexual in every respect and who never think of homosexuality, but who have been guilty while drunk of carrying out homosexual deeds such as are entirely repulsive to them in the sober state. I had under my care a teacher who while intoxicated—the first time in his life—attacked a boy and was guilty of committing a crime. When he came to himself he felt so disconsolate, his remorse was so great, that he wanted to take his life and it was only with the greatest difficulty that he was prevented from turning himself over to the authorities. Later he was denounced by some one. But I was able to squash the inquiry for lack of positive evidence. In his favor stood his exemplary previous life history and the fact that he had always been an admirer of ladies and had never taken any interest in men or boys. I have already remarked before that a large number of those who uphold temperance or abstinence are really afraid of alcohol because it releases inhibitions and permits the aggressive outbreak of repressed sensuousness.

I. E. Colla has reported on *"Three instances of homosexual deeds during drunkenness,"* in the *Vierteljahrschrift für gerichtliche Medizin und öffentliches Sanitätswesen,*[1] as follows:

The first case was a 29 year old inebriate who had had a wide experience with women and carousals; after a prolonged period of abstinence he became intoxicated while in a sanitarium, was seduced by a homosexual, and immediately after that, while in

[1] 3rd Ser., vol. XXXI, 1906.

an intoxicated state, he attempted to attack a servant. Repetition of similar episodes when under the
influence of drink but when sober exclusive breaking
forth of heterosexual feelings. A clear proof in
favor of my view about the relations of latent homosexuality to satyriasis.

In the second case a controlled homosexual leaning breaks forth overpowering the subject when
drunk. A similar picture in the third case: A prot-
estant minister, 37 years of age, drinker, loses his
self-control while drunk and by his offensive behavior in a public place attracts the attention of the
authorities.

Numa Praetorius, that thorough expert on homosexuality, relates: "In many cases homosexual deeds
are committed under the influence of alcohol. Thus,
for instance, I know a former police officer, a homosexual, who when drunk attempts homosexual deeds
upon heterosexual comrades, who excite him, although he is acquainted with the homosexual circle,
is intimate with many homosexuals, and in his sober
state he carries out relations only with persons with
whom he is safe. On account of these attacks on
heterosexual persons during his drunken condition
he has lost his position as police officer as well as
his later position in a factory.

"Another homosexual, a merchant, thirty years of
age, when drunk finds this inclination uncontrollable
and has tackled the wrong persons while in that

state. There is a great deal of truth in the contention that during the inebriate state man's true character comes to surface,—at any rate his true sexual character certainly reveals itself in that state, since the customary inhibitions are curtailed. Here '*in vino veritas*' certainly holds true." (*Jahrbuch f. Sexuelle Zwischenstuffen*, Vol. VIII.)

These cases, with the exception of the first, show only an increase of an already existing homosexual inclination otherwise under control. But frequently it happens that heterosexual persons carry out their first homosexual aggression during the inebriate state.

Thus *Praetorius* remarks in another passage: "As is disclosed in various published biographies as well as in certain communications which have reached me orally, there are young persons, otherwise apparently normal in feeling and conduct, who when drunk are attracted to their own sex with a great feeling of pleasure thus disclosing more than a pseudo-homosexual attitude. But their proper heterosexual nature does not appear to be changed materially by these occasional homosexual episodes and emotional sprees."

Hugo Deutsch [1] has reported a very instructive case, which, although far from unique, as the author believes, may be mentioned in this connection:

[1] *Alkohol und Homosexualität. Wiener klinische Wochenschrift*, 1913, No. 3.

"An intelligent workingman, 39 years of age, appeals for advice and information to the clinic for alcoholics. As a child he suffered of rachitis and began walking only at four years of age; excessive masturbation as a small boy and young man; later, occasional intercourse with girls; he married two years ago and is the father of two children. No illness, with the exception of minor complaints. Uses alcohol moderately, drinks now and then one-half to one litre of beer on the occasion of some reunion or meeting. But this always excites his sexual passion; specifically he feels impelled to take advantage of young male persons [1] so as to touch and feel their sexual parts. He has been able to withstand this desire but once while on his way home from a meeting where he had again taken a couple of glasses of beer he met a young boy whom he invited to have a drink with him and while they were sitting at a table in the saloon he touched the boy's genitals. A customer saw this and denounced him to an officer who arrested him. He was in despair over the occurrence and only the thought of his wife and children prevented him from committing suicide. He has not touched a drop of alcoholic drink since because he

[1] Krafft-Ebing also mentions a young man who carried out his first homosexual aggression under the influence of alcohol. A man who previous to that time had successful intercourse with prostitutes while intoxicated grabbed hold of his friend's genitals, they masturbated . . . and since that time he is homosexual.

recognizes how dangerous even a small amount of drink may be for him. So long as he is sober his libido is directed exclusively to women, in fact he feels only *disgust and aversion for any homosexual deeds*. When the contrary feeling first arose in connection with drink he cannot recall. There is nothing relevant in this connection in his family history and there is nothing "womanly" in his physical appearance."

Deutsch believes that this is a case of bisexuality brought to surface because the use of even moderate doses of alcohol suspends the existing inhibitions.

Hirschfeld, too, has also made a few pertinent remarks on this subject (l. c. p. 209). He mentions the case of a government official who attacked a baker's apprentice after a "heavy celebration" of the Kaiser's birthday; also the case of an apparently heterosexual high school teacher who during a prolonged carousal attacked a waiter. He also mentions a report he was requested to make about an officer who after a carousal requested his servant boy to help him take an enema and used that opportunity to seduce him. In his report *Hirschfeld* found this complaint, if it be true, contrary to the defendant's whole personality, and recommended annulling the complaint because at the time of the alleged misdeed the accused was in a peculiar and morbid mental state. But we must look upon these occurrences as

proofs of man's bisexual nature and as outbreaks
of latent homosexuality made possible through the
removal of customary inhibitions.

Otto Juliusburger, in his *Psychology of Alcoholism*,[1] has given us an exhaustive and masterly exposition of this problem. That author reports that he
has been able definitely to trace the outbreak of unconscious homosexuality in cases of dipsomania and
discusses most instructively the relations between
alcohol and homosexuality.

Juliusburger describes the case of a dipsomaniac
who during the drink episodes betrayed most clearly
his homosexual love for his uncle. During those episodes the subject felt impelled to accost men—and
only men—ordering for them anything they wished,
—"frankly a symbol, to show his affection." "One
source of the anxiety and unrest which ushers in
the so-called dipsomaniac episode or which may
entirely replace the attack," states *Juliusburger*, "I
see in the struggle and the resulting intrapsychic
tension between the various psychosexual components of the individual." I shall have occasion to
refer to *Juliusburger's* views concerning the relationship of the jealousy episodes of the alcoholics and
sadism in the chapter on "Jealousy."

It is even more interesting in connection with our
present subject to find that homosexuals are easily

[1] *Zur Psychologie des Alkoholismus, Zentralbl. f. Psychoanalyse u. Psychotherapie*, vol. III, p. 1.

induced to carry on heterosexual deeds while under the influence of alcohol. Of course this is not the case in every instance but the fact is undeniable. Neither do all heterosexuals lend themselves to homosexual acts when drunk. Often the inhibitions are more powerful than the releasing effect of alcohol.

I have made inquiries of about one hundred homosexuals regarding the circumstances under which they indulged in intercourse with women. Many hesitated to answer, but I have found that a high percentage of cases have had the experience. Some answered saying, practically: "I can do this only if I am under the influence of drink;" or, "while I was drunk a girl seduced me." We must not suppose that homosexuals are impotent with women. There are among them many more bisexually disposed than are willing to recognize this fact, because they prefer as a rule to assume the rôle of innocents before others and for that reason they claim that intercourse with a woman is positively impossible for them. I have had circulated in the Viennese homosexual circle a small questionnaire which contained also a question covering this point. Many confessed dislike for woman, others admitted a platonic attitude, but there were also such answers as: "In my 34 years I have had intercourse with a woman, this I found very pleasurable, but after four months I turned again exclusively homosexual;" or, "now and than I have intercourse with a woman": further.

"after pleasant personal relations lasting for some time I am able to have intercourse with a woman"; another writes: "Once I had intercourse with a woman and it was a very pleasurable experience but never repeated it since that time;"—Others write as follows:

"Have had intercourse previously; do so no longer."

"No intercourse; presumably would be impotent with woman."

"Intercourse previously pleasurable; sudden disappearance of feeling now makes intercourse impossible."

Another writes laconically: "bisexual."

At least one-fourth of my overt homosexuals are really bisexual with subsequent modifications of their bisexuality brought about through causes which will be discussed in a subsequent chapter of this work.[1]

We now turn our attention to the next case. It

[1] Interesting is also the case of a high school teacher whose feelings were predominantly homosexual during the stage of depression and heterosexual during the stage of exaltation induced by the addiction to morphine (*Hirschfeld*). There are persons who live a double, alternating existence: homosexual and heterosexual. Their conduct suggests that they are persons continually in search of a bisexual ideal. Krafft-Ebing also describes a hysterical (*Jahrbuch f. Sexuelle Zwischenstuffen*, vol. III) who is attracted to men each time that her neurosis improves after a sojourn at a sanitarium, while during the height of her trouble she is homosexual. What does this mean but that the heterosexual cravings are repressed during her neurosis! For notwithstanding her extensive homosexual gratifications she has become a victim of severe hysteria while every time she improves she feels the love for man.

shows clearly that heterosexual tendencies arise in the homosexual under the influence of alcohol and it also proves that under the pressure of danger the homosexual craving by drawing on the greater libido turns into the heterosexual channel:

D. S., a clerk, 35 years of age, has been homosexual for the past fifteen years. His father died when he was 7 years of age. He hardly remembers his father. His mother was always very severe, and very energetic as well as exceedingly nervous,—she had to go frequently to sanitaria to recuperate. He admits having had feelings predominatingly homosexual ever since childhood. He interested himself only in boys and his mother brought him up in girlish ways. He began masturbating at an early age and already at the age of 12 he carried on mutual pederasty with his comrades. At 17 years of age he attempted intercourse with girls. That was not easy, his *potentia* had to be roused by them first through manual stimulation, then he felt some pleasure, which was curbed partly because he could not help thinking of the possible danger of venereal disease, of which he had seen some illustrations in a museum of wax figures. He was also thinking about his mother reflecting, what would she say if she knew what he was doing! From that time on and until he was about 21 years of age he had intercourse with women regularly about every month. Then he fell in love with his office chief, who was an

extraordinarily attractive man. (He gives a romantic description of his first ideal. This account,
of course, is not trustworthy. In fact the photo of
his latest ideal, also praised by him as an Adonis,
shows the stolid, expressionless, rather common face
of a very ordinary man, a soldier in the artillery
branch of the army).

His chief was a homosexual who easily seduced
him and brought him into the homosexual circle.
Then he became aware of his condition and maintained relations only with adult and well educated
men. He had a delicate taste and not every man
could please him (here he shows me the photo of the
soldier, mentioned above). Unfortunately he had
the misfortune to be caught in a park in the act of
taking hold of the *membrum virile* of a driver. His
case is now pending in the court. He would be happy
if he could return to his former mode of gratification. When asked if he had had no intercourse with
women during the whole period from the 22nd to the
35th year he becomes uneasy and confesses that
this has happened a few times but when he did so
he was always under the influence of drink. While
he kept sober it never happened. And every time
after intercourse with a woman he had such a terrible
after-effect that *his own mother to whom he always
confessed everything had advised him to seek intercourse with men, because she noticed that he was al-*

*ways feeling fresh after doing so, while if he went
with women he was always depressed for days.* Experienced psychoanalysts need not be reminded that
the mother used this means to keep her son from
contact with other women because she was jealous
of them and therefore she drove him to men. She
was never jealous of men. That was something else.

This occurrence is far from rare. The mother of
a homosexual once told me: "I am never jealous
when O. finds a new friend, although he falls romantically in love with them. But the thought of his
giving himself up to a woman is something I cannot
bear. . . ."

D. S. listened to his mother's advice. He says:
"I gave up drink after that and became a fanatic
homosexual."

As the subject, a high governmental employee,
could easily lose his position, I advised him to have
intercourse only with women and in view of his desire to free himself of the trouble through psychoanalysis I was able to wrestle him out of the clutches
of the law. He attempted contact with women, always after partaking of small quantities of drink,
and he gradually improved so that he finally married,
his wife being, in fact, a woman 20 years older than
he. That woman was a *locum tenens* for his mother!
Further observations on the psychology of similar
cases will be recorded in subsequent pages. Here I

propose to draw attention merely to the influence of alcohol. Drink enabled him to adopt the heterosexual path.

In the last case the heterosexual act was possible only after neutralizing the inhibitions. Similar influences are responsible for the well-known morning erections of those who are psychically impotent. Homosexuals, too, have heterosexual dreams before awakening in the morning but they cannot—or will not—remember those dreams. I need mention here merely that every night the dream operates in the sense of lifting the inhibitions and that the inhibitions are fully suspended only towards morning. During the first sleep hours the dreams are full of inhibitions appearing as "warnings," but towards morning the dreams are relatively free of these inhibitions. That is why we often hear that "genuine" homosexuals are able to have intercourse with women, if at all, only towards morning. At that time most inhibitions which stand between them and woman have been overcome in the dream! This obvious fact is given a different interpretation by *Hirschfeld* who states:

"The erection of the *membrum* with which many men wake up during the early morning hours has nothing to do with the sexual instinct, but is due solely to the mechanical effect of pressure by the full bladder. Some time ago I was consulted by a homosexual, married, father of six children and expecting the arrival of a seventh. I asked him how that was possible. 'That is very simple,' he answered, not without a certain feeling of self-consciousness, 'I always took advantage of my morning erections.' Thus the children owe their existence not to the father's sexual instinct, but to the operation of his full bladder. The much-praised aphrodisiacs, are probably also nothing more than diuretics; in other words it may well be that the renown which certain remedies and articles of diet have acquired as stimulants of the *potentia coeundi* may well be due to their stimulating effect upon the bladder function and its genital reflex.

"Alcoholic drinks, when taken in small quantities have a similar effect and rouse the sexual function. Excesses *in Baccho* and venereal excesses have always been looked upon as belonging together. This is so because alcohol has the effect of lowering the inhibitions and at the same time it appears to weaken the mental acuity. We may thus see why occasionally heterosexuals confess that they have taken up with some man under the influence of drink, and homosexuals that, *when intoxicated*, they can have intercourse with women." (*Hirschfeld*, l.c., p. 189.)

But the fact that homosexuals are capable of heterosexual activity under the influence of drink is for me a proof of their bisexuality, a proof that that they have repressed the heterosexual component of their sexual instinct.

The hypothesis that the morning erections are due to a full bladder will be discussed more fully in my work on *Male Impotence*. I do not believe that erection is due to reflex action from the bladder.[1] *But it is an incontestable fact that the dream operates until the existing psychic inhibitions are overcome.* Hirschfeld's patient is able to have sexual intercourse with his wife only mornings, because through the day and evenings he is under the domination of inhibitions which make him impotent with women.

That the impotence in such cases does not always denote weakness is illustrated by the following case: C. H., a homosexual physician, tells me that he abstains from touching all drinks because he fears he might commit criminal acts. He is homosexual since childhood and had never felt any inclination towards women. Masturbation began at 9 years of age. It began when his uncle once lifted him upon the shoulder. That gave him a strong pleasurable feeling and soon after that he began rubbing his genitals and while doing so he always fancied that his uncle or some other man was carrying him. He had never felt any desire to be carried similarly by a woman. Such a thing would strike him as degrading and vulgar. His experience in houses of

[1] Cf. author's contribution, *Die psychische Impotenz des Mannes*. Zeitschr. f. Sexualwissenschaft, 1916.

prostitution, from 19 to 24 years of age, filled him
with disgust for all women who can be hired. Perhaps he might have been able to have intercourse
with a girl of better class but a certain timidity prevented him from ever approaching such a girl.
Emancipated women fill him with horror. He maintained relations with a certain colleague for some
time. *Coitus inter femora.* At 28 years of age,
after a carousal, he met a girl whom he took to a
hotel. Powerful erection and prompt coitus. *But
with the onset of the orgasm he felt an overwhelming
inclination to strangle the girl.* Suddenly a tremendous hatred mounted in his soul against the poor
creature. He hurried away from the scene as
rapidly as possible. He thought he wanted to revenge himself because through the act of coitus she
degraded him.

Here we see a sadistic attitude towards woman
under the cover of timidity. He really feared himself, his criminal tendencies. Problems rising out
of the struggle between the sexes (specifically, out
of man's instinctive sex hatred of woman) play a
certain role in this case. The significance of this
attitude will be explained fully later. This case
shows the outbreak of a heterosexual-sadistic instinct under the influence of alcoholic drink. Alcohol seems to dissolve here the defences raised by consciousness against the sadistic tendencies.

Very interesting is the case reported by *Moll* in his work on *The Contrary Sexual Feeling* (3rd edition). I give here the case in brief extracts from its history, as it contains points of significance in connection with our present subject:

Miss X. is 26 years of age. Her father she describes as a healthy but very irritable man. Already at the age of 5 she had carried on certain sexual plays *with a small boy*. She admits having attempted intercourse at the time with the boy who was four years of age. The intercourse consisted of *mutual cunnilingus*. At six years of age she was sent to school and here she soon began intimate relations with small girls. With a number of them she carried on mutual *cunnilingus* as she had done with the boy. From the time when she first began this with the girls her heterosexual inclination disappeared completely; after that she never again went through a similar experience with a boy. We shall see that later she did allow herself to be used occasionally by men; but we must note in that connection that the heterosexual acts took place without the cooperation of sexual feelings on her part. At 12 years of age she began to menstruate. At that time she had as playmates the children of a neighborly family who had a governess with whom she soon entered into close intimacy. The governess prevailed upon her to carry on sexual acts, particularly *cunnilingus*, and the active part was taken now by each in turn from time to time. In the course of these relations she experienced for the first time sexual gratification, so far as she is able to recall. Their intimacy lasted for some time. Miss X. differs from other women of her type in that she is not averse to other forms of gratification. Soon she sought also *anus feminarum amatarum lambere,* in addition to the genitals. The thought of carrying out such an act with a man was repulsive to her. Just as we know that occasionally perverse men want *urinam feminæ dilectæ in os proprium immitere* so we see that Miss X. likes to have the same thing done to her by other girls. For a number of years already Miss X. has been in the habit of allowing *fæces amicæ in os proprium iniciǔre;* the act produces in her gratification and orgasm. She had first indulged in these acts during her intercourse with the governess above mentioned, which lasted several years. Miss X. is also tremendously roused when she *sanguinem menstruationis amicæ lambit et devorat;* but, she explains that she is able to carry out these disgusting acts only when there is complete mutual confidence and only if the relationship has endured for some time. She declares further that she is sexually roused also when she is struck with a whip. When asked how she came to acquire this habit she answered that she knew a man who required to be thus treated by a former sweetheart. But, to secure her any sexual excitement the whiplashes must fall upon her from the hands of a woman. She has allowed herself very often to be flagellated by her friend with whom she has also been carrying on the disgusting acts mentioned above. It may be mentioned also that when they kiss each other Miss X. wants to be bitten by her friend, preferably upon the ear lobe. This may be carried so far as to actually cause pain and swelling of the ear.

It is necessary to delineate more clearly the attitude of Miss X. towards the male sex. She does not remember having ever felt any attraction towards the male. But during a celebration where much drinking was had a man prevailed upon her to spend the night with him. She had always wondered why she never felt any attraction towards the male sex and the desire to find out definitely about this as well as the don't-care-attitude brought on by drink induced her to spend that night with the man. Coitus brought her no satisfaction. Some time later another man became interested in her and fell in love with her but she did not reciprocate his feeling in the least. Nevertheless she wanted to try once more whether she could learn to care for a man's embrace. She therefore permitted herself to be induced by that man to have intercourse a few times; again she found that ordinary coitus did not rouse the least sexual feeling in her. She requested the man to carry on *cunnilingus* with her. This roused her sexually and thereupon she experienced gratification; but, without being asked specifically about it, she declares at the same time, that it was necessary for her to imagine that the person performing *cunnilingus* on her was a woman; otherwise even *cunnilingus* would have yielded her no satisfaction. The thought of carrying on any of the disgusting acts mentioned above with a man, Miss X. found in the highest degree repulsive. (*Moll*, l.c, p. 565.)

This case appears to me very noteworthy. It supports my contentions regarding the influence of alcohol upon the homosexual. Miss X. beclouds the fact and thinks she was actuated by the desire to find out definitely whether man had any attraction for her. Absence of orgasm during her intercourse with the first man shows clearly that even indulgence in alcohol was unable that time to release the inhibitions. But she allows herself the experience a second time and this time *cunnilingus* by the man yields her gratification. It is interesting that her first experience of this kind was with a boy. This corresponds exactly with my observations. In other ways, too, man plays in her condition a greater role than she is willing to recognize. Flagellation she adopts because she knew a man who was treated that way by his previous sweetheart. The relationship of this paraphilia to the strong, irritable father is fairly obvious. Her misophilic acts with women show that *she does not want to belittle herself before man, but that she looks upon subjecting her-*

*self to woman as a manner of paying homage to her
sex.* In my study on *Masochism* I go further into
this subject. The other acts indicate a sexual infantilism, rarely seen in a more discreet polymorph-
perverse form.

Fleischmann[1] also records a few cases showing
homosexual seduction carried out during a state of
intoxication. He relates also the case of a homosexual who when intoxicated was able to have intercourse with women. "At 28 years of age," relates the author about this subject, "he visited a
house of prostitution for the first time and, animated by drink, he was able to carry out coitus once
with a woman; when sober a twenty-horse team could
not drag him into such a place," according to the
urning. But after drinking he was always able to
have coitus.

We see that the incentive to drink is obviously
due to an ungratified craving. Psychoanalytic experience reiterates again and again that almost
every craving to become drunk or otherwise to lose
one's senses betrays an ungratified sexuality.
Among the inebriates, the morphine and cocaine ad-
dicts, we always find pronounced paraphiliacs and
bisexuals who have repressed a portion of their sex-

[1] *Beiträge zur Lehre von der konträren Sexualempfindung.*
Zeitschr. f. Psychol. u. Neurol., vol. VII, 1911.

ual instinct. In the same way every unprejudiced investigator will find a similar condition true of homosexuals who, according to my experience, are bisexuals who have repressed the heterosexual component of their instinct. I cannot agree with *Naecke*,[1] who contends that urning as such is a moderate drinker and seldom inebriate. Nor do I believe that in homosexual circles moderation in drink is the rule. Of course, I do know a number of temperate homosexuals, but the data under my observation as a whole and the material supplied through the objective accounts of physicians, reveal an entirely different situation.

A great deal of what takes place during states of intoxication never comes to the attention of those not immediately concerned. Possibly infantile experiences with drunken parents may have a greater role in the psychogenesis of homosexuality than we are aware of at the present time.

Now and then it happens that parents, drunken or otherwise debauched, attack their own children. I have had occasion to observe that some very curious habits are still prevalent in the nursery, here and there. One subject related to me that his mother had the habit of playing with his penis until he was six years of age. His wife also found this a con-

[1] *Alkohol und Homosexualität.* Allg. Zeitschr. f. Psychol. und gerichtl. Medizin, vol. LXVIII.

venient way to lull their child to sleep. He thought
it was as harmless a practice as it seemed efficacious
in quieting the child.

H. T., a homosexual chemist by profession, who
has a theoretic interest in psychoanalysis, writes
me: "The contribution that I am able to make may
be of some use to you. I have often tried to think
whether dreams have had any influence upon the
development of my sexual life. But I could recall
no experience which I could correlate to my condition. I have felt early an interest in the *membrum
virile* and this interest abides with me to this day.
The sight of the penis in a state of erection is
enough to rouse in me the strongest feelings of
pleasure. While walking on the street I always try
to observe the respective region in passers-by and I
try to estimate the size of the organ by outward ap-
pearances,—my fancies are full of such reflections.
I have always masturbated in front of the mirror
watching my penis during the act. But it took a
very long time for me to overcome my shyness enough
to find companions for these acts.

A few days ago I had a dream in which I saw
my father who has been dead for ten years. He
was the best man in the world, but unfortunately a
periodic drinker. When in the inebriate state he
treated mother very roughly. I dreamed a scene
which scared me so that I awoke. I saw my father

give me in hand his *membrum erectum*. And suddenly there flashed through my mind the recollection that he had done repeatedly this very thing when he was drunk. But with every fibre of my being I cling to my mother who is for me the ideal of womanhood such as I shall never again find the equal of in all this world! Beyond that my love is directed only to the male and specifically I am attracted to common men. Can you explain my riddle? I feel myself attracted to ordinary drivers, men of vulgar tastes such as one finds in the dram shops. Only once was I able to have intercourse with a girl. I was so "soused" at the time that I then did something which I could never carry out while in my ordinary senses. . . ."

I emphasize once more: The outbreak of heterosexual excitations after indulgence in alcohol proves the presence of that tendency and shows that under ordinary conditions the heterosexual tendency, though continually present, is subjected to suppression. The tendency is preserved in some closed-in compartment of the soul, the door to which may gape open under certain circumstances. Occasionally alcohol acts as a master key which opens up every enclosure.

It is interesting also to observe the sublimation which the heterosexual love undergoes among homosexuals. They endeavor to de-sexualize the other sex, at the same time have recourse to heterosexual friendships by preference. I know quite a number of homosexuals of this class, men who maintain motherly, sisterly, or even grandmotherly friendships and to whom these friendships are positively indispensable. We psychoanalysts are in a position to appreciate the source of these sexual attachments. They are due to repression and are also the result of an inhibition which extends merely over sexuality but allows the *sublimated* eroticism to manifest itself. Among the homosexuals there are many women haters (misogynists).

They often hate all women with but one exception: their mother. Occasionally some sister, aunt, or some friend of their mother's is also exempted. They never fail to emphasize: this is an exception! But the law of bipolarity teaches us that alongside this tremendous hatred there exists an equally powerful love. Occasionally the dislike is hidden and the homosexuals pose as completely indifferent towards the other sex. A little close analysis shows that this attitude is an artefact, that the assumed indifference really covers the fear that the true attitude will be betrayed otherwise. Beyond the apparent indifference stands the fear of woman and back of that fear there may be hidden, in its turn, a sadistic attitude towards woman. It is thus that the homosexual learns to cover his feelings with one another, to change them, or else he transforms, substitutes,

overstresses here and assumes indifference there, until
his actual state of feelings is completely hidden from
view. Superficial observers merely remark of some
man: he hates women! . . .

What stands back of such a dislike has been
pointed out by *Bloch* (l.c.) with considerable insight. He mentions the famous misogynist of
Classical Greece, Euripides, and in that connection
makes a very appropriate observation. He states:

"The strongest invectives against the female sex
are found in *Ion, Hippolytos, Hekate,* and *Kyklops*
of *Euripides.* (*Verses* 602-637, 650-655.) (Here
he introduces the actual quotation.)

"These verses contain the whole quintessence of
modern misogyny. But *Euripides* also discloses the
ultimate background for this attitude: 'The most
wanton creature,' he says in a fragment, 'is woman.'
Hinc illæ lacrimæ! Only men who are not accustomed to woman, men who cannot endure to have
her act with them as a free personality, and who are
so little certain of themselves that they fear an in-
road into their own personality, some irreparable
damage or possibly complete annihilation, only such
men are genuine women haters." (*Bloch,* l.c., p.
533.)

Here *Bloch* has come close to a solution of the
problem having plainly adopted the view developed
later by *Adler,* who traces homosexuality to the fear

of the sexual partner. Unfortunately he has failed
to draw the further inferences which this excellent
observation is capable of yielding.

*Hate, fear, disgust and shame are the inhibitions
which keep the homosexual away from the sexual
partner.*

Let us examine first the feeling of disgust. How
does the feeling arise? In my study of *Anxiety
States* I have explained this matter more fully. But
there is a form of disgust whose action is positive.
Disgust need not always be necessarily repressed desire. If I should see today a woman covered all over
with furuncles it may inspire me with disgust to hear
that she is an old aunt whom I must greet with a
kiss. In a case of this kind only the super-analyst
in his folly might be able to discover suppressed
components of the libido.

But we do know that occasionally homosexuality
may be aroused through episodes which enlist the
negative reactions (hate, fear, disgust, shame).
These revulsive effects then protect the individual
against their own positive tendencies. Disgust
covers craving, hate covers love, fear covers longing;
and shame—boldness.

But indulgence in alcohol is capable of turning
revulsive effects into positive. Disgust is turned
into desire, hate into love, fear into longing and
shame turns into daring. If the fearful, repressed
sadism is also added to this transformation of the

negative into positive affects, when it cannot be sublimated into lasting love, the moral man is turned into a criminal who represents but a stage in the development of the human race.

VI

May Disgust Produce the Homosexual Attitude?
Cases by Krafft-Ebing, Fleischmann, Liemcke—
Observation (personal) and Case by Bloch.—
Late Trauma as Cause of Homosexuality—Personal Observation of a case of Late Homosexuality—Two Cases of Bloch—Further Discussion of the Problem—A Case of Pfister's with
the Analysis of several Dreams.

Wären nicht die Details unseres geschlechtlichen Lebens so unendlich mannigfaltig und läge es nicht bei den meisten Menschen fast in allen wichtigen Erscheinungen und Fragen unterhalb des Bewusstseins, und wäre es nicht eine Wesenheit der Liebe, immer wieder die Schleier des Mysteriums über unsere sexuellen Empfindungen zu werfen, so dass allen stark empfindenden unverdorbenen Menschen, namentlich in der wichtigen Periode der Geschlechtsreife, Zynismen and Offenheiten über das geschlechtliche Leben sogar als unwahr erscheinen (Frauen und keusche Jünglinge sind schon beleidigt, wenn man über die Liebe auch nur wissenschaftlich anders als schwärmerisch, allgemein oder poetisch metaphorisch redet) und hatten wir nicht endlich mit der grossen Heuchelei und Verlogenheit der Gesellschaft in erotischen Dingen zu rechnen, so dass sogar die Anomalen und Perversen von ihr angesteckt werden, die es gar nicht mehr nötig haben, zu lügen und unwissend zu bleiben; kurz könnten wir unsere Erotik in seelischer und körperlicher Hinsicht bis zu den letzten Zusammenhängen analysieren, dann würden wir vielleicht mit Schauder erfahren, einen wie kleinen Bruchteil unseres Lebens wir unserem eigentlichen Geschlecht angehören.

Leo Berg.

VI

*If the details of our sexual life were not so end-
lessly manifold; if they did not belong for the most
part and in their most important aspects to the realm
beyond ordinary consciousness; if it were not a peculiarity of love continually to throw the cover of
mystery over our sexual feelings, so that all normal
persons of strong feeling, particularly during the
period of their sexual ripeness look upon frankness
in sexual matters as untruth (women and shy young
men feel insulted if one speaks about love even scien-
tifically, in other than romantic or poetic and false,
metaphorically veiled, language); and if we did not
have to consider the tremendous hypocrisy, and
falsehood of society in all matters pertaining to
sex, so that even the abnormal and the perverse, who
no longer need to lie and assume ignorance, are inspired to assume a similar 'chaste' attitude; in short,
if we could analyze our eroticism in its physical as
well as in its psychic aspects down to the last details, we should then probably discover with horror
to what a small extent we truly belong to our own
sex.*

Leo Berg.

The form of homosexuality which develops late in life is perhaps best suited to serve as an introduction to our inquiry into the psychogenesis of homosexuality and may help us understand the origin of the more complicated cases.

There are, in fact, a number of cases, in which homosexuality appears to have developed in consequence of a feeling of dislike for the other sex. Many authors consider the development of homosexuality among prostitutes as due to this cause. *Bloch*, for instance, writes:

"The naturally heterosexual prostitutes are driven to homosexuality for one of two reasons: First through the contact with and the influence of their truly Lesbian comrades, which strengthens the inner feeling of solidarity common among all prostitutes; Second, through their dislike of intercourse with men which grows with their experience and with the passage of time, the more so because they see man only in his brutal and raw aspect. The continual compulsion under which they find themselves of satisfying the animal sensuousness of oversophisticated men often by means of disgusting procedures, rouses in them eventually an unconquerable dislike of the male sex, and therefore they devote to their own sex the nobler feelings of which they may be capable. The homosexual relationship appears to them as something 'higher, something nobler and more innocent,' something pertaining to a purer realm than sexual contact with men, a fact which *Eulenburg* (*Sexuelle Neuropathie*, p. 143-144) has rightly observed." (*Bloch*, l.c., p. 603.)

Krafft-Ebing (*Neue Studien*, l.c.) also holds this view and thinks that, "many prostitutes endowed with great sensuousness, repelled by contact with perverse or impotent men who misuse them in connection with detestable sexual deeds, turn to pleasing members of their own sex."

In connection with my discussion of the Messalina type I have already shown that latent homosexuality is what drives many women to prostitution. They run away from woman and into the arms of man, into the arms of a great number of men! They expect quantity to replace what quality fails to supply them. We have additional reasons to assume that the women who lean most strongly towards the homosexual side are those who supply the ranks of prostitutes. That of course is true of the largest number though by no means holding true of every case. For there are prostitutes who are attached to their lover (cadet), and who experience orgasm only during intercourse with him, while the embraces of other men leave them unaffected. Here and there the factors pointed out by *Bloch* and *Krafft-Ebing* may also enter into the situation. In the presence of an already avowed homosexual inclination disgust

brought about through a number of possible circumstances may act as an effective barrier against heterosexuality.

This is revealed to us through the life histories
of certain homosexuals. We often come across the
statement that certain men, and women too, became
homosexual after an infection, particularly gonorrhea. The fear of infection also plays an important
role in the psychogenesis of homosexuality.[1]

Krafft-Ebing mentions (*Late Homosexuality,*
etc.) the case of a young man, 27 years of age, who
after masturbating since 7 years of age, at 19 years
had intercourse with women and enjoyed it. After
a gonorrheal infection he became so disgusted with
women that when frequenting houses of prostitution
he found himself impotent. Old masochistic-homo-
sexual phantasies reappeared and before long he was
attracted to the respective circle and seduced.[2] I

---

[1] It is not true that homosexuals are exposed to no dangers
of infection. I have examined a homosexual druggist who
acquired in Venice a serious gonorrhea of the anus. He
confessed to me that he had infected other men, because the
thought of having fallen himself a victim made him angry.
But on the whole infections are not so frequent an occurrence
as during heterosexual intercourse, which is what would be
expected, considering that *copulatio analis* is relatively rare.

[2] I must also emphasize that the first homosexual activity
often takes place in the twenties, if we omit from consideration the mutual gratifications between boys and between girls
which—with but very few exceptions—are found to occur
during the childhood of all persons. Between small children
(4-8 years of age) homosexual activity is very common, then
in many cases a period of latency seems to set in. During
the period from the 10th to the 15th year nearly every boy
passes through homosexual love (either purely platonic or
grossly sexual). After the onset of puberty there are nu-

must draw attention particularly to the fact that this man was able to experience orgasm during intercourse with women. Nevertheless his experience was so impressive that it intensified his revulsive attitude towards heterosexuality by generating a feeling of disgust. (In other cases under similar circumstances there arises a dislike for prostitutes, and the subject seeks as sexual partner a healthy woman.) The infection often becomes the root of a phantastic hatred of women without leading all the way to the development of a manifest homosexuality.[1] The next case which has come under my own observation belongs to this category:

I. P., engineer, 30 years of age, appears to me a typical anxiety neurotic. He is unable to leave his room, a personal servant must accompany him wherever he goes. For the past ten years has been sexually abstinent, because he had the misfortune to acquire a very serious luetic infection from a so-called "respectable" woman. Since that experience he feels a tremendous hatred for the sex. He reads with interest *Strindberg*, gloats over *Weininger* and he has translated into a foreign language *Moebius'*

merous variations: persons who later become homosexual continue heterosexual activity, try all sorts of experiments and then withdraw into homosexuality in consequence of some unpleasant heterosexual experience (infection, claim of parenthood, etc.) or on account of impotence.

[1] As is well known *Bloch* has endeavored to show that *Schopenhauer's* antifeminism and pessimism are traceable to syphilitic infection acquired during youth.

"*Der physiologische Schwachsinn des Weibes.*"
Homosexual activity does not inspire him with disgust but he claims that it has no attraction for him. Analysis discloses that the anxiety attacks appear as a defence against homosexual deeds. After the syphilitic infection he was for a time in danger of becoming homosexual. Now he protects himself against that tendency by various defensive measures. The path to woman is effectively blocked for him through his disgust and hatred of the sex.

The cure of his anxiety state was not very difficult. A few years later I found him a married man. He had married a woman who was 10 years older than he and who lacked every womanly characteristic. He is entirely potent in his marital relations, claims to experience orgasm satisfactorily, and believes his orgasm would be even greater if he did not have to use precautionary measures against pregnancy. As a syphilitic he wants to avoid bringing sickly children into the world. For coitus he prefers the *a posteriori* position and *situs inversus* and justifies this theoretically on the basis of the structure of the female genitalia. . . .

Concerning the relationship between sexual infection and homosexuality we also have an illuminating observation by *Fleischmann.*[1] This case is an *urlind* (homosexual woman):

[1] *Beitrage zur Lehre der kontraeren Geschlechtsempfindung.* Zeitschrift f. d. ges. Neurol. u. Pathologie, 1911.

She is an illegitimate child. Father a heavy drinker. She was badly brought up, neglected and persecuted. As a child she avoided work and was unruly. Prison experience. "At 16 years of age I had to earn my own living. My first position was in a restaurant serving beer. There I met Mr. X., the man who seduced me and gave me a sexual disease.

"At the hospital I saw and heard things that opened my eyes. From that time on I worked no longer. Years passed in struggle with suffering and want; prison life; house of correction; solitary confinement. In the house of correction most girls handled one another at night and from that time on no man could interest me any more. I have intercourse only with girls who are pretty. For the past year I have been a prostitute,—mostly drunk,—for I wanted to forget what has become of me and the morbid inclination to which I have fallen a victim."

The first sexual experience of the poor girl an infection! Then followed the homosexual seduction and the heterosexual channel was blocked. We see here the characteristic homosexuality of the prostitute, already mentioned; then alcoholism, obviously to forget her longing after true love. It must be clear also that her hatred of the father played a certain role and that this feeling towards the drunkard who brought her into the world a bastard she transferred towards all men.

The two cases reported by *Ziemke* [1] are also fairly clear:

An artist; between the age of 16 and 17 years a relative taught him to masturbate and he kept up the practice regularly every week. At 18 years of age first intercourse with woman; acquired gonorrhea; later, once more coitus, this time with a prostitute; never took any particular interest in the female sex; on the other hand as a boy 9 years of age he already was pleased at the sight of the *membrum virile* so much that it brought on erection. First sexual dreams were definitely of homosexual import, according to his own declaration, and continued of that character. Later has had repeated sexual experiences with other men, always feels fresh and well after that, while normal sexual intercourse fills him with disgust. His sexual partner he seeks among men of middle age; he is familiar with the literature on homosexuality.

Another case: Former officer, 38 years of age, mother said to have been a very nervous woman. Very shy and bashful as a child in the presence of older persons or strangers. At high school had to repeat the same class twice, was coached and succeeded at last to pass the army examination for officer. After a few years was dismissed from the army because he had mishandled his man-servant,

[1] *Zur Entstehung sexueller Perversitaten und ihrer Beurteilung vor Gericht.* Archiv f. Psychiatrie, vol. LI, 1913.

went to South-West Africa, there settled as a farmer, and as a volunteer participated in several small riots.

His first sexual feelings arose around the 12th year; he contends that till that time he knew absolutely nothing about sexual matters. At that age an experience brought his attention to the subject of sex for the first time; he played circus with a younger sister and with his 10-year old uncle and sat on the latter's back. While imitating a rider's movements he noticed that his penis became stiff and he had a pleasurable sensation wetting himself in front. He did not know the meaning of this occurrence but was too shy to tell anyone about it. Shortly after that he tried deliberately to reproduce similar situations; whenever he succeeded he also tried to attain ejaculation. He insists that he was not attracted particularly to his uncle, whom alone he had used for this form of gratification, nor to any other boy or man, his only desire at the time was to achieve ejaculation. Later during his high school years, when he had opportunity to gratify himself in the same way, he met a young colleague of his own age, a strong and beautiful boy, who appealed to him very strongly and with that boy playing the passive role he indulged more and more frequently in sexual deeds. In fact as soon as he met that particular boy the thought occurred to him that he would like to have him for the gratification of his

sexual feelings in the manner peculiar to himself.
During play he used all manner of excuses to climb
upon his friend's back and to imitate a rider's gal-
loping movements until he had ejaculation. Subsequently he found frequent occasion to use other colleagues in the same way. After drinking it was
particularly difficult for him to restrain himself;
that is why he frequently had to do with soldiers
while intoxicated and one day he was caught and
this led to his dismissal from the army. In order to
get rid of his unnatural inclination he took up a girl,
had normal intercourse with her a few times but
without any pleasurable feeling on his part, although
in order to accomplish this he had to suppose himself
riding a man in the manner customary with him, and
eventually he acquired a gonorrheal infection. Then
he migrated to South-West Africa, but even there
was unable to master his inclination, felt himself impelled to maintain relations with young Hottentots,
was caught at it, sentenced to jail, and finally banished from the Country.

In this case the gonorrheal infection seems to
have put an end to his heterosexual period.

I recall a number of other cases in which homosexuality broke out after gonorrhea, according to
the testimony obtained during my consultation
hours. In fact, there was a time when I was a firm
believer in the theory of inherited homosexuality, in

Hirschfeld's sense, so that I turned down all these cases and did not care to undertake a psychoanalysis of them. In the homosexual circles I had quite a reputation at the time as a man worthy of their confidence. But since I have found that homosexuals are really bisexual neurotics who have repressed their heterosexuality, these men come to me more rarely and consult me chiefly when they get into conflict with the law. The solidarity of homosexuals and their will to hold on to the notion that their condition is inborn goes hand in hand. Their secret organisation is thorough, and even where formal organisations are lacking, homosexuals know each other and they are always ready to introduce to one another their friends and colleagues.

Dr. S. K., physician, 32 years of age, relates that he has a pronounced heterosexual past. At any rate his longing previously was purely physical and psychically he was completely indifferent. As ship surgeon he acquired a severe gonorrhea in a port and this trouble lasted some six months. He suffered all possible complications: epididymitis, a posterior prostatitis and finally, a gonorrheal rheumatism of the joints. Since that trouble he has felt a terrific disgust for women. In Alexandria while entering a cabin he saw one of the ship lieutenants committing pederasty with a local boy. He knew that at the various ports young boys visited the

ships and offered themselves to the homosexual officers. The scene evoked in him a terrific nausea and
he wanted to drop that officer from among his acquaintances. But the latter spoke up frankly confessing that he became homosexual after being seduced and since then he was completely impotent in
the company of a woman. He begged the physician
to keep his secret and not to betray him. He was
the only intellectual man on board that ship with
whom it was pleasant to have relations. In a few
weeks the two men became intimate with each other:
"Then, for the first time, I learned what love was and
I had never before been as happy as that. My
heterosexual past now seemed unbelievable. But
in *Platen's* diary I came across a passage telling
that as a young man he too had been in love with a
girl named Euphrasia and that he learned only later
the true direction of his sexual instinct. It was the
same with me. I was born a homosexual although I
had to go through some experiences before my eyes
opened."

In this case the gonorrheal infection and the
trivial incident during the journey through the
Orient furnished the occasion for the outbreak of
homosexuality. But is not the subject in error regarding the strength of his homosexual predisposition? It is interesting to note that his homosexual
attitude is promptly beatified and idealized through
the addition of psychic factors. Indeed, the homo-

sexuals display a greater love intoxication than
the heterosexuals. Such a degree of love frenzy as
is displayed by the homosexuals is hardly ever seen
among the heterosexuals. Homosexuality represents a harbor of refuge, an attempt to lose one's
self exclusively in one direction, which must be conceived as an attempt on the part of the psyche to
neutralize all other tendencies by the over-emphasis
of that supreme passion.

We find frequently that the homosexuals contend
that their previous heterosexual leanings were exclusively physical.[1] Psychically their love relations
must be exclusively homosexual. In fact it is common to find men sublimating into friendship their
craving for psychic love while woman remains with
them merely an instrument for sin (*instrumentum
diaboli*).

A certain homosexual whose history is of particular interest because he recalls clearly his heterosexual period told *Bloch*:

"At what age my sexual feelings first arose I am
unable to recall. My sexual desires are directed
towards the male. *Before and during my puberty
the actual direction of my desire was not clear, in*

[1] We shall see later that this attitude is due to the fact that
these persons fix their whole heterosexual psychic eroticism
upon the immediate members of their family. Heterosexual
men in this situation often experience merely physical gratification during intercourse with prostitutes; with the other
type of women they are wholly impotent.

fact I believe I did entertain at the time a wish to have once intercourse with a girl. But it was not love, what I felt was merely a physical longing,— the psychic counterpart of the instinct was entirely absent at the time. Now I feel myself inclined exclusively towards young boys. I have had no intercourse thus far either with males or females, but I believe I would be able to carry out the sexual act in a normal way; I know, however, that it would not be pleasurable to me, it would not amount to more than masturbation so far as I am concerned. Towards the female sex I am completely indifferent, I feel neither disgust nor any dislike. My love dreams are always concerned with persons of my own sex." (*Bloch,* l.c., p. 566.)

Homosexuality often develops also in women following an infection:

Miss Erna, 42 years of age, writer, shows preeminent male features, behaves peculiarly like a male, smokes, drinks, is a preëminent champion of women's rights. She claims to be innately homosexual, even as a child she assumed a male role, and was wilder than her brothers. She always passed for an uncontrollable tomboy. Had no intimation about her homosexual condition. Masturbated very early and already at the age of 15 she maintained clandestine relations with an army officer who had seduced her. But she claims that her experience was exclusively physical. She has experienced orgasm with men. At 19 years of age another army officer gave her a venereal disease. *Since that time she feels a tremendous dislike for all men.* At 22 years of age she conceived a romantic love for a woman friend. They kept up a relationship during which she maintained the male role. She even procured for herself an artificial phallus and wore male clothes in the house. It was like a genuine marriage. "I know only since then what love really means. Formerly I only felt a liking for men. It was merely a physical attraction. But for the past 20 years my love has been exclusively for women." After the first "homosexual marriage," which lasted only three years because her friend deserted her and married, she had numerous relations with other women.

Very convincing are the cases in which the homosexual outbreak occurs first after some powerful trauma! It is not always gonorrhea. Often various other experiences furnish the inciting moment as I can easily prove on the basis of my own observations. But first I must quote a case reported by *Krafft-Ebing* which is illuminating on this score:

Miss X., 22 years of age, is considered a beauty, men flock around her whenever she appears in society; she is decidedly of a sensuous nature, seems born to be an *Aspasia*, but rejects all advances. One of her admirers, however, a young scientist, she looks upon with some favor, becomes intimate with him, allows herself to be kissed by him, *but not like a loving woman;* and when the young man believes himself close to the consummation of his supreme desire she begs him with tears in her eyes to desist because she is utterly unable to yield to him, not on account of moral grounds so much as for deeper psychic reasons. In the course of the exchange of written confidences which followed that unsuccessful meeting between the two the homosexual character of her inclination was clearly revealed to her.

Miss X. had a father who was addicted to drink and a hysteropathic mother. She herself is of a neuropathic constitution; has full breasts, and generally the outward appearance of an unusually attractive woman but reveals boyish ways about her and various male peculiarities,—she fences, rides horseback, smokes and has a decidedly mannish way of standing and walking. Lately her romantic attachment to young women has become quite noticeable. She has a young woman with her sharing her apartment.

Miss X. claims that up to the time of puberty she was sexually indifferent. At 17 years of age she became acquainted at a summer resort with a young foreigner whose "majestic" figure made a tremendous impression upon her. The privilege of dancing a whole evening with him made her happy. *The following evening, at twilight, she witnessed a horrible scene—from her window she saw that wonderful man in the bushes futuare more bestiarum mulierem quandam inter menstruationem.*

Adspectu sanguinis currentis et libidinis quasi bestialis viri Miss X. felt shocked, she seemed powerless and crushed, could hardly recover her psychic equilibrium and for some time after that could neither sleep nor eat; from that time on man stood in her mind for the quintessence of bestiality.

Two years later a young woman approached her in a public garden, smiled and glanced at her with a very peculiar look which penetrated deeply into her soul. The following day Miss X. felt impelled to visit again that public garden. The woman was there, in fact, she seemed to have been expecting her. They greeted one another like old acquaintances; they talked and joked pleasantly and thereafter met by appointment daily, first in the garden, and later, when the weather became unpleasant, in the woman's living apartment. "One day," Miss X. relates confidentially "the woman led me up to her divan and allowed me to glide to the floor while she seated herself. She lifted her shy eyes at me, stroked the hair off my forehead softly with her hand, saying: 'Oh, if I could once love you the real way, may I?' I consented, and as we sat close by gazing into each other's eyes, before we knew it we passed to that love from which there is no drawing back. . . She was bewitchingly beautiful. For me the whole experience was something new and intoxicating. . . . I do not believe that man is ever able to feel such delicate, bewitching, exquisite intoxication. . . . Man is not sufficiently sensitive, he is not delicate enough for that. . . Our foolish abandon lasted until I fell back exhausted, helpless, intoxicated. In this exhausted state I was lying on her bed when suddenly an exquisite feeling thrilled through me and awoke me from my half dreamy state, something unspeakably sweet and unlike anything I had ever experienced before; I found J. on top of me, *cunnilingus perficiens*—that was her highest pleasure, *tandem mihi non licebat altrum quam osculos dare ad mammas*—and with every motion she shook convulsively."

Miss X. acknowledged further that during her homosexual relations she always assumed the male attitude towards her womanly companion and that once, *faute de mieux*, she allowed one of her male admirers to perform *cunnilingus* on her. (*Krafft-Ebing*, l.c., Obs. 165.)

Let us consider closely the case of an exalted nature like that girl. She goes through her first graceful love fever, she is about to become a true woman, she thinks "him" a princely man, a "majestic" personality when unexpectedly she undergoes the experience of witnessing that very God-like man behave like a common beast. . . . Jealousy and a revulsion of feeling unite in her at the terrible sight rousing such a tremendous affect that forever after she feels an unspeakable horror of all men.

Many women must have become *urlinds* as a result of just such experiences. One must also take into account that among many women homosexual love shows itself merely in kisses and embraces and that it seems to them something nobler and much more esthetic than the manifestations of heterosexual love. Fear of the phallus is something that may be roused by a relatively slight infantile occurrence. In her homosexual indulgences Miss X. is not particularly esthetic by any means, nevertheless even she remarks: "man is not delicate enough!"

This highly interesting case illustrates the development of homosexuality following a trauma which must have had a tremendous effect upon so sensitive and romantic a nature as this young woman and which could not but strengthen the existing predisposition to homosexuality. But in spite of all she is still bisexual and I do not think it impossible that she should yet overcome her tremendous horror of man. We must consider that the father was a drinker and that she had probably witnessed in the parental home scenes like the one she has described. What a pity that the case has not been analyzed. *Traumatic incidents during later life are particularly powerful in their effect if they resemble and therefore re-echo infantile memories of similar childhood experiences.* It may even be possible that the woman did not actually witness the scene at the time she states but that she experienced merely a hallucination, repeating in her mind a scene which she may have witnessed only during her childhood.

A remarkable parallel is furnished by the next case which I record from among my own observations:

Miss K. S. is 32 years of age and calls to consult me about her various compulsions. She confesses that she is an *urlind* and that she had never felt herself attracted to men. Her father, a heavy drinker, died three years ago; her mother lives quietly and is not neurotic.

Our subject has had a number of chances to get married but she withdraws coyly from every man the moment one comes close to her. She feels a certain inclination towards older married men and she understands in consequence how a woman might become interested in a friend's husband. "When I did find a man whom I liked, I was unlucky," she declares, "for I discovered that he was already engaged to a friend of mine." Truly she fell in love only with girls and women. Her first romantic attachment was to a woman school teacher, whom she also visited at her home. That teacher wanted this wealthy girl to marry her brother and brought the two into contact as often as possible. She liked the brother because he looked so very much like her beloved friend. But if the sister was not in the room their conversation lagged and she could talk only in monosyllables. She sent flowers and costly gifts to her teacher. Her supreme desire was to sleep once in the same bed with that teacher and she often dreamed of it. She even proposed to take her on a journey. The teacher could not go and hesitated also because she found her pupil's attentions too oppressive. The teacher actually suffered on account of her admirer's deep jealousy, for the girl turned ill if she so much as found other girls visiting her. At any rate, quite a circle of girls in the class admired the teacher.

Later she fell in love with a girl friend whom she embraced and kissed warmly numberless times because it gave her a wonderful warm feeling to do so. On the other hand the kisses of an uncle made no impression on her whatever. No man interested her in the least. For a long time she did not know that she was homosexual, but she was well aware since her childhood that she was unlike other children. She was always as wild as a boy and her mother frequently said to her: "there are ten rough boys in you!" She climbed trees, ran around wildly and always preferred to play with boys, did not care for dolls, coaxed to be given a saddle horse and a gun until her father was driven to despair over her and exclaimed sometimes: "you are really a spoiled boy!"

During the analysis she recalled a number of homosexual and heterosexual experiences. Already at 12 years of age she had an experience with an uncle who came to her in bed and played with her. She could not recall whether they indulged in coitus that time. With girl friends she also had various adventures. She confesses in fact that she has been in the habit of masturbating since her 12th year, when she was taught by a girl, and that at one time she often indulged in the phantasy that a man was having coitus with her. In fact, as late as her 16th year she fell "heels-over-head" in love with a friend of her father's. He was much younger than her father but belonged to the same circle.

While she talks at first only in favorable terms about her father (his drinking habit was not so very excessive) and dwells mostly on his lovely qualities, his mild character, his imposing appearance, etc., at the same time she begins to show underneath a growing hatred. The father had in fact left her in critical circumstances. Every one considered them millionaires, because her father had kept up a very big house. After his death it turned out that he had been spending his capital and that there had been left practically only her share which was, however, large enough to permit her and her mother to live in comfort. Her mother had always endured the life of a martyr. The father had maintained relations with the cook in the house during the last ten years. She was a fat, shapeless vulgar person. In fact, mother and daughter were just tolerated in their home. Once her mother endeavored to dismiss the cook and the father was mad and grew almost violent showing her mother the door threatening that she might leave and take along her daughter if she did not like it in the house. After that the cook was naturally more arrogant and unbearable than ever so that the poor mother passed her days weeping until finally she reconciled herself to that state of things. It was possible to throw that cook out of the house only after her father was lying ill in bed. That daring woman started a law suit claiming that the father had promised to settle on her a home and an income. . . She lost that suit because the father testified upon his death-bed that the woman's contentions were false. The subject relates a number of other relevant incidents but does not recall having ever witnessed any intimacies between her father and the cook.

However, her dreams seem to point in that sense. Thus, for instance, among others she had the following dream:

I go carefully into the kitchen and do not find the cook there. Then I tiptoe slowly up the back stairs to the garret and through the key hole I see the cook lying in bed with the driver.

She recalls that that particular driver was in their service when the cook was a younger woman and that her father had dismissed him. He watched for her father once, as he was coming out of a restaurant to waylay him. But her father was stronger and threw the servant to the ground with such force that the fellow fractured a bone. But she thinks that the neighborhood did not know the true reason for the battle, every one naturally thinking that the servant planned the attack out of revenge.

Finally she confessed to me that there was one experience of which she had not thought before for a long time which she must tell me about. She wanted to tell me about it for some time but an inexplicable shyness prevented her. She was 16 years of age when she once heard her father leaving his study room to steal upstairs to the garret. It was the maid's day out and her mother was lying down not feeling well. She took her shoes off and followed him quietly up the stairs. The door to the servants' room stood open. The father was somewhat under the influence of drink and so was also the cook, who always managed to secure some liquor for herself on the sly. A candle was burning in the room and the stairway was dark. She could see plainly everything that was going on. She now saw *pater membrum suum in os ancillæ immisit.* The sight of his reddish face now distorted under the influence of passion was so repulsive to her and struck her so powerfully that she could never forget it in her life. Even to this day when she thinks of it she feels nauseated. (While she is telling the incident she is struggling against the impulse to vomit.) After that episode she developed a nervous complaint of the stomach, chiefly a nervous vomiting. Even during the year just passed there were times when she could not swallow a morsel of meat and she had attacks of uncontrollable vomiting.

It was after that occurrence that she fell in love with her teacher. That episode was what had determined the course of her sexual development and what drove her to homosexuality because it made her look at all men in the light in which she had seen her father. Her inclination towards elderly married men (always platonic) is also traceable to her father *Imago*. She was aiming to find a nobler and more delicate father.

Whenever a man tried to get closer to her it reminded her of the painful incident she had witnessed, which summed up in her mind all the misery in her home, the whole outrageous situation, the humiliation of her mother, and her father's morbid passion. For her father who did have some splendid qualities and who enjoyed an enviable position in society she once had as great a love and as deep a respect as for her noble mother. Then she had to go through the disastrous situation in the house. That experience could but serve her as a warning against men, a warning and a lesson! It could not but implant deeply in her soul a lasting dread of man and of man's terrible passion. She naturally shrank back from any close contact with man for there was always a picture before her mind which plainly carried the message: "do not trust any man lest you should go through what your mother did!"

What might have been the future of this brave girl if the father had not acted in that way, if the marriage of the parents had been a happy one, if she had not witnessed that terrible scene which impressed her the more painfully because she had no inkling whatever of the brutal side of sexuality? I make bold to assert that she would have developed into a quiet pleasant housewife and she would have given vent to her homosexual tendencies along quiet and innocent paths. But as it was she devoted herself to girls and avoided men more and more. She did permit herself to be attracted by men. But they had to be married and unattainable. Thus there could be no danger for her. When the husband of a friend of hers of whom she also was very fond declared that for her sake he would be willing to divorce his wife, she fled and presently found some other unreachable ideal to which she attached herself. All her ideals were practically desexualized while her sexuality she exercised exclusively on women. *The love among women loomed up in her mind as pure and elevating, while the love of men*

*she considered brutal. Even coitus seemed to her
a disgusting brutal act.*

The traumatic incident occurred after puberty
yet it had a very tremendous effect. The question
rises whether the traumas occurring during childhood may also influence the particular direction of
sexual development. This question has long since
been solved in harmony with *Binet's* view and psychoanalysis has taught us some additional facts regarding the influence of traumas. The narrower
Freudian school has gone so far as to overvalue the
influence of traumas and has designated as traumas
certain relatively trivial experiences which do not
deserve that designation. I want to sound again a
warning against underestimating the role of traumas. Certain minor fetichistic tendencies are
easily and sometimes fairly satisfactorily explained
on that basis, although the more complicated forms
of fetichism, such as we shall study later, are not to
be explained solely upon the theory of traumatic
causation. Here the association hypothesis of *Binet*
completely breaks down. We must bear in mind that
the neurotics conceive many traumas which in
reality did not occur and that their phantasy turns
innocent incidents into alleged traumas whenever it
suits the trend of their emotions to do so. The
neurotic's memory serves him poorly and that is
also true of the homosexuals who construct a purely
homosexual life history for themselves.

But are not first impressions of fundamental determinative value for future development? *Jean Paul* very appropriately declares: "*All first impressions persist forever in the child!*"

I wish to add here a couple of observations which we owe to *Bloch* and which illustrate very well the influence of first sexual impressions:

"I was about five years of age when during a walk accompanied by the nursemaid I saw at some distance a man in the act of masturbating; without knowing what it was, the picture persisted in my mind for years. In my dreams until my fourteenth year a playmate occupied the chief role. At thirteen years of age I fell in love with a school comrade who took but little interest in me; what roused my interest in him in particular was probably the fact that he was the one who brought to the class information about sexual matters. We removed to another City and I lost sight of the boy. Although I knew nothing specific about sex at the time I sought contact with those who roused my feelings.

"A stranger, a man of about 35 years of age, enticed me and as soon as he had me he carried on pederasty with me. I felt that there was something repulsive in what he was doing, but I was too weak to oppose myself against his influence. In about three months he disappeared. Now I knew what masturbation was especially as there had occurred a number of orgies at school.

"At eighteen years of age I left school, and while the others among my comrades began showing an inclination towards the female sex I found myself attracted in every way exclusively to man. Often at the insistence of some of my friends I tried to come into contact with women of the half world but every time the attempt filled me only with disgust and aversion. When I see a woman taking an interest in me I am filled with a horrible feeling. That was one more reason why I felt attracted to the male sex. When I love a man I do not think (only) of sexual attraction, but I seek to find in him precisely what I, in turn, feel myself ready to give; exclusive devotion, loyalty, tenderness; when I love a man, everything else pales into insignificance for me." (*Bloch,* l.c., p. 565.)

It would seem that in this instance the memory of the masturbating man, an incident which the boy had witnessed during childhood, determined for him the actual course of his sexual development. In the previous case the trauma acted as a warning. In this case it seems to have acted like a perpetual stimulus, since a child does not possess the usual moral scruples, and the first excitation (the sight of the erect organ) must have been tremendous. That picture stayed in his memory for years, it fixed it-

self and persisted permanently in that young man's
memory. In the K. S. case, mentioned above, the
trauma was associated with disgust; it served as a
revulsion against heterosexuality.[1]

In this particular case the memory of the incident
was associated with desire. It was utilized in
positive form as an inciter to homosexuality. Thus
we find that the problem is rather complicated. I
confess that for some time I was unable to see my
way clear in the midst of these facts so long as I
was one-sided in my views and thought that the condition arises exclusively in one way. But I know
now that a number of paths may lead equally to
homosexuality and that this is a subject which requires a much more thorough study. We must find
out whether psychic factors are invariably at work
behind every case of homosexuality or whether there
is an exclusively psychic and a specially organic
homosexuality. Such cases could be called pseudo-
homosexuality.

[1] The following statement of *Hirschfeld's* illustrates this
point (l.c., p. 315): "An urning, writer,—*unus e multis*—writes
me: 'The homosexual inclination developed in me in spite of
the fact that the first sexual aggression was of a heterosexual character—a nursemaid seduced me—in spite of the
fact that through training from childhood on I was taught
to look at the female sex and my reading of literature showed
me that woman was the object of love.'" I add: this tendency
developed because the first sexual experience was associated
with disgust on his part and because the domineering of
woman led him to hate that sex.

As a contribution to this question I find of interest the following case, reported by Bloch, as the history reveals the trauma and the bearing of the trauma upon the development of the condition. It is a case of male homosexuality:

"From my early childhood I was aware of something peculiarly girlish in my whole nature outwardly as well as inwardly (the latter in particular). Sexual excitation I experienced also very early. *I was about 6 years of age when I remember that a private instructor seated himself on the edge of the bed where I was lying ill with fever, petted me and then membrum meum tetigit with his hand; the pleasurable sensation which thus arose was so intense that I cannot get it out of my mind to this day.* At school where my conduct and studies were always excellent I indulged occasionally in mutual 'touching games' with other boys. I do not know on what side of the family I may have inherited the unusual intensity of my sexual desire, but I remember that around my 12th year the flaring up of the instinct caused me a great deal of unrest and when a comrade once showed me how to masturbate it proved a welcome relief. This 'paradisaic' state did not last long and when I learned about the dangers and forbidden features of my habit I had a terrific and useless struggle with myself.

"I remember that as far back as my memory goes I had the habit of *gazing at older, vigorous men*

almost involuntarily and with a feeling full of longing, without knowing what it meant. As to masturbation I thought that I fell into the habit because
I had no chance to come into contact with women.
As a matter of fact I did occasionally entertain
friendly relations with certain girls who appeared to
be strongly attached to me; *but I always saw to it
that these love excitations were 'nipped in the bud'*
because I was *afraid I should be unable to carry out
my role* to the end. Finally I decided to seek relief
among prostitutes, who were otherwise repellent to
my esthetic and moral sense, but the attempts proved
useless: either I found myself unable to carry out
the normal sexual act at all or if I did it, I experienced no satisfaction and thereafter I was also
plagued with the fear of infection. I did have rather
frequently the opportunity to enter into amorous
relations with married women but I never did so even
though I inwardly scorned my shyness and my over-
sensitive conscience. Although these facts are true,
I must not omit to mention the chief thing responsible for the whole situation, namely, the fact
that I am homosexual in my inclination and that the
other sex has hardly any attraction for me.

"I believed myself totally unfit for ordinary sexual
relations when I found one day that the sight of the
membrum virile alone made the blood boil in me with
excitement. I then recalled that this had occasionally happened before, although not to such a re-

markable extent. Secretly I had to face the plain fact that I was 'not like others.' This fact which I had previously suspected and of which I grew more and more convinced, brought me to the brink of despair.

"Then it happened that a simple little girl fell deeply in love with me, and I made up my mind to start relations with her. During the time while this lasted, a period of several months, my inclination towards the male sex persisted though occasionally I tried to subdue it; but to overcome it completely was for me, I found, impossible. I was still keeping up my relations with the girl when I once noticed in a public lavatory an elderly gentleman who appealed to me very strongly; he scrutinized me carefully and bent over in order *membrum meum videre*, came close by, moved forward his hand shaking with excitement and . . . *membrum meum tetigit*. I was so surprised and scared that I ran off at once and for some time after that I avoided passing by that place. But my impulsion was the greater on that account to meet that man again; this was not at all difficult. . . In this continuous struggle, so meaningless and so useless, against an instinct, which was at least partly inborn in me, I have squandered my best energies, although I have long ago reached the point of realizing that in itself the instinct is neither morbid nor sinful." (*Bloch*, l.c., P. 545.)

Does not this case illustrate clearly the influence of first impressions and the significance of the bi-sexual foundation in the homosexual attitude? The man is seduced by an elderly man and after that he longs continually to be seduced by an elderly man, in a manner recalling that unforgettable scene. Although capable of heterosexual acts, this side of his nature persists as a sort of compulsory tendency and drives him again into the arms of elderly men to seek that form gratification which was the first he had ever experienced in his life. His heterosexual leanings are repressed. He himself admits that he always saw to it that all such love affairs were nipped in the bud. In other words he is deliberately fighting off all heterosexual stimuli and encouraging the homosexual excitations. Then he arrives at the realisation that he is not like others. . . In fact he is bisexual and has the capacity to act as a bisexual being. A careful analysis would have disclosed many interesting features. We wanted only to show how this young man was continually seeking to find his teacher (father?), and what a great deal of neurotic overgrowth stood back of this desire.

The next case quoted from *Krafft-Ebing* is also very remarkable:

A merchant, 34 years of age, mother neuropathic; at 9 years of age was taught masturbation by a schoolmate; also, homosexual relations with a brother; fellatio; urolagnia; at 14 years of age first love for a school colleague.

At 17 years of age his love ideal changes completely. He is no longer attracted by young, beautiful boys, but by decrepit old men.

T. traces this back to the fact that he had once overheard his father in the next room uttering pleasurable exclamations after he retired for the night and this excited him tremendously because he thought his father was. . . .(weil er sich den Vater coitierend dachte).

Since that time old men carrying on various homosexual deeds play a predominant role in his dream pollutions and during masturbation. But even through the day the sight of an old man is enough to excite him, especially if the man is very old and decrepit when his excitement may be so tremendous as to end in ejaculation. Attempts at intercourse with women in houses of prostitution proved unsuccessful and ordinary men and boys do not rouse him. From the age of 22 years on he carried on a platonic love towards an old gentleman whom he met on the latter's daily walks. During these walks T. had ejaculation. In order to free himself of this peculiar dependence after several unsuccessful attempts at intercourse with prostitutes *he took along with him a decrepit old man whom he induced to have coitus before his eyes. The scene so excited him that he in turn proved potent. Later on he was able to dispense with the old man's presence and could carry out the act successfully without that aid. But this improvement did not last long; soon he became impotent once more.*

This case is in every way interesting and of great significance for our problem. It proves to us the great determinative role of a childish reminiscence and the persistence of a scene which is continually repeated in memory. The whole of that young man's libido is centered around that particular scene. He stages it also in the brothel when he hires an old man to have intercourse in his presence. That old man assumes then the role of the father, the prostitute is the mother, while he is once more the onlooking child. The act of looking on so excites his passion that with that aid he proves potent in his intercourse with the prostitute. But that continues only so long as the exciting influence of the scene persists. After that he reverts to his former impotence and he again . . . seeks his father. It is perfectly plain, and only the blind could fail to see that T. seeks his father. His wish was obviously that his father should also start something sexual with him. It is possible that he had identified himself with his mother. But we have no direct proof of that. This is particularly significant because *Sadger* and the others who belong to *Freud's* narrower circle place great emphasis upon the role of the mother in the genesis of genuine homosexuality while neglecting ruefully the role of the father. This case shows us a "Japhet, who seeks his father." The promenades with the respectable old gentleman are repetitions of the walks with his father.

This patient does not recall any heterosexual experiences during his youth, probably because the memory of them has been repressed from consciousness. In the other case which I shall now quote from *Krafft-Ebing* the heterosexual period is clearly recalled. I refer the reader to that author's *Observation* 144. Here I quote the first part of the history of that case:

"I am at the present time 31 years of age, lean yet well built, devoted to male love, therefore unmarried. My relatives were in good health, mentally normal, there were two suicides in our family, on mother's side. My sexual feelings arose when I was about seven years of age, the sight of the naked abdomen being particularly exciting. I gratified my instinct by allowing my sputum to trickle down the abdomen. When I was eight years old we had in our house a little nurse maid of about thirteen years. I found it very pleasurable to rub my genitals against hers, but there could be no coitus on my part at that time. During the ninth year I went to live among strangers and went to the gymnasium. A colleague showed me his genitals and that filled me with disgust. But in the family where my parents arranged for me to board there was a very beautiful girl who prevailed upon me—I was but little over nine years old at the time—to sleep with her. I found the experience most pleasurable. My penis, though small, was already capable of erection and I had intercourse with her almost daily. This continued for several months. Then my parents transferred me to another gymnasium; I missed the girl very much and during my tenth year I began to masturbate. But the act inspired me only with disgust. I masturbated but moderately, always felt deeply remorseful afterwards, although I could discover no bad consequences."

Here is a man who actually felt disgust at the sight of a friend's genitals and who found intercourse with women pleasurable. He is excellently on the way to become a heterosexual. At fourteen he falls in love with a school colleague, an experience which every person goes through at about that age, the "normal," no less than the homosexual. After the final examination (high school) he has intercourse with girls and great pleasure in the act, but he is already making use of some homosexual makeshifts. Soldiers must precede him in the act of using the prostitutes and the thought of having access to a vagina which had just been in contact with another penis, stimulates him. "At the same time I can never kiss women without feeling disgust; *even my relatives I kiss only on the cheek.*" . . . *Hinc illæ lacrimæ!* He protects himself against the sexual excitations emanating from his family circle. His homosexuality is somehow linked to his family. The peculiar action of a boy who allows sputum to trickle down his abdomen, imagining that it is spermatic fluid could probably be traced by means of analysis to a definite childhood trauma. Particularly clear in this case is the heterosexual attitude which under certain influences and inhibitions merges almost imperceptibly into the bisexual and homosexual.

Whether late homosexuality is determined every time through definite traumatic incidents, I am unable to state, because I have not had the opportunity thoroughly to analyze such a case. The next case seems to me to show that strong emotionally toned episodes may turn a latent into manifest homosexuality:

An army officer, 46 years of age, consults me for complete impotence with women. The impotence is of four years' duration. He has become acquainted with a lady of whom he is very fond and who enjoys an excellent financial status. He could now be a happy man, if he only were a complete man. Asked about his morning erections he blushes. The trouble is not with erections, they do not fail him on other occasions. He is impotent only in contact with women. Finally he admits that since his 38th year he has been carrying on homosexual relations. Since that time his interest in women gradually vanished and he has become impotent. His anamnesis reveals some significant facts. He recalls no homosexual deeds or excitations during childhood and before puberty. He was sexually precocious, masturbated already during the primary school period and was attracted by girls. First coitus at seventeen in a house of prostitution. After that he felt he wanted women very badly but had no homosexual inclination. Then a tremendous experience came into his life which agitated him and after that he was depressed for some time. That was just before his first homosexual act.

"Can you tell me something about the nature of that agitation?"

"I find it painful to speak of it."

"But you expect help in a rather difficult situation. How should I appraise the situation in its true light if you won't furnish me the necessary information?"

"You are right. But there are things of which it is almost impossible to speak. It is about my mother. But I suppose I cannot help myself otherwise. I must tell you all.

"I have always honored and respected my mother. I was 38 years of age when I received a telegram calling me to her sick bed. She passed away shortly after my arrival. As the only son it was my duty to put everything in order after her. I went through her old correspondence and in a box I came across a mass of love letters. First I was not going to read them. But curiosity got the best of me. I said to myself: 'every married person loves once in his or in her life some one else, why should not that be permitted to my mother when father died while she was still very young.' If I only had not done that! I found not one letter, I found hundreds of letters and . . . they were not all from one man. The letters were so vulgar, so plain, so cynical, so revolting that I wished myself dead. I lost the holiest thing in my life. Before then I always dreamed of finding a woman like mother, and her type of womanhood always stood before me as the ideal. Now I found that she could be bought and she was to be had for ordinary degrading purposes. The tone which her lovers assumed in those letters was so revolting that I imagined the worst. Since then I feel a deep scorn for all womanhood. Shortly after that I yielded to the temptations of a homosexual friend. . . .

"Do you believe that my impotence has some relation to that occurrence? I have often thought of it. Whenever I go to a woman I cannot help thinking of the box in which I found mother's letters. After such an experience how is it possible for one still to consider marriage?"

A late homosexuality induced by a very tragic experience. Naturally the man was always latently homosexual. But it was that experience which turned him into a manifest homosexual. Unfortunately I am unable to state whether he married the woman and became heterosexual again or not, because I never saw him after that.

The reader will observe that in this chapter I have quoted quite a number of cases culled from the reports of other practitioners. I do this for a double reason. First, I want to prove, on the basis of other material than my own, that homosexuality has its psychogenesis; and, in the second place, I aim by this means to disprove the contention unfortunately rather widespread in some circles and actually expressed by some critics, that my case histories correspond to the "genius loci." As if the Viennese differed in sexual matters from the North-German or from the Englishman! My material is derived from the world at large. *I have been unable to discover thus far any difference with respect to sexual matters between any two nations, except that one may keep things under cover more cleverly than the other.*

This series of cases aiming to illustrate the rôle of psychic trauma in sexuality may be concluded with the following case, reported by *Pfister* (l. c. p. 169):

A 28-year-old woman, member of an educational institution, of high moral repute, is in despair because she fears she is no longer able to control her homosexual longings. If she meets a young girl she is nearly overpowered with the impulse to kiss her then and there. The unknown girl's face haunts her for weeks afterwards and she can not sleep tortured with regret because she did not gratify her impulse to kiss the girl as she does with her acquaintances. She is particularly distracted at the thought that with her tendernesses and attentions, she may mislead into homosexual counter-affection a fourteen-year-old girl who is close to her, although nothing out of the way has happened between them. But the little friend already trembles with excitement when she is embraced and her great affection leads her to tears if she does not see her beloved often enough.

Our homosexual girl had a physically attractive but otherwise insignificant, nervous father who left the conduct of his business to the capable hands of his energetic and intelligent wife. The little daughter learned early to admire her mother and to look upon her father as a "light weight." As a small girl she was normal. She played equally with boys and girls. With her playmates of both sexes she underwent various sexual experiences: the girls played the game of doctor and this gave them an opportunity to touch the sexual parts, and a small, ailing boy who was one of the girl's playmates between her seventh and ninth years, did the same thing. Around the age of eight years she fell in love with an uncle who had

the habit of throwing her playfully into the air, a
game which always gave her a very peculiar feeling.
*At ten or eleven years of age a 40-year old house-
keeper abused her repeatedly.* Definitely homosexuality broke out when the girl was thirteen. She
was at the time a great deal in the company of a
teacher who resembled her mother in many ways but
who was better educated. That passionate woman
was distinctly homosexual and for two years she
treated the girl with greatest affection. During that
time her passion for kissing developed while the
grossly sexual cravings which the sensuous housekeeper had roused in her gradually quieted down. A
few love affairs with boys also led to kisses but she
experienced no particular passion in that connection.
Those affairs she took up as a pastime and to be
in fashion rather than because she was interested.

At the boarding school her one-sided erotic inclination was further developed in the course of
passionate friendships. At the age of nineteen she
made a couple of heterosexual erotic attempts but
they proved unsuccessful. The first affair was with
a hot-blooded artist of womanly appearance. Her
love was deep, the young girl floated in ideal conversations and gladly exchanged kisses with the
young man. After his departure they maintained
a warm correspondence full of tenderness but without giving one another any formal promise.

Five or six weeks after parting from the beloved

friend she became engaged to a smart young man because she was in despair and she had given up the plan of a higher education for herself as she was not getting along at all well with a relative at home. She thought she loved her young man but soon after the engagement she began fearing that she had perhaps undertaken more than she intended to carry out. The soft, shy young man apparently resembled her father. For seven months she played at being in love, vomitted every morning and wished she were dead. Finally she gave up her engagement and concentrated all her feelings upon members of her own sex. She maintained however her delicate womanly sensitiveness throughout and always gave the impression of a girlish creature. So long as she found homosexual gratification, she took little interests in a career, or in nature, art and religion; but as soon as her inclinations were thwarted, her ideal interests came strongly to the foreground. She herself compared these vacillations with the movements of a pair of scales.

When she felt deeply in love she was fairly free of grossly sexual excitations. But during her loveless engagement *she felt herself sexually roused a number of times when the young man played with her in a thoroughly respectable manner.*

Pfister then relates that the young woman interrupted the analysis just as she was making rapid progress towards recovery. But he adds a number of interesting details, including her first dream, which usually contains the nucleus of the neurosis.

The first dream is as follows:

A cat bit me on the left index finger and held on to it for some time. The finger swelled and burst down to the bone. The tendon was broken and a great deal of fluid was oozing out. It meant I shall always have a stiff finger. I said to myself: "What a pity! Now I won't be able ever to play the piano again."

I woke up and found my finger so fast asleep that I could not move it.

Just before the dream the girl in her despair had offered a fervent prayer which made her feel a little easier. Before the analysis the girl was extremely restless and longed for her beloved, but she said to herself that she would only bring misfortune upon that poor girl's head.

The analysis of this dream, which *Pfister* unfortunately, did not carry out with complete success, shows that her whole emotional life is governed by the infantile experience with that housekeeper. The first recollection brought up by the free associations with this dream relate to the housekeeper, who in the dream is represented by the cat.

I have discussed elsewhere in a lengthy contribution, the *Representation of the Neurosis in Dreams.*[1]

[1] *Die Darstellung der Neurose in Traume.* Zentralblatt f. Psychoanalyse. vol. III, p. 26.

In this dream the trouble is symbolized by a stiff finger. "Playing the piano" is again a symbol for sexual intercourse as well as for masturbation. Probably the symbol here has acquired its emotional coloring from the masturbation habit. But the heterosexual meaning is also obvious (piano playing—coitus). If we interpret the dream we have:

The housekeeper, that false cat who played a dependent rôle towards my parents, made me ill with her long-continued tendernesses (A cat bit me on the left index finger and held on for a long time). The trouble grew worse, something valuable tore in me (the ability to love a man) and the homosexual form of love established itself permanently (stiffening). Now I am incapable of loving a man, I cannot be a mother or raise a family of my own,—a wish that has already cost me so many tears (the water flowing out of the wound).

Perhaps this interpretation will be doubted as something artificial and rather forced. But the subject recalls further details of the dream and relates them subsequently. Such additions are of extraordinary significance because usually they contain the censured, the repressed material. She recalls that the cat was going to bite her at first on the foot (significant because of the proximity of the sexual parts). Further on she relates a continuation of the dream:

The water flowed down the steps. I ran to a friendly woman physician for aid to my wound. On the way I met her unexpectedly in the neighborhood of a merry-go-round. Then my sister speaks up saying: "She will fix your finger in good shape right away." The woman physician retorts: "I am sorry, but I do not operate." She sends me instead to a surgeon (male).

The interpretation is not difficult. There is a great deal of weeping. Her tears inundate her whole soul (House as symbol of soul). At first she is looking for a woman healer. A woman shall cure her trouble. Life is a merry-go-round, everything in life revolves, she may yet be happy. But the woman physician gave her the correct answer. You need a surgeon. *Only a man can heal thee.* I do not operate. I am not the one to awaken your femininity (defloration?).

A further supplementary account shows that the finger became the muzzle of a repeating revolver. *Pfister's* interpretation that this is a phallic symbol and that it shows the dreamer's phantasy that she was a male with a phallus, may be correct. Every homosexual woman has the wish to transpose the psychic state into an actual physical condition. But another possible meaning of the repeating fire arm seems to me more plausible. The subject's traumatic incident had the effect of facilitating subsequently other homosexual experiences. *The traumatic experience required repetition.*

I pass over for the present the other meanings of the dream (over-determination), which *Pfister* discloses with keen insight. I am concerned here merely with pointing out the determining influence of a trauma. Naturally there are other factors at work along with the traumatic incident, it would be necessary to find out why the incident influenced her in that particular manner, the precise constellation of her family circle ought to be taken into consideration, etc. But the dream points so clearly to the cause of the psychic trauma that the cross section it furnishes enables us to reconstruct the whole picture of her trouble.

The case is convincing also from another standpoint. The subject gave up early her psychoanalysis because she felt in a short time that she was well. These apparent cures which serve to circumvent the danger of a thorough psychoanalysis, are well known occurrences. The subject is unwilling to acknowledge that she is also heterosexually predisposed, that her whole longing, in fact, is directed towards the fulfilment of motherhood. The dream says plainly: "*I want to be a woman, like all other women, I want to bear children! Save me from the danger of homosexuality!*"

But her consciousness is unprepared to acknowl-

edge this desire. She meets difficulties upon the heterosexual path. *Pfister* believes that she identified
herself with her father. In that sense the kissing
episodes (with girls) signify: *I let father* (who was
a very handsome and well appearing man) *kiss me!*
But her mother was also in the habit of kissing her
with great show of affection. It appears thus that
the most varied forces were at work to determine
the fixation (stiffening) of her emotional attitude.

In fact homosexuality does resemble ankylosis.
The free operation of sexuality appears to be re-
stricted, a single point is fixed and every movement
takes place thereafter only within the range of that
point of fixation.

Is it possible for psychoanalysis to loosen up
such psychic ankyloses and to free once more the
bound-down energies? In this particular case can
psychoanalysis remove the fear of man and the
woman's doubt whether she can fill a woman's rôle?
How far reaching are the possibilities of psychic
orthopedics in the case of homosexuals?

I must ask the reader to follow me patiently
through the complex inquiries which follow before
attempting to answer these questions.

VII

Die Knabenliebe ist so alt wie die Menschheit und man könnte daher sagen sie liege in der Natur, ob sie gleich gegen die Natur sei.

Goethe.

VII

Boy love is as old as the race and therefore it may be said to be part of nature, although against nature.
                                                    Goethe.

Investigators interested in the problem of homosexuality point out that the condition occurs in families and see therein a support for the contention that this condition is inborn. Homosexuals usually have a homosexual brother or sister, or one or the other of their parents is similarly afflicted, in spite of marriage. But if we think of neurosis and of homosexuality (which is a particular form of neurosis) as a retrogression, if we bear in mind that all neurotics show a marked overemphasis of sexual traits, the reason for these facts is plain. What is inherited is not the homosexuality but the powerful bisexual disposition which leads to morbid tendencies. Furthermore we must bear in mind that the influence of family life is practically the same for all children. Yet one child escapes lasting injury while another is tremendously handicapped.

Before looking more closely into the influence of family life upon the development of homosexuality we must point out two very significant considerations.

One of these is the division of all love into spiritual and physical; the next point is the double attitude of every homosexual as male and female. For the present I need only emphasize the fact that persons readily adjust themselves so that one sexual component is expressed on the spiritual, the other upon the physical plane. Let us call spiritual love, "erotism," and physical love, "sexuality." The average homosexual applies his erotism to male friendships and his sexuality he places in the service of heterosexual love; the progress of culture consists therein that heterosexual love is also gradually sublimated, that is, turned more and more into erotism. The homosexual, for instance, turns his erotism towards women, and applies his sexuality in his relation with men. But at times he may turn his whole erotism into the homosexual channel and suppress his whole sexuality. Or he may endeavor to find certain spiritual qualities in his sexual ideal, trying to turn also part of his erotism into the homosexual path. Thus we meet most remarkable variations. For an example we may mention the homosexual who is interested only in coachmen, soldiers, servants and peasants. His sexual ideal he finds only among the lower orders. Such a man has turned his whole erotism towards women. He seeks the friendship of mature women, sometimes also the company of fine men, but sexually he can be active only in contact with men of low order.

This peculiarity already indicates a judgment-attitude in sexual matters. Sexuality is perceived as degrading, as compelling a return to the first aspects of "natural" life. The attitude is further complicated by the homosexual's overemphasis of one or the other sex during his acts. If he is an active homosexual he preserves his individuality, identifying his selfhood with some male ideal, the father, the brother, the teacher, etc. On the other hand, if he plays a passive rôle, he identifies himself with a woman, the mother, or her polar obverse, the prostitute. Occasionally he carries on both rôles and the relations between sexuality and erotism become reversed and transposed. That is what complicates the problem so tremendously. The urning transfers his erotism to men and his sexuality is roused in relation with women only, but the latter is soon turned into disgust. Or the urlind loves spiritually only women and finds all men repulsive, unbearable and disgusting.

In order to acquire a psychologic insight into every case as it presents itself, and to judge of its significance, it is necessary to answer the question: what does the homosexual aim to accomplish with his actions? What does the homosexual act represent in the subject's fancy. In most cases of this character reality does not enter into consideration.

Some obscure and baffling paraphilias lose their
extraordinary character once we get at the specific
act which the subject repeats vicariously through his
overt action. For *Nietzsche's* law of the eternal return of sameness applies to the neurotic.

The acts which the neurotic carries out are either
something experienced or something wished, some un-
reached yearning. It is part of human nature that
the unattained experience exercises a stronger driving power than what has been experienced. Experience acts as a retrospective tendency, craving
is prospective. (One might say, therefore: the most
severe traumas are those which have never been experienced.) The unsatisfied craving is the motive
power of most neuroses. The "world pain" of all
those who are weary of life and who struggle in vain
to accomplish the impossible is due to the eternal
craving, the *eternally Lost*, the *perennially Unreachable*. All the dream fancies of the neurotic are
shattered in contact with reality. For that reason
the neurotic overlooks the world's standards and
builds a world of his own, wherein he is master and
attains all his wishes as dreams. The *unattained
experiences* furnish the material for *perennial
dreams*.

The formation of man's character traits begins
during the first years of life. He tests his powers
upon the surroundings and his environment furnish
him the picture of life. In the eyes of children who

are not self-reliant the father must be a giant because he overawes them with his genial appearance and his image generates in their soul a feeling of inferiority which marks them for life. Every child has an ambition: to excel his father. This wish may express itself first in the desire to attain father's size, to be as strong and big as he. But later the wish shows itself in that quiet but determined competitive struggle which has always existed between father and son, or mother and daughter. The strong son takes after the powerful father. But suppose the father is weak and the mother is the one who dominates the house? What sort of picture of life becomes imprinted upon the child's mind under the circumstances? Can it help believing that women dominate the world, can he escape taking the attitude either of wishing to be a woman and rule, or of fleeing from woman when she clashes with his "will to power" as man?

In the conflict that follows, sexuality becomes mixed up with erotism, the soul of the child is bewildered, a definite outcome is delayed and meanwhile the child's soul is filled with anxiety and doubt.

Alfred Adler, who has followed this line of inquiry with great keenness, has conceived it an important factor in the dynamics of the neuroses and he has described this picture as "*the male protest.*" All reactions and protective constructions or fictions of the neurotic, according to him, lead back to the desire to be "*a complete man.*" Homosexuality displays this protest under a peculiarly cryptic form. The homosexual cries out: *I want to be a woman!* He may even go so far as to dress himself like a woman and become a transvestite. *Adler* here gives a far fetched explanation, saying: *this is a male protest under the use of female means!* He holds that the homosexual attempts to heighten by this means his feeling of personality; the latter turns away from woman because he fears his inferiority, he avoids decisions. That is true of some aspects but not of the whole picture. The problem of homosexuality as a whole shows *Adler's* position to be untenable.

The important thing is that there arises in the child's soul a wish which gravitates in the direction of the parallelogram of forces exhibited within the family circle. If the mother plays the upper rôle, the wish becomes: *I should like to be like mother! I should like to dominate and rule as she does!* Love for the mother increases this tendency to become identified with her and turns it into a directive ideal. The child begins at a tender age to imitate its mother, acts womanly, wants to play with dolls and cook, wears gladly girls' clothes. The child may overcome these tendencies or it may grow up with them or return to them later and become a pronounced homosexual. (*Late Homosexuality.*)

For the sake of simplicity I am now speaking of

boys. The same effect may be brought about when a brutal father trods down the mother, the child sees its mother suffer and comes to look upon his father as an abhorrent example. Under such circumstances the child's *"will to power"* may turn into *"ethical will."* The child's wish then is: *I would not rule and be like father; I would rather be like mother!* If the child loves his tyrannical father he may become homosexual and passive: a woman and a strong man.

These are a few examples taken at random from life. I have brought them out, because one often hears that homosexuals have had an energetic mother, and a father who played a submissive rôle. Of course, the contrary may also be the case. Frequently we hear that the mother was strongly neurotic. . . . There are no definite rules in the psychogenesis of homosexuality. Each case requires an individual solution. That is why *Sadger's* statements on the subject cannot be taken as absolute axioms. Every third case or so disproves his notions.

Many paths lead to homosexuality. It would be impossible to describe all. We can only get at a few typical examples.

We turn our attention now to the important question: what is the attitude of the neurotic towards his mother? We have seen that psychoanalysts correlate homosexuality to the repressed love for the mother. Let us give a glimpse at my few statistical data. The question: "Are you specially fond of your mother or your father? Or are you partial to some brother or sister?" was answered by my 20 homosexuals as follows:

"Only of mother—mother—no particular preference—both alike—mother—father—no preference—on the whole, more fond of mother—love the whole family passionately—father—mother—my father mother—mother—mother—mother—specially fond of a brother (indifferent to all the others)—father—mother."

Approximately one-half confess a greater fondness for the mother. I have mentioned the preferences in these cases because in one of them, at least, I am able positively to prove that back of love for the mother is hidden really a powerful aversion against the father; another subject had failed to mention his fondness for his sister which played a tremendous rôle in the development of his homosexuality. Such a statistical inquiry really requires documentation through psychoanalysis. But even on the face of the statistical figures we find a certain percentage of cases showing a greater fondness for the mother. This is also true of some of the cases in which the predominant love had been declared in favor of the father.

Hirschfeld holds that the attachment of the urning to his mother is a common occurrence. He states:

"The homosexual is attracted to one woman with particular tenderness; *this is his mother;* and here we also find the analogy of a particularly intimate relationship between the urning daughter and her father. The homosexual's attachment to his mother is so typical, that the *Freudian* school has described this mother-complex as the cause of homosexuality. *I hold this deduction for a false one.* The homosexual does not become an urning because he was so passionately attached to his mother as a child; on the contrary, he leans towards the mother instinctively rather than knowingly, at first, this being the direction of his weakness and peculiarity and often his mother, also instinctively, makes him her favorite child. . . ."

This conclusion of *Hirschfeld's* I find myself unable to accept. The urning is often the mother's favorite child before his birth. The child responds with the most tender love for his mother with whom he identifies himself in the end. Sometimes the mother wishes a girl and brings up her boy as one. I know one urning who was never dressed in pantelets by his mother, who was always kept by her side and whose mother was in the habit of folding his external genital over with his skin, saying: *you are a girl!* Even as a grown up boy he was frequently put in girl's clothes and he preserved for some time a tendency to transvestism.

Undoubtedly there are many cases, in which direct

love for the mother has absorbed all love for the female sex.

One urning, for instance, as quoted by *Hirsch-feld*, states:

"My mother was everything to me, she was my one best friend, the *alpha* and *omega* of my existence. I had built many pretty plans for her, desiring to make her comfortable in her old age. . . . Then, there came the terrible catastrophe, which nearly wiped out my whole existence, death robbed me of my much-beloved mother. The report of her illness, which made me fear the worst, found me in the North of Ireland and the tortures which I endured during the two days and two nights that it took me to reach home, could not be described in mere words. On the train folks avoided me suspecting that I was insane. . . . For three weary weeks I took care of my mother day and night, then God took her from me, and I remained a lonely wanderer, broken in mind and body. It was a blow from which I could never recover. In the endeavor to forget I returned to my England to take up my former work but it was use-less. Forget I could not, day and night I was a prey to mental and physical suffering. I could not stand it any longer. So I returned to the old home where my people had lived for 100 years. Sometimes I was nearly insane and felt a little more quiet only when visiting the cemetery and hovering around my parents' resting place. Unable to find peace I decided to travel. In the churches and cathedrals of every City and in the chapels of every village through which I passed I prayed to God for the soul of my beloved mother. The gnawing anguish in my heart over the death of my beloved mother had shattered my nerves all to pieces. . . . I felt myself paralyzed on account of my deep depression, I could no longer think, I fell into melancholy although I sometimes tried to rouse myself. I abandoned all correspondence because no one could write me a consoling word. When the world which existed between mother and myself shattered, life ceased to have any interest for me."

The relationship of the urlind to the father and of the urning to the mother *Hirschfeld* summarizes in the following table:

I. *Urning boy*	*Urlind girl*
Prefers girls' games, avoids characteristic boys' games, has many girlish features in his character and behavior, Sometimes also in his appearance. Observers remark: "He is like a girl."	Prefers boys' games, dislikes handwork, confections, is 'boy-like' in behavior, in acts and, often, in appearance. Remark: "She is like a boy!"

II. *Attitude towards the other sex*

Prefers the company of girls.

Preferably plays rough games with boys.

Emotional fixation on the mother.

Attachment greater to father.

III. *Attitude towards own sex* (as erotically colored in the unconscious)

Instinctively inhibited and bashful in relation to boys.

Greater bashfulness in the presence of girls.

Dreamy attachment to teacher or some school mate.

Similarly attached in dreams to some female person—teacher or school mate.

The powerful influence of the mother in bringing up the child is illustrated by the following passage from one history:

"A young lieutenant relates: as soon as I was out of the school room I used to rush to my girl friends. My mother was fond of taking me along when she went shopping and always asked me how I liked this thing and that, before making a purchase. For every new hat which mother bought I served as a model, that is, every hat was tried on my head, and mother purchased for herself the hat that looked best when tried on me. 'You look like a little girl,' mother often would say to me while the hats were tried on, 'too bad, that you are not a real girl!' " (*Hirschfeld*, l. c., p. 113.)

The expression, "too bad, you are not a real girl," shows how the mother influenced the child's soul at a time when it is so very plastic. But *Hirschfeld* maintains that the conditions were reversed; that the parents had suspected the child's homosexual inclination and treated it accordingly:

"Often the disposition towards homosexuality is fostered in children by their elders who treat them according to that leaning. The fathers feel specially attracted to the urning daughters—the mothers fondly give their urning boys girlish tasks about the house. The feminine and the virile peculiarities are not brought out through training at first; the mother would not expect girlish tasks of a boy who was not in the first place inclined that way. When *Krafft-Ebing* relates in his description of the case of the *Countess Sarolta Vay:* 'it was her father's whim to bring up S. as a boy; he let her ride, drive, hunt, admired her virile energy, called her Sandor. On the other hand this foolish parent allowed his second son to be dressed like a girl and to be brought up very much like one'—we must credit the father with the intention of meeting deliberately an outspoken tendency on the part of his children." (*Hirschfeld*, l. c., p. 112.)

Naturally when one explains everything so arbitrarily and tries to interpret in the parent's favor, suggesting that the father displayed great psychic insight, anything may be proven.

But when one looks with open eyes at this observation and at another case of *Hirschfeld's*,—an important contribution because it illustrates the whole inner condition of the homosexual,—it is not difficult to draw one's own conclusions. One urning relates about his mother:

"In the midst of his worries he was suddenly embraced and kissed—his mother held him tightly in her arms; she drew his little face to her cheek and their tears mingled while she consoled him until his eyes again mirrored a smile. These were unforgettable experiences in the life of the homosexual child. He felt that his mother was his truest friend, and in his grateful heart he planned to recompense her above all other mothers. His whole life and hope was centered in her; it was for her sake that he was willing to prepare his school lessons, and because of her he avoided arousing his father's wrath; he did not want her to be scolded on his account. To make her happy was his ambition in life. Because she was not happy, he felt as if it were his fault and with redoubled tenderness he clung to her, the quiet sufferer.

"He reached 16 years of age, he became sexually ripe and a perplexing unrest troubled him. His comrades told him about their gallant adventures. But he remained unresponsive to everything that seemed to make them so happy. On the contrary, he was terribly distressed when his best friend 'betrayed' him in favor of a girl. He began to be aware of his peculiarity and the terrible thought that he must hide his awful feelings made him tremble. He tried very hard to turn into the right path. But he could not live at home while harboring his secret; his mother, whom he loved above all else, he wanted to spare; he felt he had to leave; so he abandoned his home and went into the world trying to direct properly his sexual feelings. While away he received most tender messages from his mother to whom he wrote as to a beloved. After an absence of two years he returned home. From that time on his life developed *under the eyes of his mother, in whom he saw the highest quintessence of all womanhood*. His relations with women were marked by timidity. He adored them and felt he would like to serve them. He became early their confessor for his womanly soul made him their natural comrade. But in the midst of all he was very unhappy, his feelings for them never turned into physical love—*the sexual attraction was absent*." (*Hirschfeld*, l. c., p. 105.)

This urning actually confessed, in his own words, that in his mother he saw the quintessence of all womanhood. The condition is obvious. Every woman represents the mother, in part. At first I had occasion to observe cases of this kind and that is how I came to the hasty conclusion that every homosexual is emotionally fixed upon his mother and avoids women because his inhibition towards them is due to the mother *Imago* which he carries within him.[1]

Another observation of *Hirschfeld's* seems to me of very great interest:

"The great attachment of homosexuals to their mother as pointed out by *Sadger* and other followers of *Freud* is really a fact and holds true of nearly all homosexuals, the attachment reaching far back into their own childhood and extending over the mother's whole life. We have seen that many who lost their mother at an advanced age, for a long time were unable to recover from the blow. But it seems more proper not to look upon this great attachment to the mother as the cause of homosexuality, but as a consequence thereof. Aside from this more feminine nature, absence of a home of his own keeps the homosexual for a longer time than usual close to his mother, especially when she possesses a more pronounced personality, which is rather not unusual where the children are homosexual.

[1] In a novel which is an autobiography and a confession at the same time, the hero relates that during his first visit to the brothel he had to think of his mother. (*Erlebnisse des Zoeglings Taxil.* Wiener Verlag.) This book is interesting also because it describes accurately the homosexual practices in a school of cadets. The fact that young boys are impelled to think of their mother when visiting the brothel for the first time is often the cause of total impotence. Cf. *Weininger: Geschlecht u. Charakter*, chapter: *Mutter u. Dirne.* The work has been translated into English.

Urnings who contract marriage are not wound up emotionally in their mother quite to such an extent and often their love is transferred to their wife." (*Hirschfeld*, l. c., p. 344.)

With these words and the admission of the transference of the love for the mother to some other female person *Hirschfeld* recognizes the possibility of healing the condition, which is the psychoanalyst's task. But I must warn against any tendency to solve the problem of homosexuality on the basis of any single finding.

In the first place I must point out that the history of these cases discloses two types of motherhood: the strong mother and the weak mother. Both types are common and either or both may determine the growth of the child. *Hirschfeld* states that the urning becomes readily attached to the mother who is strong. This corresponds with my practical observations and shows one type of homosexuality which I shall presently describe. The strong mother dominates a weak child throughout his life, he never escapes her and she determines his relations to other women.

It will be of interest to record on this question the opinion of a man who is looked upon as the spiritual leader of the homosexual circle in a cosmopolitan city, a man who has organized them and who has had considerable experience. This gentleman writes me:

"My Dear Doctor:

"In conformity with your wish I am sending you herewith a number of life histories.

"First I wish to report to you the result of a questionnaire; I have reached with the questionnaire 800 persons. It is noteworthy that none of them knew that the answer to the question was of any particular interest to me, for the question and the answer came up unobtrusively in the course of ordinary conversation. This disposes of the criticism sometimes heard in medical circles that the answers to interrogatories are of little or no worth because the respondents unconsciously report things in a manner to favor themselves if they do not deliberately tell falsehoods with that end in view.

"Among the 800 persons interrogated 65% stated that the mother was unusually energetic and self-reliant, while the father was mild and easy going, as well as diffident and easily influenced.

"In my opinion these 65% represent the hereditary cases; there may be some also among the other 35% due to hereditary transmission but this, of course, I am unable to ascertain and it would be interesting to conduct a medical inquiry into the subject.

"In favor of a hereditary predisposition as the most general factor stands also the fact that in many families the homosexual's sisters or brothers show a similar tendency."

Illustrations

U. Sch., 26 years of age, a merchant. The mother extraordinarily self-reliant and the one who determines the course of action in every family emergency. Father good-natured fellow, easily influenced. U. Sch. has been several years ago under the care of Prof. Pilz. At the time he had some intercourse with women, but the act always caused him disgust and did not diminish his need to get into contact with men. At first he tried to oppose this leaning towards men, but after two months of struggle—during which he lost considerable weight—he had to give in again and today he maintains relations exclusively with men. His brother, six years younger than he, is an actor and is also homosexual. An older brother, also a merchant, is completely normal in his sexual life, but far from self reliant and very moody. His sister is also heterosexual, but has male traits and physical features, hairy growth on the face and a bass voice which would be considered very low even in a man.

Count X., 25 years old; a very energetic mother. His gait and movements are exceedingly feminine, he is careless and has been mixed up already in a number of unpleasant affairs from which the writer successfully helped him extricate himself. Two of his three brothers are also homosexual, and of his family circle in the wider sense, two uncles.

Karl W., 28 years of age, bank clerk. For the past six years has maintained relations with his older colleagues. He is very strikingly feminine and anxiety appears to lend zest to life in his case. He is continually living in dread lest some one in his family should find out about his peculiar inclination, although he is a stranger here and has no relative living nearby. But if he has no reason to fear anything on this score he finds some other reason to keep his mind in torment. For instance, he fears he will be run over by an automobile, even when he strolls along the safe side of a side walk, etc. As he is otherwise mentally normal I conclude that he has a strong masochistic tendency which he satisfies thus by conjuring up absurd fears. There is no expression of the masochistic tendency in any overt acts. On the other hand K. has relations only with persons belonging to the lowest social stratum (plasterers, drivers, etc.) and it is probable that the greater danger in that connection serves as a stimulant for him.

His mother is normal, but a very energetic woman, always taking care of her own affairs and when a couple of thieves once broke in at her home she grappled with them, threw them to the ground and held them. She has married a second time, has a slight downy beard growth, and in her house often puts on male clothing.

We need not be surprised that the expert emphasizes the fact that in many instances homosexuality occurs in groups in the same family. The same conditions bring about similar effects. Even the fact that 65% of homosexuals have a very energetic mother need not be in itself of any particular significance as typical of the psychogenesis of homosexuality. The expert really means that these are mannish women so that they naturally bring into the world womanly boys.

INDEX

353

Moebius, 283
Moll, 18 *passim,* 20, 22
Monosexuality *vid.* Bisexuality
Mother complex, 213, 339
    Imago, 186, 246, 335
Motherly feeling, 161
Mutterschutz, 230

Naecke, 20, 184, 269
Narcissism, 102, 227
"Natural" life, 333
Nausea, 226, 230, 236, 290, 303
Necrophilia, 131
Nervousness, 257, 286
"Neuropathic" constitution, 294
Neurosis, 17, 22, 27 *passim,* 41 *passim,* 45, 48, 55, 58, 96, 106, 122, 145, 215, 223, 237, 305, 324
Nietzsche, 334
Nutrition, 216
Nymphomania, 163

Object, sexual, 11
Obsession, 113, 120
Onanism, *vid.* Masturbation
Ontogenesis, 45
Orgasm, 74, 82, 184, 263, 267, 281, 293
Outbreak (of H.), 223
Over-compensation, 46
    determination, 327

Paranoia, 39, 95
Paraphilia, 58, 146, 156, 268
Parents, 30
Passion, 89, 97, 144
Paul, Jean, 306
Pawlow, 35
Pederasty, 81
Perversion, 69, 102
Pfister, 320, 323, 326
Phallic symbol, 217

Phantasy, 70, 130, 300
Phobias, 68
Piety, 190, 200, 219, 235
Pilz, 349
Platen's Diary, 290
Plato, 56
Pollution (dream), 212, 227, 313
Polygamic neurosis, 124
    tendency, 176
Potentia, 133, 217, 257, 261
Polygamy, 237
Praetorius, Numa, 250, 251
Precocity, 45 *passim,* 47, 318
Predisposition, 31, 34, 36, 39, 41, 290
Preference for widows, 98
Priapism, 131
Prognosis, 216
Progression, 44
Prostitute, 61, 163, 178, 184, 217, 280, 285, 316
Prostitution, 57, 85, 106, 281
Protection, *vid.* Defence
Pseudo-Cassanova type, 99
    Homosexuality, 24, 25, 247, 308
Pseudonym, choice of, 65
Psychic Homosexuality, 85
    Urge, 183
Psycho-Analysis, 26, 27, 39, 47, 70, 109, 150, 158, 172, 190, 202, 225, 241, 244, 248, 268, 284, 300, 312, 328, 338
Psychosis, 58
Puberty, 31, 33, 124, 291, 294
Pursuit, 186, 191

Quest for sexual object, 164, 172
    father, 312
Questionnaire, 255 *passim,* 348

Rationalization, 72, 247
Reality, 60
Recessive type, 45